Hello there!

Basically, there are two types of survivalists. The first survivalist is the person who can go into a forest with a piece of string and a match stick and construct a shopping mall. These individuals live off the land – eat spiders and centipedes – climb trees and eat coconuts - forage in the underbrush for edible twigs, sticks and rocks and build a shelter on top of a cactus. This type of survivalist should be envied – respected – and admired. But this type of survivalist is not me.

The second survivalist is the person who purchases supplies <u>in advance</u> for emergency pantries that can be used during a disaster – and hopefully, this survivalist can live through the disaster <u>in their home</u> *without* eating bugs, climbing trees and eating coconuts, living on top of a cactus or scrounging for twigs, sticks and rocks to prepare the next meal. *I am this type of survivalist.*

There are seventeen important elements affected by consequences that occur during a disaster. In this book, I will introduce you to them. In addition to learning about basic emergency principles, you will learn about important strategies, insights, tips, guidelines and lists on the elements that can be impacted by a crisis.

As you begin the journey, at first it may seem overwhelming – there is so much to learn and so much to do. <u>Remember - not everything discussed in this booklet is something you must have in your emergency pantries. Based on your individual situation, you can review the information and make a *realistic* and *smart* decision on what would be good choices for your family</u>. And in many cases, much to your surprise, you will discover you already have many of the suggested supplies in and around your house!

An important point to be made with emergency preparation is to take it very seriously but don't take yourself so serious when doing it! Consider it to be a project and a challenge, but have fun doing it!

As a beginning student to emergency preparation – it seems like the hardest part is taking that first step. And since you are reading this book, it tells me that you are serious and committed to getting your emergency pantries in order. We all have to begin somewhere – sometime. <u>The time is right</u>. <u>The time is now</u>. So let's get crackin!

TABLE OF CONTENTS

TERMS

TERM	DEFINITION
Consequence	Produced by a cause (disaster) having important affects or influence over the earth and its inhabitants. Examples include disruption of electrical power, flooding of neighborhoods, destruction of homes and hospitals or broken bridges and roads.
Disaster	A state of extreme ruin and misfortune. An act that has consequences. An unexpected natural or man-made catastrophe of substantial extent causing significant physical damage or destruction, loss of life or permanent change to the natural environment. Examples include *earthquake*, *thunderstorm*, *nuclear meltdown* or *volcanic eruption*.
Element	Components essential to our survival on this planet and standard of living. These elements are made up of various agencies and organizations that provide goods and services to the human population. Examples include *Administration, Operation, Sanitation, Transportation, Communication, Nutrition, Medication, Immunization, Financial Institution, Documentation, Commercialization, Inspiration* and *Protection*.
Health	*Physical*, *Mental*, *Emotional*, *Psychological* and *Spiritual* well being for all living creatures on earth.
Team	Individuals in a group who purchases and consumes supplies in emergency pantries and will share in responsibilities and duties associated with implementing the overall emergency plan. Examples include a family living in a home.
Layers	Alternatives for an element. If one type of alternative isn't realistic or possible for a specific situation, another alternative could possibly be used. Examples of layered supplies that provide <u>light</u> include a *candle, lantern, flashlight*, and *lamp*.
Level	A classification of disaster scenario based on the elements that are affected, the severity of the consequences and the duration the element is compromised or disrupted. There are three emergency levels including Level 1, Level 2 and Level 3.
Pantry	A facility, room or container used to store various sources and items assigned to each element. Examples are pantries located in the *primary residence, place of refuge, auto, work* or an *evacuation* kit.
Place of Refuge	An alternative location for the team in the event the primary residence is damaged or destroyed <u>or</u> the pre-selected primary location for team members to reside during the disaster. A place of refuge could be a *motor home, trailer house, camper, cabin, summer home* <u>or</u> some other location (including a *church, school* or designated *public shelter*) pre-determined by the team.
Primary Residence	The building or structure and location where the team members will store, use and consume emergency preparation supplies and items. During a disaster, the team will congregate and remain at this location as long as the residence is habitable.
Resource	A manmade or natural source that is available to us for use in emergency preparation. Examples include the *sun, water, wood, wind* and *rain* or a *grocery store*.
Supply	A man-made or commercial product or service that is available to us for use in emergency preparation. Examples include *flashlights, clothes, radio, grain,* and *gloves*.

PREFACE

During peaceful as well as disaster times, the protection of team members is a continual and persistent mission and must be aggressively pursued at all times. As team members continue to build their emergency supply pantries, it becomes even more important to see measures are in place to protect the lives and well being of team members, the primary structure and its contents and the health and safety of pets and livestock who count on us for their health and well being.

As I have researched emergency preparation and the various agencies and organizations responsible for responding, assisting and protecting the general public in an emergency or disaster, I have discovered several interesting facts about their perceptions and assumptions regarding a disaster. Obviously, these perceptions are derived from past experiences, mathematical analyses and projections and observing actual disaster occurrences. As a result, their overall disaster plans are created based on what has been learned from past events and conclusions of what might occur in the future. For example, an emergency or disaster will:

- Only occur in a **specific area** or **region** of a city or state, country or continent, i.e. the west end of New York City; the northern part of Washington; the entire state of California; the entire east coast of the United States; the entire United States; or the entire African continent

- Have a **finite time period** in which it will be destructive based on the type of disaster, i.e. an earthquake generally lasts less than 5-10 minutes; a tornado starts and finishes in less than an hour; a drought lasts for several years

- Have a **finite amount of property damage, destruction and loss of life** based on the type of disaster, i.e. a wildfire damages and destroys 1,000 acres of forest, six homes and kills ten people

- Generally not include more than **two disaster types at a time**, i.e., earthquake and the resulting tsunami

- **Not create such a cataclysmic disaster** that it cannot be "handled". Emergency personnel and government agencies, charitable organizations, medical personnel and other responders will be able to respond to the crisis and effectively perform their duties so a "normal" environment can be restored in the foreseeable future

Frankly, as I have studied various disasters that have occurred in my lifetime and over the past several millenniums, I can think of only two disasters that were so catastrophic - the affects were felt around the entire globe. The first one supposedly occurred sixty-five million years ago when a comet hit the earth and took out all the dinosaurs, and the second one occurred about 4,500 years ago when a man by the name of Noah was warned about a pending rain storm.

With the exception of these two events, up until now, all other manmade and natural disasters seem to fall in line with the above conclusions, including all the wars, nuclear meltdowns, chemical and biological attacks, nuclear bombs, volcanoes, earthquakes, droughts, famines, pestilence - and all the other countless tragedies, crises, emergencies and disasters that have happened over the centuries.

So, based on past disasters, at least on the surface, it would seem realistic and logical to assume future disasters would also mimic the behavior of their predecessors. Since government, religious and charitable administrators and the scientific community responsible for the safety and security of the overall population *before*, *during* and *after* a disaster relies on the fact it is highly unlikely another comet or big rain storm will happen again, there would be no reason they could not jump in and save us all from certain death and destruction.

Let's review the specific areas or regions around the world where an *encompassing* disaster could happen and how others outside of the disaster region can easily come to their aid. As you can plainly see from the below maps, it doesn't matter what type of disaster, when it happens, how long it lasts or where it occurs - **IN ALL CASES** - government, religious, charitable and scientific agencies and communities (as demonstrated by the arrows on the maps) come to the rescue and support the troubled area or region.

There will be shelter, food, water, money, medical and pharmaceutical supplies, clothing, building materials, generators, toilet paper and all other possible supplies brought to the disaster site. Corporations also provide financial assistance and citizens bring donations and/or travel to the area to help with rebuilding and cleanup.

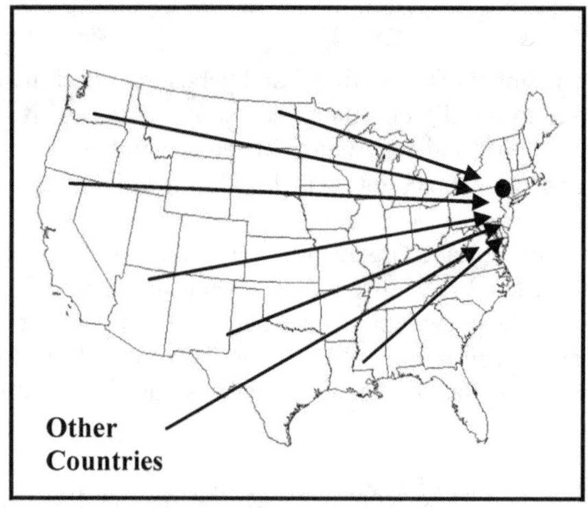

West Side of New York City

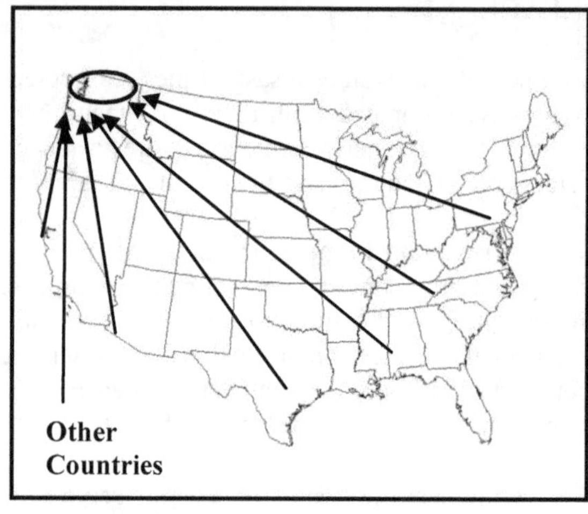

Northern Region of the State of Washington

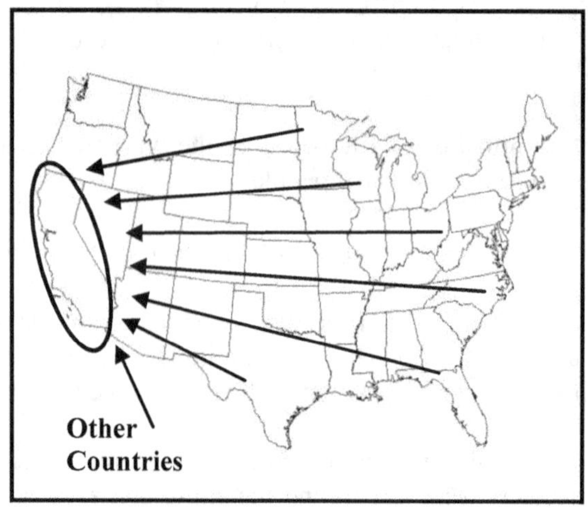

Entire State of California

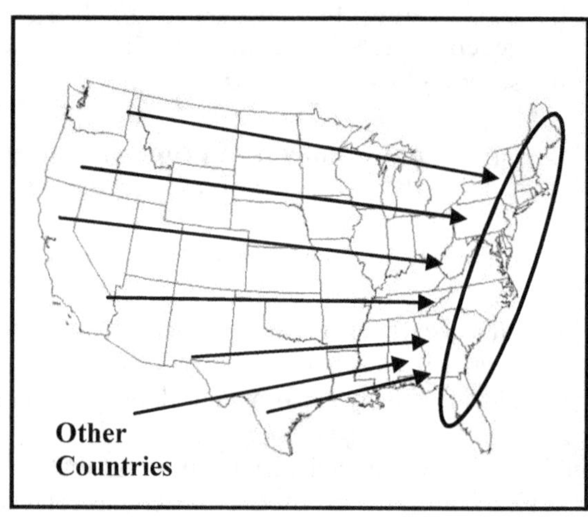

Entire East Coast of the United States

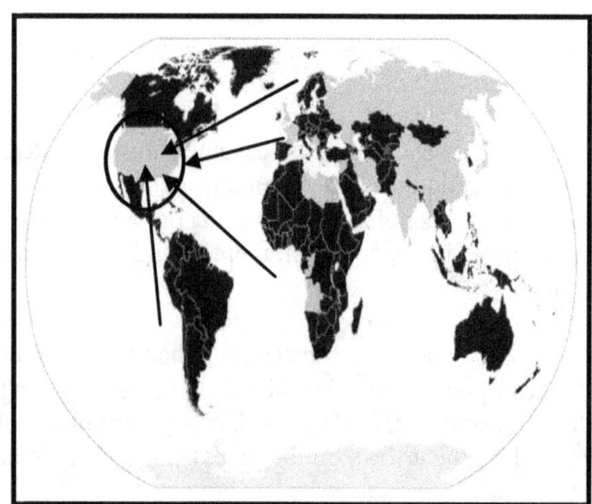

Entire United States

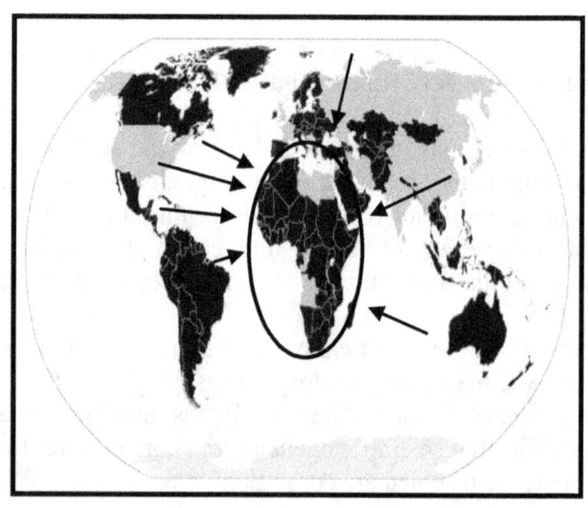

Entire Continent of Africa

But what happens if there was such a cataclysmic disaster it affects the entire planet again? Could such a disaster <u>really</u> happen during these current times? The answer is YES. For example, although somewhat unlikely, there could be another comet hit the earth, but more likely, this type of serious and long-term disaster could include a combination of both manmade disasters (nuclear war, electro-magnetic pulses (EMP), nuclear meltdowns, terrorist threats and chemical and biological attacks) and/or natural disaster (drought, famine and pestilence, earthquakes, tsunamis, volcanoes, flooding, heat waves and cold temperatures).

These types of events could occur - within a short period of time or over a longer period of time. And as a *consequence*, **all** vital *elements* would certainly be affected and everyone would have to fend for themselves. Imagine being faced with no electricity for an entire year. No lights. No heat. No gas pumps. No computers. No cell phones. No transportation. No stores or markets. No banks. No food. No water. No hospitals. No medications. No toilet paper. No government.

This is the reason when *planning in advance* for disaster <u>ALWAYS PLAN FOR THE WORST CASE SCENARIO</u>! We need to prepare to be <u>self sufficient</u> and vigilant in stocking emergency supplies that would maintain our health and keep us alive for a <u>long term</u> disaster.

IF FACING A LARGE SCALE AND CATACLYSMIC DISASTER LASTING MORE THAN A YEAR

- Loss of electricity
- Loss of communications
- Large scale destruction and damage of infrastructure
- Large shortages of food, water, medical supplies, fuel etc.

As part of *planning in advance*, it is important to understand how various state and local government officials (including governors, mayors and town council members) may react to various types of disaster scenarios. Obviously, depending on the level of the disaster (1-3), these elected officials will assess the situation based on <u>many</u> factors, including:

- *local* damage or destruction (consequences) to the surrounding <u>infrastructure</u>, including homes, hospitals, transportation modes, electrical grids, fuel hubs and communication equipment

- *local* damage or destruction (consequences) to the important <u>operational elements</u>, including the food, water, shelter, heat etc.

- *local* injuries and deaths of local population and ability to support the population

- length of time disaster is anticipated to last, e.g. several days, weeks, months or even a year or longer

- *local* availability of emergency supplies to support population, including food, water, clothing, medical

Some politicians who may still command the respect and support of local citizens will attempt to manage the disaster in a fair and equitable manner. However, depending on the severity and longevity of the disaster, there will be a large number of elected officials who will make decisions that will benefit and protect themselves from not only loosing their elected position but also to ensure adequate emergency supplies are available for them and their families and friends.

One method to ensure adequate emergency supplies for a select few would be to either order or convince large numbers of the local population to move to other locations where "large amounts of emergency supplies" would be available for them. A lie - of course. But convincing or forcing local citizens to move to other locations, the "problem" of dealing with these citizens becomes the responsibility of someone else down the road as well as ensuring more emergency supplies will be available for those in power and their families and friends.

As these citizens are forced out of their homes and ordered to evacuate the local area and travel (more than likely by foot) to another area down the road, stress, strain, apprehension and tension will escalate, tempers will flair and violence will happen - not only among themselves, but with the unsuspecting towns, cities and villages who see an infusion of new refugees coming into their communities. Will they be welcome? Yes. No. Maybe. It all depends on how *these* citizens have assessed the disaster situation based on the above factors.

GEORGE WASHINGTON VISION OF FUTURE WAR IN USA

In 1777, while at Valley Forge, George Washington recorded in his journal a visitation by an angel who showed him the destiny of the United States:

"And again I heard the mysterious voice saying, 'Son of the Republic, look and learn.' At this the dark, shadowy angel placed a trumpet to his mouth and blew three distinct blasts; and taking water from the ocean, he sprinkled it upon Europe, Asia and Africa. Then my eyes beheld a fearful scene: from each of these countries arose thick, black clouds that were soon joined into one. Throughout this mass, there gleamed a dark red light by which I saw hordes of armed men, who, moving with the cloud, marched by land and sailed by sea to America. Our country was enveloped in this volume of cloud, and I saw these vast armies devastate the whole country and burn the villages, towns and cities that I beheld springing up. As my ears listened to the thundering of the cannon, clashing of swords, and the shouts and cries of millions in mortal combat, I heard the mysterious voice saying, 'Son of the Republic, look and learn.' When the voice had ceased, the dark shadowy angel placed his trumpet once more to his mouth, and blew a long and fearful blast.

Instantly, a light as of a thousand suns shone down from above me, and pierced and broke into fragments the dark cloud which enveloped America. That same moment, the angel upon whose head still shone the word "UNION" and who bore our national flag in one hand and a sword in the other, descended from the heavens attended by legions of white spirits. These immediately joined the inhabitants of America, who I perceived were well nigh overcome, but who immediately taking courage again, closed up their broken ranks and renewed the battle. Again, amid the fearful noise of the conflict, I heard the mysterious voice saying, 'Son of the Republic, look and learn.' As the voice ceased, the shadowy angel for the last time dipped water from the ocean and sprinkled it upon America. Instantly, the dark cloud rolled back, together with the armies it had brought, leaving the inhabitants of the land victorious.

Then once more I beheld the villages, towns and cities springing up where I had seen them before, while the bright angel, planting the azure standard he had brought in the midst of them, cried with a loud voice: 'While the stars remain, and the heavens send down the dew upon the earth, so long shall the Union last.' And taking from his brow the crown on which blazoned the word "UNION", he placed it upon the Standard while the people, kneeling down, said 'Amen.'

The scene instantly began to fade and dissolve, and I at last saw nothing but the rising, curling vapor I had at first beheld. This also disappearing, I found myself once more gazing upon the mysterious visitor, who, in the same voice I had heard before, said, 'Son of the Republic, what you have seen is thus interpreted: Three great perils will come upon the Republic. The most fearful is the third, but in this greatest conflict, the whole world united shall not prevail against her. Let every child of the Republic learn to live for his God, his land and the Union. With these words, the vision vanished, and I started from my seat and felt that I had seen a vision wherein had been shown to me the birth, progress and destiny of the United States."

- *George Washington - Valley Forge - 1777*

I see in the future a crisis approaching that unnerves me and causes me to tremble for the safety of my country. Corporations have been enthroned. An era of corruption in high places will follow, and the money power of the country will endeavor to prolong its reign by working upon the prejudices of the people, until the wealth is aggregated in a few hands, and the Republic is destroyed.

- *Abraham Lincoln - prior to his assassination in 1865*

CHAPTER ONE

INTRODUCTION

OSTRICH SYNDROME

A common belief is that whenever an ostrich senses danger, instead of facing the threat – he immediately buries his head in the sand. If he cannot see the danger – then the danger cannot see him. Only a very small percentage of citizens in this country are concerned about being prepared, educated or ready for any crisis. Some people don't believe that any disaster is going to happen here in the United States. Others believe that disasters may affect only those people who live outside of the country. Still others believe disasters may happen but they are powerless to do anything about it. There are countless individuals throughout the world and here at home – including right in your backyard, who are not worried about any type of disaster happening to them. They truly believe that it is best to eat, drink and be merry – for tomorrow they still won't die! These individuals are convinced that in the event of any unlikely disaster – the government, church, employer, charities, relatives, friends, neighbors and co-workers will shoulder this burden for them.

Regardless of individual opinions about possible future disasters, it is important for all citizens to recognize the following:

> **NO PERSON OR GROUP IS RESPONSIBLE FOR THE SAFETY, WELL-BEING OR HEALTH OF YOUR HOUSEHOLD DURING A DISASTER.**

Survival planning is nothing more than realizing a disaster could happen that would put everyone in a survival situation and with that in mind, take steps to increase chances of survival. Although helping others is certainly meaningful, worthwhile, and in some cases, necessary – the main emphasis for all team members should be to *purchase*, *gather*, and *store* resources and supplies for your *own team members*. Everyone must be encouraged and expected to provide for themselves. We have been encouraged through religious, education, scientific and government media to prepare for these future events.

Survival planning means being organized, having survival supplies and knowing how to use them. Emergency preparation requires *physical*, *mental*, *emotional*, *psychological*, *spiritual* and *monetary* sacrifice, but in the end, survival planning is essential.

PROBLEM

There are many types of emergencies and disasters that can occur in your city, county, state, country or around the world. Depending on the type and location of the disaster, the consequences can affect each of us in a *direct* or *indirect* manner. Because of the thousands of scenarios that can take place during a disaster, my approach to disaster planning focuses not on the actual *disaster* (earthquake) but on the *consequences* (power outage) to the *elements* (Operation) that most likely will occur as a result of the disaster and the *length of time* consequences will remain in place.

ELEMENTS

All seventeen elements are essential to our survival on this planet and current standard of living. These elements include:

ELEMENT	WHAT IT COVERS
Administration	Governmental agencies and their role and responsibilities to the general public during normal and disaster situations. The administration includes organizations assigned to the federal government (military, national guard, FEMA, federal freeways, railroads, airports, prisons and post office etc.); state government (national guard, coroners office, state roads, prisons, environmental quality etc.); county government (fire, police, sheriff, ambulance, trash collection and county roads etc.); and city government (sewer, electric, water, EMT and fire etc.).

ELEMENT	WHAT IT COVERS
Commercialization	Public, private and charitable manufacturing, processing, distribution, retail and wholesale companies, organizations or systems providing goods and services, including Proctor and Gamble, Johnson & Johnson, General Motors, Wal-Mart, McDonalds, Home Depot, Bob's Family Farm, Foster Farms, Syscon and Red Cross.
Communication	Public, private and commercial communication modes including land line phones, cell phones, ham radios, television, radio, newspapers, written correspondence, postal service, satellite, Internet and written correspondence.
Documentation	Legal and personal documentation including birth certificates, death certificates, marriage certificates, home and auto titles, mortgages, leases, wills and living wills.
Emotion	Human reaction to stress, anxiety, fear, confusion, anger and depression that becomes prevalent during a crisis – both as individuals, groups and entire populations.
Financial Institution	Banks, credit unions, financial firms and stock brokers who have access to and/or controls government, public and private money sources around the world.
Fuel Consumption	Energy sources used for all public and commercial vehicles and transportation modes, food preparation, lighting and heating equipment, tools and oil-based goods. Examples include gasoline used for all vehicles, natural gas and propane used in furnaces, gasoline used for generators and chain saws, wood, coal and other oil-based fuels used in cooking stoves and lanterns and oil-based goods such as plastics.
Immunization	Vaccinations required minimizing the possibility of contracting diseases.
Inspiration	The faith in a Higher Power to assist team members with the spiritual means to prepare to meet and survive future disasters.
Medication	Hospitals and medical centers, medical care providers, first responders, insurance carriers, prescription and over-the-counter drugs and first aid supplies.
Nutrition	Food nutrition, processing, distribution, preparation and storage requirements.
Operation	Basic shelter, electricity, light, heat, clothing, tools and water needs.
Production	The means of producing the food supply and other goods and services and the relationship between these goods and how they can be affected by a disaster.
Protection	Spiritual means and physical weapons (guns, knives) to provide protection.
Recreation	The means of providing enjoyment, pleasure and relief from stress during a disaster including games, music, books and sports.
Sanitation	Basic personal hygiene, toilets, sewer and septic tanks, public and individual trash collection and disposal, mortuary services and death issues.
Transportation	Public, private and commercial transportation including air, roads, waterways, subways and rail; all private transportation including walking, motorcycles, cars, snowmobiles, mopeds, boats, ATV's and bicycles; and freeway, highway and road accessibility.

Our focus must be on what happens to our **health** as a consequence of a disaster. For example, during a hurricane, one family received ample warning and was able to seek refuge in an underground shelter. Once the hurricane passed through the area, all family members were able to leave the shelter and come to the surface. The family was now safe, alive and their health was preserved. On the other hand, another family was unable to reach the underground shelter in time. As a result of flying debris, one family member was struck in the leg by a metal stake and another family member received severe head injuries. In this case, after the hurricane passed through the area, both families are safe and alive –

but health is threatened for the second family who did not seek shelter in time. Again - there is one and only one goal or objective for each of us to have during any level of disaster:

PRESERVE AND MAINTAIN OUR PHYSICAL, MENTAL, EMOTIONAL, PSYCHOLOGICAL AND SPIRITUAL <u>HEALTH</u>

ALTERNATIVES OR LAYERS

Another important strategy in emergency preparation planning is to have numerous *choices* and *options* in providing for the various elements. <u>The more layers – the better chance of maintaining health and safety during an emergency</u>. For example, for the **OPERATION** Element and to have light during an emergency, include a *flashlight, lamp, lantern* and *candles* in emergency preparation pantries. For the **COMMUNICATION** Element, include a solar powered and hand-crank *radio*, a *walkie-talkie* and perhaps a *ham radio system*. If possible, purchase supplies that do <u>not</u> require electrical power, batteries or other fuel sources. During many disasters, electricity, water and fuel will not be available for short-term and long-term scenarios.

LEVELS

When making an analysis of disaster scenarios, it is obvious there are millions of possibilities. As a result of any disaster scenario, there will likely be consequences that take place to one or more of the elements. For example, a 4.2 earthquake in Kansas causing minimal damage or a 9.7 earthquake in Los Angeles, California that takes out many of the power lines. The <u>consequence</u> of the 9.7 earthquake was disruption of electricity (and possibly water) for many residents. This earthquake was the direct cause of the **OPERATION** Element (electricity/water) being disrupted. On the other hand, the residents in Kansas did not have any disruption in services. Instead of attempting to prepare an emergency plan based on a <u>specific</u> disaster or combination of disasters, it is more prudent to <u>classify</u> disasters into three <u>levels</u> (1-3) based on (1) elements that are affected; (2) severity of the consequences and (3) duration the element is compromised or disrupted. Disaster levels are outlined in the table below:

LEVEL	DURATION
1	*1 hour to 7 days*
2	*7 days to 1 month*
3	*1 month to 1 year*

CONCEPT

	DISASTER	CONSEQUENCES	ELEMENTS	DURATION SEVERITY	LEVELS
EXPLANATION	<u>Disaster</u> occurs and has one or more types of disasters such as an earthquake	And as a result of the disaster, there are <u>consequences</u>	Consequences can affect one or more of the 17 <u>elements</u> maintaining our *health*	Depending on the <u>length of time</u> and the <u>severity</u> of the consequences on the affected elements	The disaster is categorized into 3 distinct <u>levels</u>: Level 1 is minimum and Level 3 is maximum
EXAMPLE	**Earthquake**	Takes out some power lines but alternatives are available	**OPERATION**	3 weeks	2
		Hospital damaged but alternate sites are available	**MEDICATION**	5 weeks	3

DISASTER TIMELINE

Depending on the <u>point in time</u> of the disaster – less or more resources will be required to sustain the health and well-being of team members. For example, if the duration of the disaster is between one month and one year, one must recognize there will be different types and amounts of resources needed at the beginning of this disaster (one month) versus at the end of this disaster (one year). As the length of time increases in a disaster and more elements are compromised or disabled – there will be less resources available and public dissention and violence could escalate to dramatic proportions.

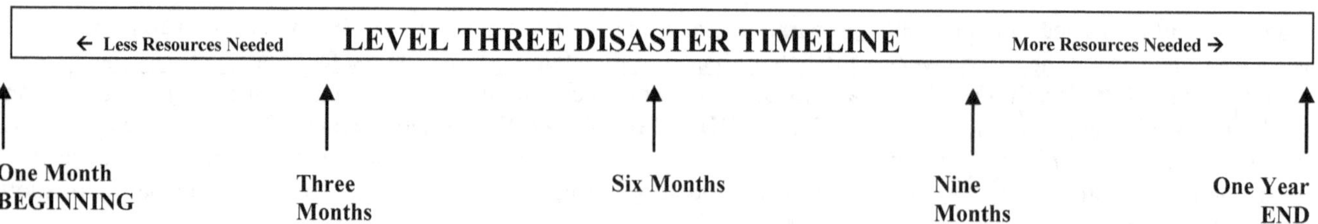

PRIMARY RESIDENCE

The primary residence is generally the main residence or house occupied by a <u>majority</u> of the team members. The primary residence could also be a cabin, motor home, trailer house, camper, office or other structure. In some cases, all team members (an entire family) will already reside at the primary residence. Team members may also reside in homes within a few miles of one another.

It is generally advisable to select <u>one</u> residence or building to serve as the primary residence. This structure will be used to store a <u>majority</u> of the emergency supplies and items. <u>The primary residence is the principal location where team members will gather and reside during</u> *some* <u>short-term but</u> *most* <u>medium-term and long-term disasters.</u>

For short-term disasters lasting only a few hours or even a few days, team members who do not permanently reside at the designated primary residence may choose to stay in their own homes and should have basic supplies stored in the home for such emergency situations. This eliminates the need to travel to the primary residence site if circumstances do not warrant the move. On the other hand, for Level 2 (lasting a month) and Level 3 disasters, it may be better for all team members to converge at the primary residence – where a majority of the emergency supplies should be stored to support disasters lasting a longer duration of time.

When evaluating the location for the primary residence, consider the following criteria as part of the selection process:

- The building is easily accessible for all team members to gather during a disaster. All persons will be able to walk (or with assistance - get there) to the location. <u>Everyone agrees this location will be the best place to designate as the primary residence.</u>

- The legal ownership of the structure is under the control and management of at least one of the team members.

- A significant amount of resources are already available at the location, i.e., fireplace, wood-burning stove, solar panels, orchard, root cellar, natural water sources, large capacity storage spaces (basement), etc.

- There is room in the structure to comfortably accommodate all team members (spacious kitchen, adequate sleeping areas, bathrooms, laundry facilities and a room to serve as the designated "shelter-in-place location).

- The building structure is sound and in good condition including the foundation, beams, roof and chimney.

- There are no obvious hazards in and around the structure or surrounding area including items that can move, fall or break during an emergency situation.

- The location is clean, uncluttered and free of debris in and around the building.

- The structure accommodates any handicapped or disabled team members.

- The utilities supporting the structure (water, gas, electricity, sewer/septic tank) have infrastructure in good condition and able to withstand damage that could occur during a disaster. All large appliances including the water heater have been secured to wall studs, all electrical panels and wiring meets or exceeds code requirements, water taps and lines are not corroded, rusty or have any leaks, toilets are working properly and in good condition, flexible gas and water connections are installed on all gas appliances, propane tanks have approved valves that operate properly and sewer and/or septic tanks do not have any obvious problems that could cause sewage backups.

When selecting the primary residence, attempt to select a location that offers the least amount of problems that could occur *before*, *during* and *after* a disaster. By avoiding potential damage and destruction to the primary residence, the team members can reduce stress, anxiety and apprehension and focus on maintaining health for the duration of the crisis.

> During a serious disaster when a family is forced to leave their home and upon returning home after the crisis, they may discover squatters have taken over the home and their possessions and may not be willing to vacate the premises. If at all possible, team members should remain in their homes or make arrangements to have trusted friends and neighbors protect the premises.

TEAM SELECTION

A <u>major</u> task when creating an emergency preparation plan is to determine who will be included in the group who will purchase and consume the emergency supplies and will also share in the responsibilities and duties of implementing the overall emergency plan. All team members should contribute to the overall plan – both with ideas and actions. Although discussion is certainly reasonable and warranted – all team members must agree and understand *in advance* on all or most of the emergency plan to be utilized by team members *before*, *during* and *after* a disaster.

The team will generally include all individuals living at the primary residence – or in other words - the family members. However, other individuals may also be included as part of the team. For example, if elderly parents, children, siblings, friends, relatives, neighbors or other individuals who <u>live in close vicinity</u> to the physical primary residence, then they could be included as part of the group.

When setting up the team, consider skills and talents that could be used by each team member in an emergency. There may be some members who will be more active in emergency preparation *prior* to the emergency, i.e., purchasing and storing supplies. Other members will become important *during* and *after* the disaster, i.e., lifting and carrying heavy items or providing medical assistance. As a disaster reaches Level 3, individual teams can then band together with other teams to create highly effective and successful groups who can work together for the benefit of all team members.

Another important consideration is to <u>carefully</u> consider the logistical probabilities of all members being able to congregate at the designated primary residence either *before*, *during* or *after* the disaster. A good rule to follow would be to ask the following question of candidates under consideration to join the team:

> **How far away does the candidate live from the designated primary residence and during any disaster that <u>impedes transportation</u> – could the candidate(s) reasonably travel <u>on foot</u> to the primary residence where emergency preparation supplies are stored or could another member of the team bring the candidate on foot to the primary residence?**

If the answer is **NO** – then as hard as it may be – these individuals should set up their own team and store all emergency supplies at their own primary residence. To ignore this important principle is to leave individuals with no emergency supplies because they are not realistically able to travel to the designated primary residence of the team. This would include candidates that simply live too far away or who are handicapped or disabled and would not be able to walk the distance.

In a <u>small</u> town – it may be realistic to include anyone who lives in the community, providing they are healthy and able to walk to the designated primary residence. However, anyone living in towns and cities further away should set up their own team. As a <u>general</u> rule, if there is at least five to ten miles separating a possible candidate and the designated primary residence – the candidate should set up his/her own team.

Encourage all other family members, relatives, friends and neighbors to set up their own respective teams to guarantee that everyone is included in a team. This will eliminate serious problems during a disaster when non-team members come knocking on the door seeking sanctuary – and request or even demand that your team members provide them with needed resources and supplies during the term of the disaster.

Carefully evaluate the willingness and ability of all members to get along with one another and be able to work together as a cohesive unit and a strong and unified team. A serious disaster can release negative attitudes and destructive opinions that can surface between team members. If there is <u>any</u> likelihood some members will not be able to work together as a unit – the time is <u>before</u> a disaster occurs to make arrangements for separate teams and a different primary residence for those members.

<u>I cannot stress enough the importance of serious consideration and deliberation in determining who will belong to the team</u>. Make absolutely certain all team members understand the significance of the team concept, the responsibilities and duties that come with their inclusion in the team and their ability to support and contribute to the overall team *before*, *during* and *after* a disaster.

COMBINING TEAM SUPPLIES

Depending on the level of the emergency, individual teams will begin to band together to form highly efficient and incredibility strong groups that can work together to maintain the overall health of all members. This is where community, church, and neighborhoods really show their stuff!

Although it is certainly practical to work with other teams to prepare for future emergencies, there are several considerations and conditions that merit careful scrutiny before combining forces. During "good" times, most team members would be willing to give a cup of sugar to a neighbor who came to the door and asked for the favor. No problem. But during "disaster" times - the line of generosity is not so clear.

There are specific emergency supplies where combining forces with other teams would be sensible. For example, when purchasing medical supplies and first aid items, it may be sensible for several teams to go in together and purchase an entire box or carton of bandages and then split the contents equally between the teams. No one team would be given the entire carton of bandages to store in their primary residence. <u>Instead, each team would store their share of the bandages in their own respective primary residence</u>.

There are also some so-called "emergency" items that could legitimately be divided among several teams, and during a disaster, the teams could exchange and share the supplies with each other. For example, although teams having recreation supplies are an important consideration, the ultimate survival of the team is not contingent on a soccer ball. In the case of recreation supplies, and in order to help tight emergency preparation budgets for individual teams - by all means - combine forces! Each team could be assigned to gather specific recreational items with the agreement that all teams would share the supplies among each other during the disaster. If one team decides to keep the soccer ball for themselves and not share - the rest of the teams will still live to see another day.

Another area where combining forces will more than likely be <u>required</u> is actually protecting team members and possessions during a serious disaster. Teams can combine together and set up schedules where each team will take turns in guarding the area or standing watch over team members, property and supplies.

Due to the overall cost of some emergency preparation supplies and equipment, individual teams may decide it would be smart to combine with other teams to purchase higher priced items and share the cost. For example, instead of a team purchasing a solar powered generator costing several thousand dollars, several teams could go into together and buy one - that way, no one team would have to pay the entire price and the cost would be spread over several teams. On the surface, this plan would seem like a good idea. But then the questions must be asked: (1) where will the generator actually be stored, (2) which team will be responsible for the safety and security of the item, (3) what happens if one team moves to another location, (4) what happens if the generator gets stolen or damaged - who pays for the repairs, *and more importantly* (5) <u>during a disaster</u>, how will the schedule be set up for each team to use the generator at their primary residence.

This is where serious problems can erupt in a very short period of time. During a disaster, the team who actually has *physical* possession of the generator may not be as willing to abide by the sharing and scheduling agreement created between teams when the generator was purchased. Parents may resist giving up the generator because of the belief their need for electric power is greater than that of other teams who have a legitimate right to also use the generator.

In order to avoid explosive confrontations and volatile situations, teams should plan to purchase, gather and store <u>most</u> emergency supplies at their own primary residence, and with very few exceptions, avoid sharing the cost, sharing the supplies and sharing the storage with other teams. By following this rule, if a team decides to share supplies with other teams, they will maintain the freedom of choice and power to do so.

EMERGENCY PREPARATION PRINCIPLES

As with all emergencies, it is essential to *prepare in advance* and eliminate excessive stress, anxiety and pressure. By addressing needs and concerns <u>prior to any emergency</u>, issues can be eliminated in getting essential supplies and resources during a disaster situation. For example, during a disaster, water could be contaminated. By *planning in advance*, we can have water stored in containers that would be available for us during the crisis.

There are thirty-two <u>general</u> principles that must be incorporated into the overall emergency plan to prepare for and in some cases eliminate problems and issues that become prevalent during a disaster situation. These general principles apply to *all* elements:

- **Create a comprehensive emergency preparation plan** for the team.

- *Plan in advance* of an emergency to substantially improve your chances of a healthy survival.

- When gathering and purchasing supplies, it is essential to make sure all **supplies and equipment are kept safe and secure, properly stored, operating correctly and you know how the supplies and/or equipment will be used** in a <u>disaster</u> environment. Do not confuse the way supplies are used in a "normal" environment with the way they will be used in a "disaster" environment.

- **Not every team will need to purchase every thing** outlined in this manual. Depending on your circumstances, analyze each purchase to make sure it will actually be needed by your team during a disaster.

- **Buy on sale and buy in bulk** whenever possible.

- **Get out of debt** and live within your means.

- **Become simple minded and uncomplicated**. Attempt to utilize simple and uncomplicated procedures, processes and methods when purchasing, gathering, processing and storing emergency supplies.

- **Purchase supplies (whenever possible) that do <u>not</u> require electrical power (including batteries), water or fuel (including gas and propane)**. Attempt to purchase equipment that can be <u>solar</u> or <u>manually</u> operated.

- **Know your inventory and where it is stored.** Know how many supplies you have and make sure they are readily available and logistically located for easy access and transport.

- **Purchase, gather and store <u>most</u> emergency supplies at your own primary residence** and with very few exceptions, avoid sharing the cost, sharing the supplies and sharing the storage with other teams.

- **All items should be packaged and stored in the appropriate packing materials or containers**. Whenever practical, package like items together and on each container, label what is inside. Alphabetize the contents on the label for ease in identifying the items in the container.

- **Analyze risks and assess talents and skills needed to deal with emergencies**. On a continual basis, be aware of your surroundings, what is happening in the world and how any changes could affect you and your team.

- **Learn to become proficient in life-saving skills** by becoming CERT certified or proficient in CPR and other life-saving techniques. Know how to start a fire, grow a garden, bottle fruits and vegetables, bake bread, prepare a meal using a campfire or use herbs for medicinal purposes.

- **Maintain consistent order and cleanliness** by keeping the primary residence and surrounding buildings in good repair; appliances and other mechanical, electronic or electrical equipment in good condition; gas tanks full in cars being used regularly, and keep the yard clean and free of debris and trash at all times.

- **Remind yourself what is at stake** and remember that failure to prepare yourself psychologically to cope with survival leads to reactions such as depression, carelessness, loss of confidence, poor decision-making and a feeling of hopelessness. Anticipate fears and begin thinking about what would frighten you the most during a disaster. The goal is to build confidence in your ability to function despite your fears.

- **Be realistic** in planning and remember during disaster, the environment, atmosphere and surroundings will be different – plan for easy and uncomplicated tasks and actions.

- <u>**All** team members must be expected to fulfill their assigned tasks, duties and responsibilities based on the overall emergency plan</u>. Exceptions would be small children and the elderly and injuries or death at the primary residence or place of refuge in the event of evacuation. <u>Women and older children should understand they must carry their own weight and can not depend on spouses, boyfriends or other male members of the team to shoulder their responsibilities.</u>

- **Every person has different priorities, values and morals** as circumstances change based on new situations and events that occur in our lives. As we move towards higher disaster levels, we will continue to change our outlook on life, death and survival issues. <u>Our priorities will change.</u>

- **Not everyone will behave the same way before, during and after a disaster.** As individuals become more stressed and fearful of a situation, and as the level of disaster increases, pre-conceived notions about morals, values and ethics may not be so clear with others and with you. Recognize not only what <u>you</u> and <u>others</u> are – but also what <u>you</u> and <u>others</u> are not – for better or for worse.

- **Adopt a positive attitude and have faith in a spiritual force.** Learn to see the potential good in everything. Looking for the good not only boosts morale but is excellent for exercising imagination and creativity.

- **Investigate and include alternatives, layers and options** when gathering resources and supplies.

- **Emergency planning is an essential, serious and worthwhile project** but at the same time, don't take things so seriously when doing it. Consider it an exciting challenge that can be accomplished day by day and week by week until the final goal is reached - a year's worth of emergency supplies!

- Always **hope for the best but expect the worst case scenario** - that way, if things are better, you can smile, but if things are worse, you have *planned in advance* - and you can <u>still</u> smile. **WIN/WIN**

- **Conduct practice drills** semi-annually so plans and tasks are done in an efficient and expedient manner.

- **Do not overly publicize your overall emergency preparation plan** to others or divulge the location of resources and supplies.

- If teams find themselves in the middle of a disaster, they may be **the last to know what is really going on.** The rest of the world will likely be informed via public media and access to information for those in the middle of the disaster may be sparse or unavailable.

- **The main emphasis is to support the needs of its members.** Although charity, sharing and compassion are important, it may not be feasible or realistic to provide emergency supplies to others outside of your team circle during a serious and long-term disaster. Everyone is responsible to prepare themselves for these events.

- **Use a <u>regimented</u> plan *appropriate for the circumstances of your family*.** Know the difference between a *need* and a *want* but recognize that in many cases, *want* items can make the difference between a healthy mental and psychological outlook or severe depression and anxiety during a disaster.

- While making preparations for these future events – **live in the present**. Appreciate every single leaf on the trees, every drop of rain falling to the ground and every sunbeam that shines on our world. Every day, get down on your knees and thank God for what you have - *and* what you <u>don't</u> have.

- **Every single day as you perform a task - step back and ask yourself *if* and *how* this task would be performed during a disaster situation**. Analyze every single step it takes to perform the task and make sure you are prepared to do these same steps in a disaster environment.

- When considering any type of emergency supply, **drill down** (analyze) any other complement items that would be required to utilize or consume the supply, i.e. for flashlights requiring batteries, you will also need to purchase rechargeable batteries and possibly a solar-powered battery charger in order to recharge the batteries.

- Depending on the type of disaster, intensity, season, weather, time of day, or location – **government assistance to individual citizens may <u>not</u> be available**.

It is up to each citizen to recognize that **SELF SUFFICIENCY** is a key factor for survival. <u>As a minimum, citizens should plan on taking care of themselves for no less than seven days and even up to one or two years in the event of a serious and long-term disaster.</u> Government officials, workers and first responders will be assigned roles to perform during emergencies. <u>The focus will be on ensuring that overall utilities are working, fires are controlled, medical services are available and roads are passable. First priority will **not** be to support individual citizens. Depending on the severity and length of the disaster, government personnel may not reach entire towns and/or individuals for days, weeks or even months after the disaster.</u>

NORMAL VERSUS DISASTER ENVIRONMENT

One of the most important concepts when *preparing in advance* for a disaster is to (1) examine the way you perform simple everyday tasks in this <u>normal</u> environment, (2) consider whether or not these same tasks could or would *realistically* need to be done in a <u>disaster</u> environment, and then (3) analyze how these same tasks could be done in a <u>disaster</u> environment - and especially without the use of *electricity*, *fuel* and *water*. For example:

- In a *normal* environment, and if we want a loaf of bread, we simply get in our car, buy a loaf of bread at the store and bring it home - walla! We have bread! In a *disaster* environment (and without electricity, fuel and water) - the market would be closed and we will either go without bread, barter for bread or make our own bread at home. To make bread, it will be necessary to purchase whole wheat (or flour), a good manual wheat grinder (if using wheat), any additional ingredients to make the bread, and everything will have to be properly stored. You must know how to make homemade bread, and more importantly, some means of baking the bread *without* electricity and fuel will have to be considered.

- In a *normal* environment, if the carpet is dirty, we grab the *electric* vacuum cleaner and within minutes, the carpet is clean again. In a *disaster* environment, the carpet will either have to remain dirty or some type of *manual* vacuum cleaner or broom will need to be purchased <u>in advance</u> for such cleaning functions.

As part of *planning in advance* - the practice of **continually** and **regularly** examining normal everyday tasks and analyzing how these same tasks could be performed in a disaster environment without electricity, fuel or water is absolutely critical. All team members must *step back*, *think through* and *drill down* to find alternative methods and processes to simple everyday tasks that will work in a disaster environment.

WANT VERSUS NEED

When preparing emergency pantries, team members must learn the difference between a *need* and a *want*. A *need* is an item you <u>absolutely must have in order to survive or there are none or few alternatives</u>, for example, shelter, food and water. A *want* is a luxury item that would be nice to have but is not absolutely necessary for survival, for example, a washing machine and personal hygiene items including toilet paper. For many items, we consider them to be essential when in actuality – they are not absolutely necessary – just convenient. Most supplies that team members will include in emergency pantries will not be absolutely essential for survival – but will simply make surviving more bearable.

A good rule of thumb is to ask if the team could realistically survive without it. If the answer is 'no' – then consider these supplies as *need* items. If the team could survive without it and there are alternatives, consider these supplies to be *want* items. Recognize that many *want* supplies, although considered as "luxury" items, are also very important to include in pantries. For example, we certainly can get along without a toothbrush and toothpaste, and there are alternatives, but these two items provide an easy, inexpensive and convenient means for dental health.

Although toilet paper is a luxury item – consider it to be absolutely essential because we would not be willing to accept the alternatives. On the other hand, if money is an issue when making purchases (which tends to usually be the case) having cologne and makeup as a top priority would be impractical. Be cautious in your selection process and carefully analyze each item. Avoid supplies requiring electricity, batteries and/or fuel unless arrangements are made to provide for an electrical power source such as solar energy.

PANTRIES AND KITS

When *planning in advance* for a disaster, it is impossible to guess every scenario that will occur during the crisis or where you will be located when disaster strikes the area. It is necessary to prepare several different types of emergency pantries – or kits – so the team will be ready for whatever consequence may come your way during an emergency situation. There are seven <u>types</u> of emergency pantries or kits to be considered:

1. **PRIMARY RESIDENCE** – the designated primary residence will include the largest and most diverse supplies to accommodate *short*, *medium* and *long-term* disasters.

2. **WORK** – located at work and would include <u>basic</u> supplies helpful to accommodate *short- term* emergencies.

3. **AUTO** – located in the automobile and would include <u>basic</u> supplies helpful to accommodate *short-term* emergencies. Depending on space available, this kit can include basic essentials and luxury items.

4. **PLACE OF REFUGE** - a place of refuge for the team *if* the primary residence has been damaged or destroyed <u>**or**</u> the *pre-selected* primary location for team members to reside during the disaster. This emergency pantry could be a fully stocked cabin or summer home, camper, motor home, trailer house, or even hidden survival supplies at a predetermined location in the nearby mountains or desert. It could also be a public shelter in the event the team has no other options. Place of refuge could be used for both short and long-term emergencies.

5. **EVACUATION** – contains <u>basic</u> supplies for each team member to survive a minimum of *ten days*. This particular kit should be ready, accessible and easy to transport. Team members could seek shelter at the place of refuge or sites such as a church, school or approved public shelter in the vicinity.

6. **FIRST AID** – includes medical and first aid supplies and is part of the five pantries and kits listed above. Depending on the kit, first aid supplies will include basic or more advanced items.

7. **DOCUMENTATION** –includes important documentation and is part of the six pantries and kits listed above. The documentation to be added will differ depending on the specific pantry or kit.

PRIMARY RESIDENCE PANTRY

The primary residence would be the main residence or house occupied by a majority of the team members and would be the principal location where team members would gather and reside during *some* short term emergencies, *most* middle-term disasters and *all* long-term disasters. This pantry contains a majority of the goods and supplies.

WORK AND AUTO KITS

These kits could perhaps hold more and heavier items because a larger space may be available for storage. Depending on how many items are included in the auto kit, they can be stored in a duffle bag, box, plastic container or large plastic tote. A small tote or hard plastic container could be used at work to store emergency supplies. If you have a locker or other assigned area, the storage container would have to accommodate the assigned space allocation. If funds for emergency preparation are scarce, do not spend a fortune on the auto and work kits! Buy or gather only the basics! This list is not intended to infer that *all* items should be included – or are even necessary. If you already have items on the list that could be included – by all means – do so, but don't spend money to stock an auto kit on "luxury" items when the money could be spent on more important supplies.

Automotive

I recognize based on the auto list, <u>not all items will be practical for all individuals</u>. For example, if you live in a region where the temperature never drops below 90 degrees – you probably don't need to worry about having anti-freeze or a heavy-duty coat, hat, socks and gloves. On the other hand, everyone should have a heavy-duty pair of gloves for work, a hat to protect from sunburn and a light pair of clean socks. Most men won't need to bother about having hair ties – this item is reserved for persons with long hair to keep it out of their face. If you use a sleeping bag – you probably won't need blankets. You get the idea.

I would also strongly recommend the purchase of <u>solar</u> powered flashlights and lanterns and a solar/hand-crank radio – that way you don't have to store batteries. Finally, <u>plan for the worst case scenario</u> – always assume you will NOT be able to continually leave the car running and the car will sit dormant during the disaster.

Survivalists may wonder about the solar garden light. No – I wasn't suggesting you create a lovely yard around your stalled car. Place the garden light outside during the day and then bring it back into the car at night for an all-night light source. You can use the light to drink the mixture of baking soda, salt and water – a recipe to reduce shock. The hammer, twine, tarp and nails may be needed to make a tent shelter if the car can not be used.

AUTO KIT

Anti-Freeze	**Map** (surrounding areas - driving and topical)
AXE	**MATCHES**
Baby Supplies (formula, diapers, etc.)	**MEDICAL EQUIPMENT** (oxygen, walker, inhaler)
Baking Soda	**MEDICATION**
Binoculars	**Motor Oil**
BLANKETS	Nails
BOOTS	**NOTEPAD**
BUCKET * (heavy-duty plastic, folding or collapsible)	**PAPER AND PENCILS**
Cards, Games, Books	Paper Towels
Cash and Coins (for telephone calls)	**PLASTIC GROCERY BAGS** (human waste)
Cell Phone	Plastic Ties
CLOTHES (practical change of clothes)	**POCKET KNIFE**
Coat (heavy-duty and/or warm)	**RADIO** (solar/hand crank)
Comb/Brush	**RAIN GEAR**
Compass	**ROPE/CORD/TWINE** (towing, rescue, shelter etc.)
Cup (paper and/or metal)	**Safety Glasses**
DOCUMENTATION (See Documentation List)	**SALT** and/or sand
Dust Mask	Scissors
Eating Utensils – Plastic (knife, fork, spoon)	Sewing Kit
Eyeglasses and Eyeglass Repair Kit (if applicable)	**SHOES – STURDY**
Fan (hand held)	**SHOVEL** (collapsible)
Feminine Hygiene Products	**SIGNAL DEVICE** (light sticks, mirror, flasher)
Fire Starter	**SLEEPING BAG**
FIRST AID KIT AND MANUAL (See First Aid List)	**Soap**
Flag (fluorescent distress)	**SOCKS** (one warm pair PLUS one light pair)
FLASHLIGHT (solar powered)	**SOLAR GARDEN LIGHT**
Flint Striker	**SPARE TIRE**
FOOD*(non perishable)	Sunglasses
FUNNEL – 2 (one for gas and one for water)	**TARP/TARP CLIPS** (tent if car unavailable)
Fuses	**Tire Chains**
GARBAGE BAGS – heavy-duty (3)	**Tire Pressure Gauge**
Gas Can	**Tissues** (facial)
GLOVES (one warm pair PLUS one heavy-duty pair)	**TOILET** (collapsible commode, bucket*, etc.)

Hair Ties	**TOILET PAPER**
Hand Sanitizer	**TOOLS** (pliers, wrench, hammer, screwdriver)
Hand Warmer	Toothbrush / Toothpaste
HAT (warm and/or light)	Toothpicks/Floss
INSECT REPELLENT	**Tow Chain**
JACK	**TOWELETTES** (pre-moistened)
JUMPER CABLES	**WATER**
Keys (extra set for home)	**Water Purification Tablets**
LANTERN (solar powered)	Weapon/Ammo
Lip Balm	**Windshield Scraper**
Lotion	

UPPERCASE BOLD items are mandatory. **lowercase bold** items are recommended. Other items listed are discretionary. *Food should be easy open cans and require no cooking.

Work

Depending on the type of disaster, the electrical power may be out, the water may be shut off and the plumbing could be damaged or destroyed. Restaurants and other commercial markets may also be experiencing the same utility problems. Transportation could be severely impacted and you may be forced to remain at work for several days.

WORK KIT

BLANKET	Keys (extra set for home and car)
Bucket with lid (you guessed it – a toilet)	**Lantern** (solar powered)
Cards, Games and Books	**Lip Balm**
Cash and Coins	Map (detailed of local area)
Cell Phone	**MEDICATIONS**
CHANGE OF CLOTHES (casual/work)	**Plastic Bags – heavy-duty** (for the bucket)
Comb/Brush	**RADIO** (solar/hand crank)
Cup	**Sleeping Bag** (light weight)
Documentation (see **DOCUMENTATION** List)	**SOAP**
Dust Mask	**SOLAR GARDEN LIGHT** (used for light)
Eating Utensils (plastic)	**STURDY SHOES**
Eyeglasses / Contact Lens Solution	**TOILET PAPER**
FEMININE HYGIENE SUPPLIES	**Toiletries** (Miscellaneous)
First Aid Kit (small)	**Toothbrush**
FLASHLIGHT (solar/hand crank)	**Toothpaste**
FOOD* (nonperishable items)	**Towelettes** (pre-moistened)
Hand Sanitizer	**WATER** (bottled)
Jacket or Sweatshirt (cold months)	Whistle

UPPERCASE BOLD items are mandatory. **lowercase bold** items are recommended. Other items listed are discretionary. *Food should be easy open cans and require no cooking.

Why are soap, toilet paper and feminine supplies on the WORK list? During an emergency, your co-workers may not be as prepared as you but will realize they need these items. Unless you can run to the restroom faster than they can – they will get it all – you will get none. And the bucket? To be used for broken toilets and damaged sewer lines!

EVACUATION KIT

As part of evacuation from the primary residence, an emergency evacuation kit will provide each family member with food, water and other necessary items to survive during the time the team remains at a refuge location. Although planning for a three-day evacuation from the home is good, it is more likely your stay at the place of refuge may be longer, and since smart

planning includes "*worst case scenario*" - attempt to prepare fourteen-day emergency evacuation kits for each member of the team.

Include children in the planning process and attempt to make the project appear as an adventure and not a fearful challenge for younger team members. Practice *in advance* with children so they are familiar with the process and understand their role in an evacuation. Parents should recognize that although it is necessary to show young children compassion and understanding while preparing the child's kit and <u>during the evacuation process</u>, it is critical for children to follow instructions and meet their responsibilities – even if strong words and a firm hand are required. Once in a public shelter, <u>management and other refugees will demand parents manage and control their children for the benefit of all who are housed in the facility</u>. Consider what items will serve to calm and comfort the child during this time, including comfort foods, blankets, games, books and favorite toys.

When preparing evacuation kits, teams should remember disasters can occur at any time - during any season - during any temperature. For example, in winter, many areas experience sleet, hail, rain, snow and frigid temperatures so survival would depend on finding an inside shelter. For safety and security reasons, public shelters will <u>not</u> allow fire or fuel inside the buildings so cooking would have to be done outside. Kits should contain food items that do not require cooking and can be eaten right out of the package or can. Teams should attempt to prepare for all contingencies when selecting food items, but to be safe, think of the <u>worst case scenario</u> (middle of winter) and include food that can be opened using the hand and does not require heating - if space is limited, this eliminates the need to carry can openers and items used for heating and/or cooking the food.

<u>**Every team member should have their own emergency evacuation kit and with few exceptions, should be expected to carry it during the evacuation.**</u> Only very small children, the disabled, or senior citizens in poor health should be assisted in carrying their kit. The emergency kits should be stored in a location that is easy to access, easy to carry, easy to identify and easy to transport out of the primary residence and to the designated place of refuge. Every kit should be <u>clearly marked and identified as to ownership</u> and every team member should know where the kits are located, recognize their own kit, know how to carry it and be able to carry it to a place of refuge. Someone should also be assigned to carry the bag containing pet supplies, if applicable. Most public shelters will not allow pets inside the building - consider other options for your pets and/or livestock including pet shelters, friends, neighbors or other family members or restraining your pet on the grounds outside of the shelter.

Items for the emergency kit must be stored in a <u>water-proof</u> backpack, duffle bag, suitcase, box or plastic container. If the storage unit is not water-proof, make sure that it is completely covered with a <u>heavy-duty</u> garbage bag in the event it rains during the evacuation. This kit is generally the most complicated to prepare because of conflicting priorities and limited space. To be forced to choose between taking one item and leaving another is a difficult – even excruciating process. When evaluating whether or not to include any item in the kit – ask yourself this question:

> **Will this item be required to preserve and maintain my *physical, mental, emotional, psychological* and *spiritual* health for the duration of this short-term disaster and is it so important that I am ready, willing and able to carry it – along with all other items - to the new location? If the answer is no – leave it behind. If the answer is yes – include the item in the kit.**

When gathering supplies to be included in emergency evacuation kits, **THINK SMALL**. If lotion and hand sanitizer are items to be included in your kit, buy travel size bottles. Avoid any item that requires batteries! ALWAYS attempt to purchase or gather solar-powered items. To save space, remove any packaging materials from supplies, cut out any important instructions on the packaging and attach it to the item using a twist tie.

REMEMBER! Every team has different needs and not all supplies will be needed by all members. Depending on the chosen location as the place of refuge, not all items would be needed. For example, if your team plans to take refuge in the desert, the fishing pole probably isn't a required item. Not every team member must have identical items in their packs. For example, a collapsible shovel is an important item to include in an evacuation kit, but not every team member must have one in their individual pack. Only one shovel would be needed – simply designate which team member will carry it in their pack. Analyze other items to see if only one is needed or if everyone should have the item in their individual pack.

One of the biggest challenges will be to have enough water in the kit. Water is heavy – one gallon weighs eight pounds. For even a seven day supply, each member would require seventy-two pounds - which is unrealistic and even a hefty male would find it difficult to carry a three day supply of water plus other supplies in a duffle bag. Due to the "heavy" requirement of carrying water, it is wise to get some sort of device to carry and transport the kits. For example, a sturdy and light-weight garden trolley or wagon is perfect. In a local sporting goods store, I purchased a collapsible heavy-duty plastic bucket used to carry water. The cost was around ten dollars. Since a bucket is an important item to be included in an evacuation kit – check out your local sporting goods store to see if you can find such an item. Good investment!

Organize supplies into groups, for example, *toiletries, clothing, cooking, food, medical, operations* (shelter, light, fuel) and *miscellaneous* supplies. Put supplies for each group into plastic bags, plastic containers or other storage units. Type up labels for each of the groups (listing the supplies in <u>alphabetical</u> order) and attach the appropriate label to the respective container. By alphabetizing the lists, it is easy to see which supplies are in the container.

As part of your overall emergency evacuation plan from the primary residence, make sure all team members understand that regardless of the emergency compromising the primary residence – all family members should take their evacuation kit when evacuating the home – NO EXCEPTIONS.

If your team plans to evacuate to a church, government building or designated public shelter, and depending on the circumstances and the extent of the disaster, officials <u>may</u> be equipped to provide <u>some</u> amenities including a heat source, water, medication, sanitation facilities and even food. However, since no one knows exactly what will be damaged or destroyed during an emergency, it is wise to <u>assume</u> that the facility would be able to provide <u>shelter only</u> with no electricity, heat or water - you should plan to provide your own water, food, light, heat, medication and sanitation supplies. (In the event a public shelter has a water fountain available, a funnel may be necessary to transfer the water from the faucet on the fountain into your own water container).

In a public shelter, there will no doubt be many people - privacy and space will be very limited. In order to provide a means of privacy for team members, a *pop-up tent* (with no stakes) is great. It doesn't need to be expensive - just simple to set up. This tent provides limited privacy when changing clothes and/or sleeping. Another important addition to the kits is a *solar garden light*. Instead of using candles, put the solar garden light outside and let the sun do its work. At night, bring the light inside and the team has a reliable light source for the entire evening. Another important item is a *tarp* or *heavy duty (2 mil) 55 gallon trash bag* that can be placed <u>under</u> the sleeping area (whether inside or outside) and will serve to "stake out" your team's space in the building. In public shelters, fire and fuel will not be allowed. It is important to select alternative methods for heat (blankets/sleeping bag, clothes), light (solar powered lantern, flashlight, garden light) and cooking (food not requiring fuel/fire for cooking).

Special care and precautions should be taken at all times while staying in any type of public shelter - watch your children carefully and guard your supplies. On the other hand, the simple fact that there are a large number of people in the shelter would discourage thugs and gang members from challenging any one individual - there is strength in numbers.

EVACUATION KIT

Axe	**Lip Balm**
Baby Supplies (formula, diapers, etc.) - if needed	**Lotion**
Baking Soda	**Map** (surrounding areas including driving and topical)
BLANKET	**MATCHES**
Bowl (used for personal hygiene)	**MEDICAL EQUIPMENT** (inhaler)
BUCKET* (heavy-duty plastic, *folding or collapsible*)	**MEDICATION** (prescription/over-the-counter drugs)
Cards, Games and Books	Nails
Cash and Coins (for telephone calls)	**Napkins (paper)**
Cell Phone	**NOTEPAD AND PENCIL**
CLOTHES (practical change of clothes)	**PAPER TOWELS**
Clothes Line and Pins	**PLASTIC BAGS**
Coat (heavy-duty and/or warm) - if applicable	**PLASTIC TIES**
Comb/Brush	**POCKET KNIFE**
Compass	**RADIO** (solar/hand crank)
Cookware (sauce pan/skillet)- if needed	**RAIN GEAR**
Cup (paper and/or metal)	**ROPE/CORD/TWINE** (towing, rescue, shelter etc.)
DOCUMENTATION (See Documentation Pantry List)	**SALT**
Duct Tape	**Sewing Kit**

Dust Mask	**SHOES – STURDY**
Eating Utensils – plastic (knife, fork, spoon)	**SHOVEL** (collapsible)
Eyeglasses and Eyeglass Repair Kit	**SIGNAL DEVICE** (lightsticks, mirror, flasher)
Fan (hand held)	**SLEEPING BAG**
Feminine Hygiene Products	**Liquid Soap**
Fire Starter	**Socks** (one warm pair PLUS one light pair)
FIRST AID KIT AND MANUAL (See First Aid List)	**SOLAR GARDEN LIGHT** - for light at night
FLASHLIGHT (solar/hand crank)	**Sunglasses**
Flint Striker	**TARP/TARP CLIPS**
FOOD* (non perishable)	**TENT** – pop up, waterproof and easy to assemble
FUNNEL – (water)	**Tissues** (facial)
GARBAGE BAGS – 55 gallon heavy-duty (1)	**TOILET PAPER**
GARBAGE BAGS - 13 gallon heavy-duty (2-3)	**TOOLS** (pliers, hammer, screwdriver)
GARBAGE BAGS - 33 gallon heavy-duty (1)	**TOOTHBRUSH**
GLOVES (one warm pair PLUS one heavy-duty pair)	**TOOTHPASTE**
Hair Ties (pull hair back out of the face)	Toothpicks/Floss
Hand Warmer	**TOWELETTES** (pre-moistened)
Hand Sanitizer	**WATER**
HAT (warm and/or light)	**WATER PURIFICATION TABLETS**
Insect Repellent	**Weapon/Ammo**
Keys (extra set for home)	**Whistle**
Lantern (solar powered)	

UPPERCASE BOLD items are mandatory (if applicable). **lowercase bold** items are recommended (if applicable). Other items listed are discretionary. *Food should be easy open cans and require no cooking.

IMPLEMENTING A PLAN

An emergency preparation plan requires organization, knowledge of inventory control and an effective money management program. A fully stocked emergency pantry provides protection against outside forces (economic, political, natural), and when you stock up on emergency supplies, your emergency pantries become your store. To begin the project, we must first determine (1) what supplies we need for each element, (2) what supplies we already have for each element, (3) what supplies still need to be purchased for each element, (4) a budget of how much money can be expended each month on emergency supplies, (5) the priority and importance of supplies to be purchased, and finally (6) a schedule of when each supply will be purchased.

Getting Started

The goal of fully stocked emergency preparation pantries can begin with your next paycheck. The ***Emergency Preparation Worksheet*** and the ***Emergency Supplies List*** (**APPENDIX A**) provides a method to determine resources, items and supplies to be included in the various emergency pantries, inventory current supplies available at the house, wanted or needed supplies still to purchase, and estimate the overall cost of the supplies. Using the worksheet and list of supplies **and a sharpened pencil**, follow these steps:

1.   Print off at least twenty pages (front and back) of the **Emergency Preparation Worksheet** located at the back of this book and identified as **APPENDIX A**.

2.   Using the **ITEM** Column, and after reviewing the list of supplies in the table (also part of **APPENDIX A**), write down (on the **Emergency Preparation Worksheet**) all supplies and items the team wants to include in the various emergency pantries.

3.   Using the **ELEMENT** Column, identify element(s) served when purchasing each item. Some items may serve more than one element. For example, an axe could serve for cutting wood to build a shelter (**OPERATIONS**), building a fire for cooking food (**NUTRITION**) or keeping warm (**OPERATIONS**).

4.   Using the **NEED/WANT** Column, review supplies listed on the worksheet and add or delete items based on an assessment of basic and realistic needs for your circumstances. Be tough on yourself in determining what is a *need* is and what is a *want* or *luxury*. Identify all remaining items on the worksheet as a *need* (**N**) or *want* (**W**).

5.   Using the **PRIORITY** Column, use a priority rating system of 1 through 3 (1 being very important, 2 being somewhat important and 3 being not important) and rate each item on how *essential* or *vital* it is to meet the basic needs of your team, i.e., if it is very important to have toilet paper, you would rate it as a "1" priority, if it is somewhat important, you would rate it as a "2" priority, if it is not important, you would rate it as a "3" priority. If an item would definitely enhance the emergency pantry but is simply unrealistic to purchase or obtain now, you could either cross the item off the list or assign a Priority "1" rating but recognize that acquiring this item would be in the future.

6.   Using the **HOUSEHOLD MEMBERS** Column, list the total number of team members in your group.

7.   Using the **LENGTH OF TIME** Column, establish the duration (length of time) you want to have supplies in your various emergency pantries. For example, as a beginner, you may consider only gathering supplies for a 3-month period of time. On the other hand, in order to have adequate supplies for a Level 3 (long-term) disaster, consider emergency supplies to sustain team members for an entire year. ***The goal is to work towards a one year supply***.

8.   Using the **PRIMARY RESIDENCE, PLACE OF REFUGE, AUTO, EVACUATION** and **WORK** Pantry Columns, determine how many of each supply listed on the worksheet will be needed for each pantry.

9.   Using the **TOTAL ITEMS NEEDED** Column, add up the totals of each item in the worksheet shown in the pantry columns (see Number 8) to determine how many total supplies will be needed to fill <u>all</u> pantries.

10.   On a <u>separate</u> piece of paper, go throughout the entire home, garage and surrounding buildings, barns, sheds or storage facilities, and inventory all items <u>you currently own</u> that are identified on the worksheet as being necessary to fill one or more of the emergency pantries. List should include the following information: (1) description of each item, (2) how many of each item, (3) where each item will be located, i.e. auto, work, place of refuge or evacuation kit, or a specific place in the primary residence.

11.   Physically move these items to the designated locations as part of your overall emergency plan. Make sure that all items are in good working condition and you know how to use them.

12.   Using the **ON HAND** Column, and based on this inventory, identify and list how many of each item on the worksheet is on hand and available to add to the various pantries.

13.   Using the **STILL TO PURCHASE** Column, *subtract* the number in the **ON HAND** Column from the number in the **TOTAL ITEMS NEEDED** Column. This will give you the total number of each item still needed to be purchased.

14.   Using the **PACKAGING** Column, identify and list the packaging type of items on hand and still to be purchased, i.e., each, box, package or pair for each item in the worksheet.

15.   Using the **UNIT COST** Column, research a practical and realistic <u>unit cost</u> for each item that must still be purchased. Cost should be based on sound purchasing practices, i.e., buying in bulk, buying on sale, buying as a co-op etc. Consider the legitimate necessity to purchase higher quality and more costly items versus lower quality and cheaper items, i.e. a heavy-duty bucket versus a cheap crappy bucket.

16.   Using the **TOTAL COST** Column, *multiply* the number shown in the **STILL TO PURCHASE** Column with the dollar amount listed in the **UNIT COST** Column. This will give you an <u>estimate</u> of the total dollar amount still to be expended on each item in the worksheet.

As you work through the worksheet and inventory your home, you will be pleasantly surprised to learn <u>**you already have many of the items on the list!**</u> The problem is that they are scattered all over the property! Some items are stored in the attic, others are out in the garage, many are stored in the shed and still others are located in drawers, cabinets and closets throughout the house. **GET IT TOGETHER!** Make sure you know the location of all emergency items and they are stored in areas easy to remember and access during an emergency situation.

INITIATING A BUDGET

In order to initiate an Emergency Preparation Budget, borrowing money or using credit cards is generally not a sound policy. However, there are some items that because of their high price tag may require a payment plan with the bank. If borrowing money is necessary, make sure you are using sound financial management principles. Begin by doing the following:

- Identify <u>net</u> income (after taxes) including *wages, interest, dividends, alimony, child support*, etc.

- Identify <u>fixed</u> expenses that are the same amount every month (generally includes *mortgage, rent, car payment, insurance*)

- Identify <u>variable</u> expenses that vary in the amount every month (generally includes *utilities, taxes, food, charitable donations, gas, clothing, entertainment, savings, miscellaneous*, etc.)

- Can net income be increased or fixed/variable expenses decreased? - make the appropriate adjustments.

Many times, we can <u>increase</u> our income by selling items no longer needed or taking on an extra job. We can also <u>decrease</u> our fixed and variable expenses in the same manner. For example, analyze your insurance policies to see if premiums can be reduced, practice conservative use of all utilities, be more prudent in driving the car, purchase clothing needs (not wants) at second hand stores, have shoes repaired instead of buying a new pair, attend movies during non-peak times and buy cheaper cuts of meat.

Another very abrupt and immediate method to cut expenses is to simply *cease* or drastically *reduce* the practice of what may be considered as luxuries and not necessities. For example:

- Agree gift giving will include items to be added to emergency preparation pantries
- Agree with family and friends to stop or modify gift giving during special occasions
- Cancel all unnecessary memberships to the spa and health clubs
- Cancel all unnecessary subscriptions to magazines, books, and other services
- Discontinue cable or satellite television
- Discontinue Internet - use free Internet available at local libraries and schools
- Do your own housekeeping
- Do your own nails and hair (including cutting your own hair)
- Drink water (free) instead of soft drinks when at a restaurant or fast food outlet
- Eliminate or reduce all school activities requiring large cash outputs
- If working outside of the home, brown-bag your lunch instead of eating out
- Make a commitment to stop smoking and drinking alcohol, soda or caffeinated drinks
- Mow your own lawn every other week instead of every week
- Run the air conditioner a little higher and the furnace a little lower
- Select either a landline or a cell phone (if possible) but not both
- Sell cars, trailers, boats, ATV's, and snowmobiles that are not needed or being used
- Stay out of the grocery and department stores unless absolutely necessary
- Stop buying stupid stuff you don't actually need
- Stop buying unnecessary clothes
- Stop or reduce going out to dinner at restaurants or fast-food establishments
- Stop or reduce going out to the movies
- Stop or reduce luxury massage treatments
- Stop taking laundry to the dry cleaners and do your own laundry at home
- Use coupons whenever possible to buy *needed* items
- Use the bus system (if possible) instead of driving the car
- Wash your own vehicles
- When grocery shopping, try to avoid processed or packaged foods, make a list and stick to it

By <u>avoiding</u> certain types of expenses, you can also manage money more effectively. For example, follow driving laws and avoid getting tickets, pay bills on time to avoid late fees, maintain the minimum amount in checking and saving accounts to avoid monthly service charges, refrain from using ATM machines charging fees, and whenever possible, repair broken items instead of buying a new one, practice preventive maintenance on yourself, home, car and other appliances to avoid more costly expenses down the road. Another possibility is to reduce or forego expensive family vacations and use the money for emergency supplies instead - remember - <u>emergency preparation requires recreational and monetary sacrifices</u>.

It is also important for <u>teenagers</u> to contribute towards emergency pantries. If teenagers are working and making wages, consider approaching them about contributing towards the dollar amount designated for emergency preparation. After all - they will certainly be using the supplies. It will also teach teens the law of budgeting, the law of contribution, the law of sacrifice and the importance of working together as a team to meet this very important objective. And when it comes time to use the supplies, they will be much less likely to waste since their hard earned dollars also contributed to purchasing the items.

Each team should determine what is *realistic* and *acceptable* for them in finding additional funds from our already stretched dollars to begin purchasing items for emergency pantries. Once the team has determined the workable amount of money from everyone's (including teenagers) paycheck to be used for emergency supplies, review the items on the worksheet and **TOGETHER** decide which supplies will be purchased on each payday. The family may decide to purchase less expensive items so that it can be marked off as "complete" in a sooner time period. On the other hand, you may decide to focus only on Priority 1 items or items that provide uses over multiple elements, i.e., matches or buckets.

Try to purchase items from all the elements (**Operation, Medication** etc.) to guarantee you are meeting *basic* requirements and have several *alternatives* or *layers* available for each element. Remember, if teenagers are going to financially contribute to the emergency pantries, include them in the priority and buying decisions and shopping excursions. Whatever approach you take in stocking emergency pantries, <u>continue to keep accurate records of the inventory</u>. This practice will eliminate over-buying some items and not buying adequate supplies of other items. Remember to buy in bulk, pay attention to sales and consider discount drug stores, garage sales, charitable outlets, wholesale outlets, membership clubs, mass merchandisers, dollar stores or Internet sites.

THE GOOD, THE BAD AND THE UGLY

As the team gathers supplies for emergency pantries, some items **MUST** be high-quality supplies while others may not need to be at the high end of the scale. Sometimes, a high quality item can be purchased at second hand stores, garage sales and charity outlets for less money than if purchasing a new item. On many items, it really doesn't matter if you purchase a high scale or high quality item. For example, if you buy a notebook for $100.00 and another one for $2.00 – both will serve the purpose.

It is not always the price paid for the item – what matters is <u>what</u> you get for your money. The reality of disaster survival focuses on the fact there would be some supplies used over and over again and for very important functions. These specific supplies **MUST STAND UP TO CONTINUAL USE, ABUSE AND OPERATION**. When creating an overall budget for emergency supplies, the table below will serve as a <u>guideline</u> on items that should be good-quality and/or heavy-duty merchandise.

Aluminum Foil	Can Opener (Manual)	Flashlight (at least one)	Hatchet	Pliers	Shoes	Step Ladder
Axe	Chain Saw	Garbage Bags	Hoe	Radio (hand crank)	Shovel	Tarps
Blankets/Quilts	Clothes Line Rope	Generator (Solar Power)	Knife	Rake	Sleeping Bag	Thermals
Boots	Clothes Wringer	Gloves	Knife Sharpening Tool	Ropes	Socks	Trash Can
Broom	Dust Masks	Grain Mill	Laundry Tub	Saws	Solar Powered Battery Charger	Wheel Barrow
Bucket	Fishing Pole/Line	Hammer	Plastic Sheeting	Screwdrivers	Stapler	Wrench

HOME HAZARDS

An important step in emergency preparation is to inspect the home and surroundings for possible hazards and take action to lessen those hazards <u>before</u> the emergency. The following is a checklist to help identify and correct home hazards:

Rooms in the Home

Look for the following hazards in each room:

- Windows and other glass that may shatter
- Unanchored bookcases, cabinets, refrigerators, water heaters and other furniture that may topple
- Heating units, fireplaces, chimneys and stoves that could move or fall
- Areas that could be blocked by falling debris
- Hanging pictures and wall decorations that could topple from the wall

Securing Appliances

Secure large appliances with flexible cable, braided wire or metal strapping and install flexible gas and water connections on all gas appliances. This will significantly reduce the chances of having a major fire after an emergency. Brace and support air conditioners and particularly those on rooftops.

The typical water heater weighs 450 pounds when full of water. In an emergency, the floor tends to move out from under the heater, often causing it to topple. The movement can also break the gas, electric and water line connectors, posing fire or electric shock hazards, and can shatter the glass lining within the water heater.

Here are two suggestions on how to secure a water heater:

(1)   Wrap at least a ½ inch wide metal strap around the top of the water heater and attach it to wall studs with three-inch lag screws. Attach another strap about 2/3 of the way down from the top of the water heater.

(2)   Wrap steel plumber's tape around the entire water heater at least twice. Then secure the tape to two different wall studs with three-inch lag screws.

Securing Items in the Bathroom

Replace glass bottles from the medicine cabinet and around the bathtubs with plastic containers.

Hanging and Overhead Items

Inspect and anchor overhead light fixtures and chandeliers, heavy mirrors and pictures hanging above beds, chairs and other places where you sit or sleep. Analyze if the full swing of hanging lamps or plants will strike a window and if so, move them. Secure hanging objects by closing the opening of the hook and replace heavy ceramic or glass hanging planters with light-weight plastic or wicker baskets.

Shelves, Cabinets, and Furniture

Secure top-heavy and free-standing furniture such as bookcases and china cabinets. Use "L" brackets, corner brackets, or aluminum molding to attach tall or top-heavy furniture to the wall, eyebolts to secure items located a short distance from the wall, and attach a wooden or metal guardrail on open shelves to keep items from sliding or falling off. Fishing line can also be used as a less-visible means to secure an item. Place heavy or large objects on lower shelves. Secure cabinet doors by installing sliding bolts or childproof latches.

Hazardous Materials

Identify poisons, solvents or toxic materials in breakable containers and move these containers to a safe, well-ventilated storage area. Keep away from water storage and out of reach of children, pets, wildlife and livestock.

Foundation

Check to see if the house or garage is securely fastened to the foundation. If the house was built before 1950, it probably does not have bolts securing the wood structure to the concrete foundation. If this is the case, use a hammer drill and carbide bit and drill a hole through the sill plate into the foundation. Holes should be approximately six feet apart. Drop a ½ x 7 inch expansion bolt into each hole and tighten the nut and washer.

Beams, Posts, Joists, and Plates

Strengthen the areas of connection between beams, posts, joists, and plates using "T" and "L" straps, mending plates, joist hangers, twin post caps, and nails and lag screws. Pay particular attention to exposed framing in garages, basements, porches and patio covers.

Roof and Chimney

Check the chimney or roof for loose tiles and bricks and repair as needed. Reinforce the ceiling surrounding the chimney with ¾ inch plywood nailed to ceiling joists. On a regular basis, make sure the chimney is cleaned to remove smoke buildup from forming on the inside walls of the chimney.

SHUTTING OFF UTILITIES

Teach **all** adult team members *where*, *when* and *how* to shut off utilities – **this includes all female adults and young adults old enough to understand the instructions and perform the task.** The natural gas should be turned off at the *meter only* if the in-house lines are damaged or if instructed to do so by a firefighter, police or gas company representative. If natural gas is turned off at the main meter into the house, a professional will be required to turn it back on. If you use propane as a fuel source – it can be turned on and off at the meter on top of the tank. Know where the main water meter and electrical box are located and how to turn these utilities on and off at the source.

PERSONS WITH DISABILITIES

For persons with disabilities or individuals on the team who require special assistance during a disaster, *plan in advance* to identify and solve issues involving these team members.

CHILDREN

A child may be afraid of injury, death or recurrence during and after an emergency. They may fear being separated from family or being left alone. A child will be less likely to experience prolonged fear or anxiety if they know what to expect and talking with children openly and *in advance* will help overcome fear or misgivings.

Although it is important to deal with the child's needs in a compassionate and caring environment, it is also important to understand during an actual disaster, the adult should take whatever steps are necessary to ensure the physical safety of the child. Once the child is safe and secure, the mental and psychological aspects can be addressed. As part of the emergency pantry, make sure toys, games and other important items are readily available for the children.

If children of team members are in school, *plan in advance* and discuss the emergency preparation plan outlined by the school with school administrators. Make sure **EVERYONE** understands what will take place during a disaster – including the school officials, parents and children.

EVACUATION PLANS

During some disasters, team members may need to evacuate a damaged area – *including the primary residence.* When creating, practicing and implementing evacuation plans, it is important to communicate with all team members *before, during* and *after* a disaster. The team will be better prepared to respond appropriately and efficiently to signs of danger or to directions by civil authorities. Take time with the team members to communicate various scenarios of evacuation plans and places of refuge.

Sketch a floor plan of the primary residence and walk through each room and discuss evacuation details. Plan an alternate approach to exit from each room or area. If special equipment is needed such as a rope ladder - buy it, install it

<u>and mark where it is located</u>. On the floor plan, mark where emergency food, water, first aid kits, evacuation kits and fire extinguishers are located and mark where the utility switches, valves or meters are located so they can be turned off. If there is time, <u>and only if there is time</u>, and if you have not received contrary instructions from local authorities, secure the primary residence *before* you evacuate the home:

- Turn off all natural gas or propane *appliances*, furnace and air conditioner
- Turn off <u>propane</u> tanks
- Disconnect all electrical appliances including television, computer and hot water heater
- Lock all windows and doors and activate the house alarm
- Move vehicles to garage, carport, shed or driveway
- Store any perishables
- Make arrangements for pets and livestock and display the appropriate signs
- Prepare windows for breakage, i.e., plywood or plastic over the glass window or door

EVACUATION LOCATIONS

During an emergency, <u>our preference will be to remain in our homes - or the primary residence for the duration of the disaster</u>. However, our home and/or primary residence may be damaged or destroyed - and the team would need to find alternative meeting places and/or shelter sites. As part of *planning in advance*, teams should designate **three** alternate meeting places and/or shelter sites as follows:

<u>Priority One Location</u>

Designate a **PRIORITY ONE** area <u>*outside*</u> of the primary residence where all team members can *meet* if the structure is damaged <u>*but the surrounding area is still safe*</u>. Make sure the meeting place is <u>not</u> directly adjacent to the home. Avoid an area close to power lines, gas lines or propane tanks. This area could be in an open field, by the mail box, or by a tree near the home.

On the evacuation plan, indicate the location of the **PRIORITY ONE** emergency outdoor *meeting place* for the team. Once all family members have reached the designated location, arrangements can then be made to move to an alternate shelter site or a place of refuge. **Make arrangements for pets and livestock!**

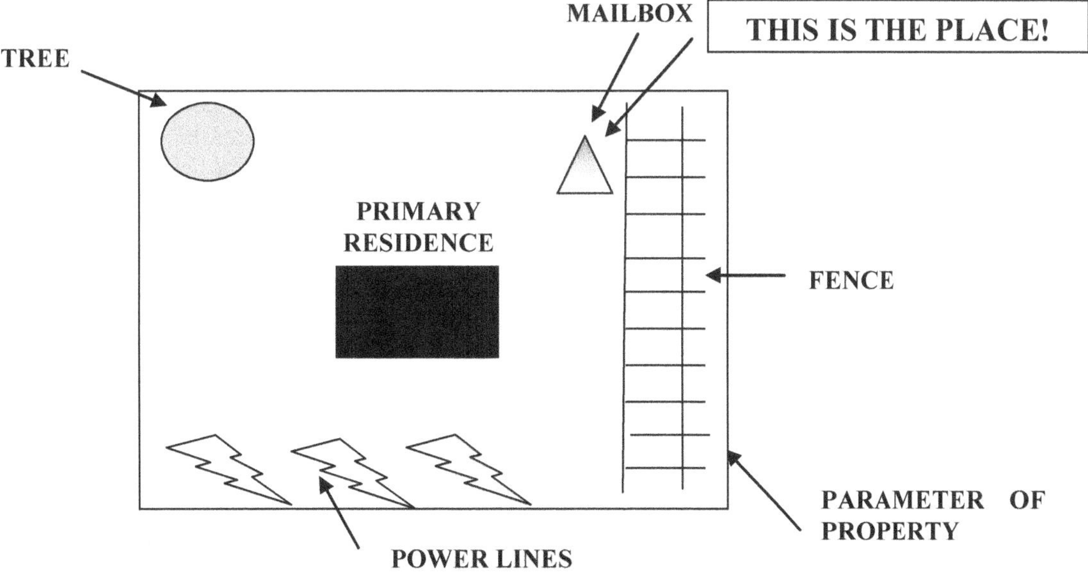

<u>Priority Two Location</u>

Evaluate the vicinity of the primary residence and select a **PRIORITY TWO** area <u>outside of the primary residence parameter</u> where everyone will *meet* <u>if</u> the **PRIORITY ONE** area is compromised <u>or</u> when team members meet at the **PRIORITY ONE** location and it is now time to move to an alternate shelter site or place of refuge. Make sure the area is away from power lines, gas lines or propane tanks. This area could be the home of a friend, relative or neighbor, park, church, soccer field or school.

The **PRIORITY TWO** location should be no more than one or two miles from the primary residence. As part of the overall evacuation plan, since team members may be at the primary residence during this emergency, make sure all members are physically and mentally capable of reaching the **PRIORITY TWO** area <u>on foot</u>. If not, arrangements will need to be made to ensure disabled members are able to join the rest of the team at the designated location. **Make arrangements for pets and livestock!**

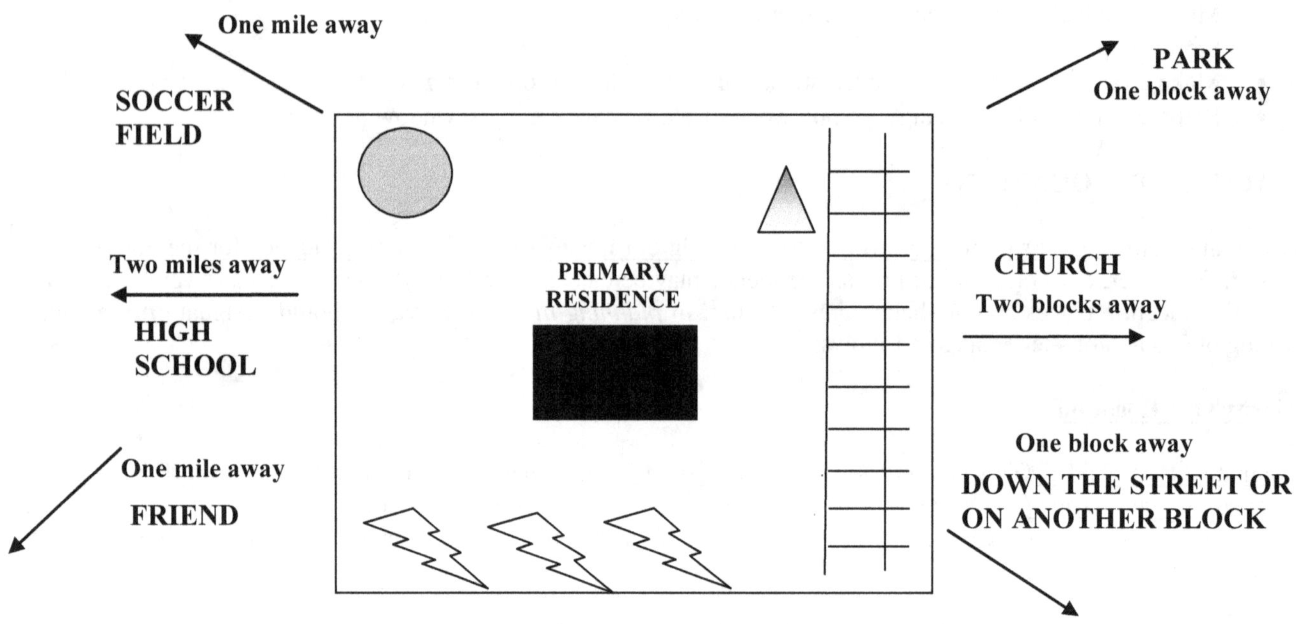

<u>**Priority Three Location**</u>

It is likely when an emergency occurs that all team members will be in different places! Both parents could be at work in the same city, in another town or even in another state. The children could be at different schools throughout the area. Teenagers could be with friends at the movies, at a soccer game, on a picnic in the canyon or shopping at the mall. The distance between team members and the primary residence could be many miles.

The situation could present an unrealistic expectation for everyone to travel to the primary residence. All roads could be impassable, power lines could be down, or a large chemical explosion could make the area restricted between team members and the primary residence. Under these circumstances, the communication systems (including cell phones and land lines) could be down and it may be virtually impossible to locate every member of the team. The primary residence could also be damaged or destroyed.

<u>As a general rule</u>, if a serious emergency happens that <u>places the **THREAT** between the primary residence and the team members or if it would be obvious the primary residence is damaged or destroyed</u> – attempt to select a meeting place <u>in the middle</u> where all team members have approximately the same amount of distance (and chance of success) to travel in order to reach the <u>meeting</u> place destination. For example, if a parent is working, the kids are in school and one of the teenagers is finally cleaning his filthy dirty room while at home – perhaps a good "middle-of-the-road" <u>meeting</u> place could be the *<u>closest</u> public building* to the primary residence. Once all team members are assembled, the team could then move to a more permanent place of refuge (public shelter or a privately owned location such as a cabin, motor home, trailer, camper or the home of a friend or relative).

If the location of the **PRIORITY THREE** destination is a government building, church, school building or building approved as a reception center or public shelter, there should be a registration system in place and *all team members should register as soon as they arrive at the building*. By doing so, this will assist agencies responsible for verifying missing or injured citizens and determine fatalities. It could also provide the team with information concerning the individual status of their team members.

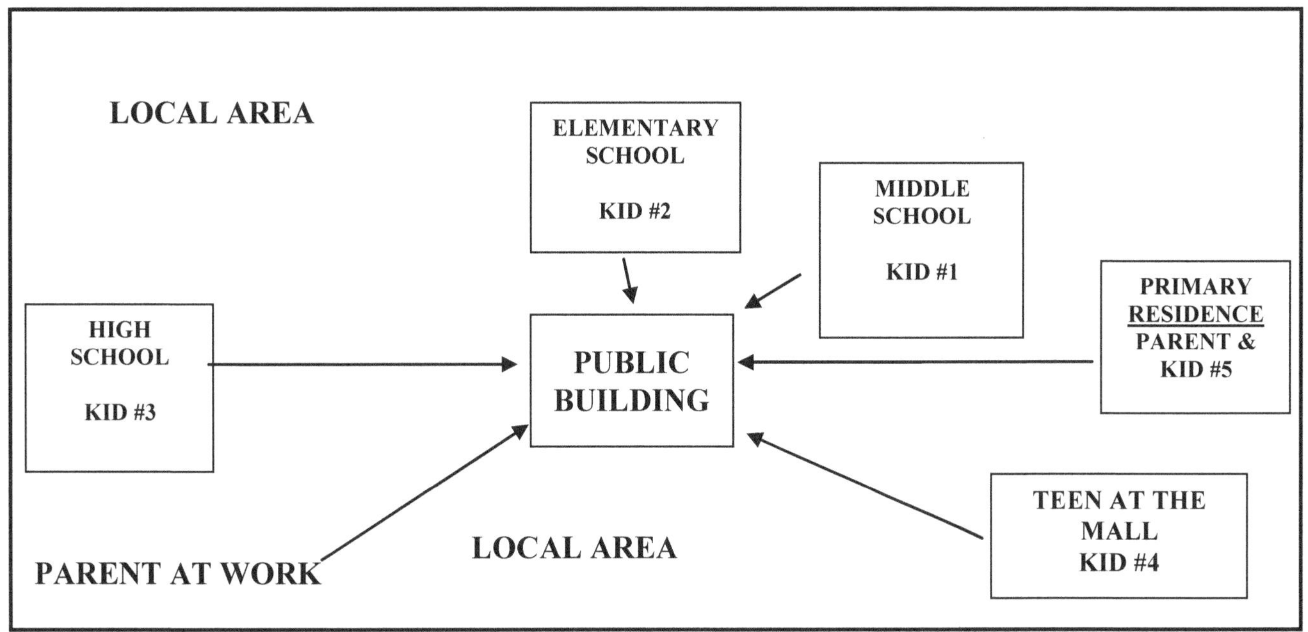

For all three priorities, all team members, including children, must understand the plan, scenarios of possible emergencies, what to do, when to go, where to go, and what is expected of them. **COMMUNICATE EFFECTIVELY** that once they are at the designated meeting place – they should stay there until **ALL MEMBERS** are accounted for – even if it is cold, wet or hot weather. Once all members arrive at the meeting place, other arrangements can be made for a more permanent, safe and secure shelter.

EVACUATION LINES

If residents are ordered by authorities to leave an evacuation perimeter, NO ONE will be allowed to cross the line and return to the evacuation area. If the primary residence or place of refuge is inside this evacuation perimeter, you would not be allowed to return to the residence. This type of evacuation is considered as a police or fire mandated evacuation and they have ultimate authority to force you out of your residence and out of the evacuation perimeter. You would not be able to assist any other team members, friends or neighbors inside the perimeter nor would you be allowed to retrieve any personal belongings, pets, or turn off utilities you may have forgotten in a panic to leave the area. If you do not know where all team members are at the time – you would still be required to leave the area. In these cases, it will be law enforcement, National Guard, military and fire fighters who will be responsible for ensuring everyone is out of the evacuation area.

PETS AND LIVESTOCK

When preparing pets for the possibility of a disaster, remember the basics for survival – *shelter*, *water* and *food*. Consider two kits: (1) everything your pets will need at the primary residence and (2) a light-weight smaller version if you and your pets are required to seek refuge. Be sure to review the kits regularly to guarantee the contents are fresh.

- **Collar/Tag/Harness/Leash**. The pet should wear a collar with a rabies tag and identification at all times. Include a backup leash, collar and identification tag in the pet's emergency kit. Place copies of the pet's registration information, adoption papers, vaccination and medical records in a clean plastic bag or waterproof container and add them to the kit. Consider permanent identification (microchipping or recovery database).

- **Crate/Pet Carrier**. To evacuate in an emergency situation, the ability to do so will be aided by having a sturdy, safe, comfortable crate or carrier ready for transporting your pet. The carrier should be large enough for your pet to stand, turn around and lie down.

- **First Aid**. Talk with the veterinarian about what is most appropriate for the pet's emergency medical needs. Most kits include cotton bandages, rolls, bandage tape, scissors, antibiotic ointment, flea and tick prevention, latex gloves, alcohol, eye drops and saline solution. Include a pet first aid book.

- **Food**. Keep 7-10 days of dry food in an airtight and waterproof container for each pet. Don't forget to pack the bowl.

- **Photo**. If you become separated from your pet during an emergency, a photo of you and your pet together would help to document ownership and allow others to assist in identifying your pet. Include detailed information about species, breed, age, sex, color and distinguishing characteristics.

- **Sanitation**. Include pet litter and litter box (if appropriate), newspapers, paper towels, plastic trash bags and household chlorine bleach to provide for sanitation needs. You can use bleach as a disinfectant (dilute nine parts water to one part bleach). Do not use scented or color safe bleaches or bleach with added cleaners.

- **Toys**. Include favorite toys, treats or bedding which will help to reduce stress for your pet.

- **Water**. Store at least 7-10 days of water specifically for each pet. Don't forget to pack the bowl.

In the event of evacuation from the primary residence and depending on the circumstances, make sure *advanced planning* is taken with regards to livestock. In some cases, it may be wise to contain and shelter any livestock. In other instances, it may be necessary to release livestock to give them a chance for survival.

Plan

Be prepared to assess the situation. Plan how you will assemble your pets and determine the place of refuge. If you must evacuate, take your pets with you if practical to do so. If you go to a public shelter, keep in mind pets may not be allowed inside. Secure appropriate lodging *in advance* depending on the number and type of pets in your care.

Options may include a motel that allows pets or a boarding facility such as a kennel or veterinary hospital near an evacuation facility or pre-determined meeting place. Find out <u>before</u> an emergency happens if any of these facilities in your area might be good options. Plan with neighbors, friends or relatives to care for or evacuate pets if you are unable to do so. Show them the location of pet emergency supplies. Designate specific locations to retrieve pets after the emergency.

Make a list of contacts, addresses and phone numbers of area animal control agencies including the Humane Society or ASPCA and emergency veterinary hospitals. Keep one copy of these phone numbers with you and one in your pet's emergency supply kit. Purchase or make "**PET ALERT**" stickers and place them near all doors and/or windows *in advance* including information on the number and types of pets in the home to alert firefighters and rescue workers. Consider putting a phone number where you could be reached on the sticker.

Before evacuating and if time permits, write the words "**EVACUATED WITH PETS**" across the stickers if you are able to actually evacuate with your pets and then place the stickers on doors and/or windows. These stickers can be purchased on-line through the ASPCA and other organizations. You may decide to make your own decal. I would also recommend the background of the sticker is <u>**red**</u> so responders can see it and laminate stickers due to fading over time.

The level and consequences will determine what to do with regards to your pets and livestock.

- Whether to take them with you
- Whether to leave them enclosed at the primary residence, either in the house or pet enclosure
- Whether to release them outside
- Whether to leave them with friends, neighbors or other facilities able to facilitate pets and livestock

There are so many factors to consider including:

- Probable length of time you will be away from the primary residence or home
- Whether others in the immediate vicinity will also be required to leave the area
- Whether emergency and rescue workers will be able to reach the area within a reasonable amount of time
- Type of dangers outside the home or shelter where pets are located, i.e., downed power lines
- Weather conditions and temperatures acceptable for survival

Livestock

In most cases, livestock can remain at the primary location unless there is probable danger of flooding or an emergency situation that would cause harm or death to the animals if they remain in place. Depending on the level of disaster, emergency and rescue workers as well as humane societies and other animal groups would attempt to access the damaged areas as quickly as possible to provide assistance.

As a responsible owner, you should do whatever is possible to provide rescue for your livestock. If circumstances merit the release of livestock in order to provide them with a chance of survival – then do so. If possible, attach some type of collar or tag to your animals with the name of the owner, address and phone number so after the crisis, livestock can be identified and returned home. In order to assist rescue workers, be sure to attach a "**LIVESTOCK INSIDE**" sticker to barn doors, sheds or other enclosures *prepared in advance* to alert them livestock are in need of assistance.

PRACTICE DRILLS

By *planning in advance* and practicing what to do in an emergency, teams can learn to react automatically. During many types of disasters, collapsing building materials and heavy falling objects such as bookcases, cabinets, and heating units cause most deaths and injuries. Learn the "safe" and "unsafe" spots in each room of the home. The "safe" spots are under tables, desks and beds. If children are in the home, get the entire family to practice going to the "safe" locations. During a drill, get under a sturdy table, desk or bed and if none are available, cover your face and head with your arms or brace yourself in an inside corner of the house or building.

The "unsafe" areas are inside a doorway, by windows and mirrors, underneath or adjacent to heavy objects standing on the floors or hanging on the walls or ceilings. Participating in an emergency drill can help children understand what to do in case you are not with them.

Practice drills should be conducted at least twice a year. Another good idea is to include using the car as part of the evacuation plan. Although a car may not be available – if it is – it provides a valuable means to transport members and supplies during an evacuation. Although the practice drills do not need to actually include the evacuation of pets and livestock, make sure each team member "walks through the steps and pretends to do the motions" of handling indoor pets and outdoor pets and livestock.

STORAGE

By properly organizing emergency supplies in containers, there will be less stress during an emergency – the supplies will be easy to locate and readily available. During an emergency is NOT THE TIME TO BE DISORGANIZED!

The best place to store most emergency supplies is in a *dark*, *cool* and *dry* environment. These storage areas should be located in areas where there is minimal chance of water, sun, fire, heat, rodent or insect damage and theft. One of the best places to store emergency supplies is in a basement <u>above the floor</u> – on pallets or shelves and away from windows and walls. *Never* store items on a concrete floor – especially food or items stored in metal or plastic cans – the lime from the concrete can leach into the containers.

The garage can be used as a storage location – <u>but not for food items, including dehydrated or freeze-dried food</u>. The extreme heat and cold environment and the possibility of rodent and insect damage and theft are reasons why a garage may not be a good choice. If no other areas are available, items such as tools, equipment and non-perishable supplies can be stored in the garage area.

When storing emergency supplies, <u>items must be stored in the right type of containers</u>. By storing supplies properly, it eliminates waste, destruction or contamination of expensive supplies. When storing *food* items, the containers must be approved for <u>food</u> storage. For example, hard plastic paint buckets purchased in hardware stores are <u>not</u> acceptable for storing food items – they contain harmful chemicals that can leach into the food.

There are many places where good storage containers can be purchased or gathered other than grocery or department stores. If buying new containers, purchase them when on sale. Check out local garage sales - you would be surprised how many people are "throwing away" perfect storage containers for your emergency supplies. Another good source is local charitable organizations or dollar stores who sell items at reduced prices or local restaurants and fast-food outlets. Make arrangements with the owner or manager to get these containers for your emergency supplies. Possible storage containers include totes or containers, barrels, buckets, boxes, sacks or bags just to name a few choices. For example, when storing medical supplies, you could place bandages, lotions, creams, medications, and tools (tweezers, thermometer, tongue blades etc.) in separate small containers or baggies. On the front of <u>any</u> storage container, place a label listing the contents.

<u>Smaller Containers Holding Items</u>

- Use only containers with tight fitting lids or strong zippers
- Label all containers listing the content type and amount i.e. Razors (2)
- List contents in <u>alphabetical</u> order (to determine quickly if item is inside container)
- Place clear plastic tape over the label (so it won't be torn or come off)
- Use containers that are sturdy but light i.e. hard plastic, metal, leather, denim
- Avoid glass containers and flimsy plastic bags
- Attempt to store "like" items in the same container, i.e. tools, lotions, creams, bandages, medications

When purchasing new items:

- Remove all packaging
- Examine item to ensure you have all parts
- Make sure the item is operational
- Know how to use the item

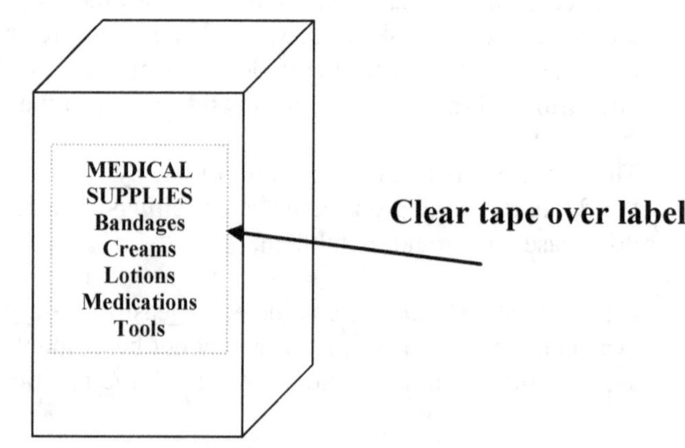

CHAPTER TWO

ADMINISTRATION

Government DOES play an important part in the control and management of its citizens. Unless you actually believe (and can justify) absolute anarchy (chaos) is the best system to "govern" a city, state or nation, *reasonable citizens* understand the need for policies, rules and regulations that everyone must follow in order to maintain some sense of order, services and protection for the general population. In fairness to the government, there are some services provided at the federal, state and local level that are <u>mandatory</u> in order to maintain an organized, secure and civil society.

In many cases, it is only a government entity that can afford to finance, operate and maintain the service for the general population. Because of the complexity of the service or the wide-range affect it has on all or most citizens, it is generally more effective to have a government entity manage these services to guarantee fairness and access for <u>all</u> citizens.

For example:

- Courts
- Environmental Quality
- First Responders
- Health Services
- Homeland Security
- Internal Revenue
- Law Enforcement
- Libraries
- Medical Services
- Military
- Parks
- Post Office
- Prisons, Jails, Detention Centers
- Transportation (roads, bridges, seaports)
- Universities and Schools
- Utilities
- Welfare

Imagine federal, state and local governments have collapsed. A collapse of government would mean serious ramifications throughout the country including:

- All prisoners in the prisons, jails and other detention centers would be released

- There would be no police or law enforcement to maintain law and order in the streets

- There would be no courts to uphold the law

- Mentally ill citizens roaming the streets without any means of assistance, control, oversight or protection

- No IRS and state and local tax commissions so all government services would be discontinued due to lack of funding

- There would be no services of the postal service

- There would be no schools or universities - so much for reading, learning and education

- There would be no libraries

- The enemy countries and terrorist groups around the world who have waited for a chance to take a punch at the United States would be pleased to learn military personnel are now out of a job

- There would be no personnel assigned to Homeland Security, the Federal Bureau of Investigation (FBI), the Central Intelligence Agency (CIA), or other agencies charged with protecting the country and citizens

- There is no more enforcement of <u>sanitation</u> regulations on meat, fruits and vegetables and other food items purchased in the supermarket

- There is no more enforcement of <u>safety</u> regulations for computers, electronics, cars, airplanes, televisions and other commodities purchased in the stores

- There is no more regulation on drug companies

- There is no funding or enforcement to preserve the parks and natural resources in the land

- There is no more driving rules on the roads or enforcement of the laws

- There is no funding for new transportation construction or to maintain roads and other modes of transportation

- There is no funding for new infrastructure or to maintain current infrastructure

- There is no oversight on banks or financial institutions

- There are no building new roads or maintenance on existing roads

- There is no Internet, cell phones or land line phones

- There is no utilities - electricity, water and gas

- There are no fuel supplies for vehicles, machinery etc.

- There is no oversight on guns and ammunition

- There are no social services for those who are <u>legitimately</u> in need of assistance

PHASES OF COLLAPSE

It is difficult to know what circumstances would actually cause a collapse of the government. It could be an event that takes place in a second such as a comet hitting the earth or even a solar flare or terrorist attack that wipes out the electrical grid around the world. And of course, it could also be the collapse of the financial institutions and markets.

The collapse could occur over a short period of time due to nuclear war, electro-magnetic pulse (EMP), terrorist attacks, chemical and biological warfare, financial meltdown, rioting and dissention. It could be an overwhelming and destructive series of natural disasters including earthquakes, tsunamis, fire, drought and flooding that wipes out the infrastructure of the country.

As one observes the present state of the union, a majority of citizens recognize the country and the government are in a crises mode. There are countless theories that account for the ultimate collapse of a government, but I have attempted to combine some of these ideas into a summary of phases that could perhaps accelerate the ultimate collapse of a government brought about by the citizens themselves, including:

Phase 1: <u>Moral Collapse</u>. Citizens begin not to trust *individuals*. Neighbors, business executives, religious leaders, law enforcement, politicians, military, and other government employees are no longer considered to be trustworthy. Crime and immorality among the population and corruption in government continues to increase. There is high unemployment, neighborhoods and cities become dangerous, and riots, demonstrations and suicides dramatically increase in the land.

Phase 2: <u>Money Collapse</u>. Citizens begin not to trust *banks and financial institutions*. Risk can no longer be assessed and financial assets may not be guaranteed. The value of homes decreases and many people are losing their homes. The price of many goods and commodities dramatically increases and savings, retirements and pensions may be wiped out and it is difficult to access capital. Citizens are beginning to remove their money from financial institutions and hoard their money at home. There is social unrest throughout the general population.

Phase 3: <u>Commercial Collapse</u>. Citizens begin not to trust *companies*. Money may be devalued and/or credit becomes scarce. Small, medium and large businesses begin to close their doors. Supermarkets post guards at their doors and food riots spread across the nation. Citizens begin to hoard and trade basic commodities and there may be widespread shortages of survival necessities. Some people begin to search for food, water, medicine and other needed supplies on the streets and in neighborhoods.

Phase 4: <u>Political Collapse</u>. Citizens begin not to trust *governments*. Official attempts to effectively manage the affairs of the country and provide survival necessities are ineffective, and corrupt and incompetent politicians lose legitimacy and relevance. Electricity and fuel sources are in short supply or non-existent for the general population. Contracts and land ownership become invalid. Starving people want your food, water, medical supplies and weapons. There is increased rioting and demonstrations in the streets. Constitution? Hanging by a thread.

Phase 5: <u>Community Collapse</u>. Citizens begin not to trust *authorities*. Institutions loose all or most of their resources and are unable to serve the needs of the population. There is a staggering increase in diseases and dead bodies. Hospitals, clinics and schools cease to function. Law enforcement loses legitimacy, can no longer maintain order within the communities and cities and is openly challenged by the citizenry – their gun against your gun. Police and firefighters are no longer obligated to protect citizens, belongings or homes. Urban cities become centers of increased crime and starvation.

Phase 6: <u>Military Collapse</u>. Citizens begin not to trust the *military*. The military forces who have been trained to protect the country now find themselves in a quandary. The fine line between protecting the citizens in the country and protecting the government (politicians) may become blurred as the military may perceive team members now as the *enemy* of the country or as *targets* competing for the same resources as themselves. And remember – they have guns and know how to use them. Depending on the circumstances <u>and whether citizens would permit the action</u>, martial law could be declared which is imposed by military forces when civil authority has broken down. During martial law, citizens could expect curfews, rationing, closed borders, confiscation of weapons and supplies, travel permits, sealed cities and even concentration camps.

Phase 7: <u>Civilization Collapse</u>. Citizens begin to lose *faith* - in each other, in religion and in God. Death is everywhere and those who still survive become scavengers and bandits to maintain life. Urban regions become death zones. Nothing is more dangerous than desperate human beings who are starving, thirty, cold, wet and homeless.

At first, there is chaos, anarchy and mayhem. However, at some point in time, good citizens will combine forces to eliminate those who would attempt to harm or steal property and supplies from others and will create strong communities to protect their members, property and emergency supplies.

During short-term disasters including **LEVEL ONE** and **LEVEL TWO** emergencies, the government will more than likely be available to assist the citizens. However, as a serious and extended **LEVEL THREE** disaster approaches the one year mark, any remaining government agencies may tell you that following their instructions will guarantee your survival. But *your* independent survival may not support *their* survival. For some reason, people think the government is obligated to take care of them after a disaster. Team members should be responsible for their <u>own</u> welfare. **<u>Do not count on the government to save you.</u>**

RECOGNIZING THE SIGNS

Depending on the circumstances, the disaster could happen all at once or over a period of time. It is possible for several disaster types to happen at the same time as was the case in March of 2011 when Japan experienced an earthquake, tsunami and nuclear meltdown – all within a few days.

The same is true of some manmade disasters. For example, it really didn't take a nuclear scientist to recognize the preliminary and obvious signs causing the 2008 financial meltdown. In retrospect, citizens should have seen it coming and yet many citizens either did not recognize or chose to ignore the signs of the pending collapse. More importantly, no one should be fooled into believing the financial meltdown is over – if you sit down and do the arithmetic, there is still plenty more fun to come.

It generally takes several years for some natural disasters such as a severe drought to take affect on the population in the area. By observing weather patterns, changes in precipitation and climate, and listening to climate and weather reports, one may be able to predict the possibility of a future drought or by watching <u>legitimate</u> news reports and observing other natural signs, it may be possible to "predict" the possibility of extreme cold temperatures or heat waves and purchase and store supplies *in advance*.

When citizens observe government politicians failing to create and pass a budget, fund the government and continue to raise the debt ceiling - these are all critical signs of a pending national financial meltdown. When news agencies report escalated confrontations between nations, the instability in the overall banking system or in specific banks or lending institutions, or when Wall Street stocks and bonds surge downhill at a frantic pace, citizens should take warning that a financial institution collapse could occur in the foreseeable future.

Continue to watch news reports, observe natural and manmade signs and listen to knowledgeable experts. There are government agencies, scientific communities, religious organizations and other private groups that provide warnings of impending tsunamis, earthquakes, flooding and even the probability of a comet or solar flare hitting the earth. Many of these same groups also provide legitimate and truthful coverage on financial institutions and prominent business and market trends.

If citizens recognize the signs of an imminent disaster occurring in the future, it is easier to *prepare in advance* for the likelihood and gather, purchase and store supplies. Pay attention to world events and listen to the opinions and counsel of <u>legitimate</u> financial experts. Become informed about possible threats, including the imminent collapse of the government and/or financial markets and take proactive steps. Watch! Listen! The signs are there.

> **THE BEST DEFENSE AGAINST GOVERNMENT COLLAPSE IS TO BECOME SELF-SUFFICIENT AND *PREPARE IN ADVANCE FOR THE WORST CASE SCENARIO* IN ORDER TO SURVIVE UPCOMING EVENTS.**

TARTAR SAUCE

1 cup mayonnaise
1 tablespoon minced parsley *or* dry parsley flakes
1 tablespoon sweet pickles, finely chopped
¼ teaspoon onion salt

Combine ingredients in small bowl and mix well. Spoon into pint jar, cover and refrigerate. Makes 1 ¼ cups.

CHAPTER 3

FINANCIAL INSTITUTION

The **FINANCIAL INSTITUTION** Element consists of banks, credit unions, mortgage and loan centers, the stock market as well as various financial instruments part of the financial systems including paper and coins, checks, debit and credit cards, precious metals and stones, and stocks and bonds. A collapse of the financial institution in a small area, in a state, in the country or even in the entire world can be a result of a manmade or natural disaster - or a combination of both - and can take affect instantaneously or over a long period of time.

The conjoined twins of the **FINANCIAL INSTITUTION** Element include the **ADMINISTRATION** (government) Element and the **COMMERCIALIZATION** (markets, businesses) Element.

THE PERFECT STORM

It really doesn't matter if we are talking about an individual – a family - a small business - a bank – a large corporation – an entire country – or the entire world. The basic principles for financial stability, financial responsibility and sound financial management are the same for everyone handling money:

DO NOT SPEND MORE MONEY THAN YOU MAKE
MAKE SOUND INVESTMENT DECISIONS
AVOID QUICK AND EASY MONEY SCHEMES
AVOID MAKING OR ACCEPTING RISKY LOANS
LIVE WITHIN YOUR MEANS
USE CREDIT WISELY AND AVOID EXCESSIVE DEBT
WHAT SEEMS TOO GOOD TO BE TRUE GENERALLY IS NOT TRUE
CREATE AND FOLLOW A REALISTIC BUDGET
INCLUDE SAVINGS AS PART OF THE OVERALL FINANCIAL PLAN

As a result of the financial crisis in 2008, the credit rating for the United States was reduced which affects the interest rate our country now has to pay in order to borrow money from outside creditors, including China, Japan and Germany. The United States is stretched militarily and is now stretched financially as well.

John Gray, political philosopher and professor at London School of Economics, wrote in the London Observer:

> *Here is a historic geopolitical shift, in which the balance of power in the world is being altered irrevocably. The era of American global leadership, reaching back to the Second World War is over. The American free-market creed has self-destructed while countries that retained overall control of markets have been vindicated. <u>HOW SYMBOLIC THAT CHINESE ASTRONAUTS TAKE A SPACEWALK WHILE THE UNITED STATES TREASURY SECRETARY IS ON HIS KNEES</u>.*

CREDIT CATASTROPHE – THE UNRELENTING DRAGON

Frugal living means carefully budgeting in order to keep food on the table, pay bills on time and still have money left over to gather emergency preparation supplies. It's time for all of us to become frugal with spending habits.

A significant problem with easy credit is the inability or unwillingness of consumers to scrutinize their purchases. In other words, there have been countless <u>greedy and stupid</u> individuals and families who purchased expensive homes that even a first grader would recognize could not be afforded based on their income. Furthermore, everyone was so zealot to get as many toys as possible, no one actually asked whether or not the toys were <u>really necessary</u> let alone whether they could afford to buy them.

As a result, the credit system was ruthlessly abused by financial institutions that <u>made</u> loans and consumers who <u>accepted</u> the loans. The bankers made out just fine with a very generous government bailout but there are many citizens who are now struggling to make payments on homes and "used" toys no longer worth the amount of money still owed on the loan. And many people are still trying to find a job.

Another type of credit that creates a similar financial storm is the use of credit cards. Unless one has impeccable willpower and resistance to withstand the seduction of impulse buying, it is simply too easy to make the argument you really need that new video game, new outfit or new bedspread for the master bedroom. After all – they all were on sale. Come on – wise up! Unless you pay off the <u>entire balance of credit card debt every month</u> – the high interest rate will eat up any savings you would have made when buying the items on sale.

In order to become financial survivalists, it is necessary to make some very difficult – even excruciating decisions about how to pay for items you purchase in the future. While still making payments to the credit card companies to pay off any balances, the way to be released from the dragon is to cut the strings that bind you to the beast. Get rid of ALL credit cards. Cut them up. Make a bonfire and roast hotdogs. Dance and sing around the raging inferno being fed by the melting plastic as you begin to acknowledge you are now on your way to financial freedom – a frustrating and chilling road to say the least and a torturous journey to reach the top of the mountain – but it is a new beginning. From now on, you will only purchase items that can be paid with cash or money you have in the checking or saving account. For services that actually do <u>require</u> the use of a credit (or debit) card, i.e. purchasing an airline ticket, staying at a hotel or renting a car – use a separate <u>debit</u> card and only carry it with you when you are going to make this type of purchase.

ORGANIZING PERSONAL FINANCES

In order to see whether team members are in jeopardy of being swallowed up by debt, possible bankruptcy or long-term financial ruin – each member should ask the following questions about their personal financial situation:

DANGER ZONE	SAFETY ZONE
Job in construction, auto sales, retail, hospitality, airlines, government or you are a low wage worker or new hire.	All other jobs
0-5 months of living expenses in cash and solid (and liquid) investments.	6+ months of living expenses in cash and/or solid investments that can easily be turned into cash.
Fixed monthly expenses are high and cannot be reduced (mortgage, car payment)	Fixed monthly expenses are low and can be reduced (mortgage, car payment)
Large amount of debt and/or interest rates are variable.	Small amount of debt and/or interest rates are fixed.
No family or friends nearby who can provide support.	Nearby family/friends who can provide support (childcare, food, transportation, housing)

If you find yourself in the "danger zone"- attempt to take immediate action to become more financially solvent. Every person will have a specific set of circumstances – the important goal is to scrutinize these circumstances and analyze if there are any reasonable or realistic solutions to relieving your debt burden and obligations while at the same time, increasing the amount of cash in your possession and allocating an amount of money each week to purchase emergency supplies.

During a Level One (1 hour to 7 days), Level Two (7 days to 1 month), and even the beginning of a Level Three (1 month to 1 year) disaster, if the financial intuitions have collapsed or are in jeopardy of collapse, paper and coins would still be used as currency since many people would assume the banks and/or government will be quickly re-established and everything will be back to normal. If electrical power is out, it will be even more important to have cash on hand to make transactions.

However, for a serious and long-term disaster, the banking system and government would have closed their doors. Teams should have some cash available in all emergency pantries, but it is also wise to include *alternatives* or *layers* of currency in the overall emergency pantry to support short-term, middle-term and long-term disaster situations that involves the intermittent or permanent disruption of financial institutions and/or government operations. These alternatives include some cash carefully protected in the home, precious metals (gold and silver) and <u>emergency items that can be bartered</u>.

EMERGENCY PREPARATION PRINCIPLES

In order to facilitate this strategy, all team members must be committed to becoming financial survivalists and be *ready*, *willing* and *able* to make the necessary sacrifices required in order to become financially solvent during disaster situations. Using this strategy, team members would apply the following principles:

- **Enjoy life and have fun** <u>must</u> be incorporated into the overall financial plan – otherwise, it will fail. Recognize that even though firm steps would now be taken to become effective financial survivalists, it is still important to <u>live a full life</u> and enjoy the many blessings that are given to us on a daily basis. The adage – "all work and no play makes a team member a cantankerous, ornery, crabby and irritable person" is an important guideline in our overall strategy.

- **Work towards having a savings account IN CASH** (paper and coins) that contains a <u>minimum</u> of six months' income covering ALL fixed and variable expenses. Consider storing a portion in the bank (safety deposit box) and the rest in a safe location at the primary residence.

- **Work towards obtaining precious metals** (gold and silver) that can be used as currency. Consider storing a portion in the bank (safety deposit box) and the rest in a safe location at the primary residence.

- **WORK TOWARDS OBTAINING A SUBSTANTIAL INVENTORY OF EMERGENCY SUPPLIES** that can be used by team members and used for bartering.

- **Establish a <u>reasonable</u> monthly budget** that includes funds to cover all fixed expenses (mortgage, rent, auto, insurance), essential variable expenses (food, utilities, taxes, gas, charitable donations and entertainment), <u>emergency preparation supplies</u> and **SAVINGS**.

- **Reduce or eliminate ALL <u>unnecessary</u> and <u>frivolous</u>** *services* **and** *activities*, i.e. cable or satellite television, Internet, telephone (either a land line or cell phone but not both), laundry and dry cleaning, nail care, massage, subscriptions, memberships, automatic car washes, lawn and garden, housekeeping, eating out at restaurants and fast-food establishments, going out to the movies, shopping for clothes and other items that are not essential, over-indulging in expensive school activities or buying extravagant gifts.

- **Consider making only the required <u>minimum</u> payments on all debt** including mortgage, credit cards, signature loans and collateral loans. Would you rather have no debt and no cash to pay for housing and food or would you rather have some debt and some cash to survive? That's why you should think about not paying down your entire debt <u>right now</u>. Under "normal" circumstances, paying down your debt is the proper strategy. But we are not in a normal environment at this time.

- **Scrutinize all essential expenses** on a semi-annual basis to ensure optimum effectiveness, i.e. insurance premiums and utility bills.

- Do everything you can to **keep your job**. In a growth economy, it's much easier to find a new job, but at the present time, we don't have that kind of economy.

- **If you have an interest-only loan but have also been making principal payments, consider just paying the interest for now**. When things improve and there is more stability, you can start paying down the principal again.

- **If you're paying a student loan, check the rules of your loan**. Many government sponsored loans do not require you to pay on it if you are a student. Take a class (one that increases your skills or employability) for $50 and find out how to stop paying on the loan for a while.

- **Renegotiate your credit card payments or interest**.

- **Consider stopping or reducing contributions to your children's college savings plans**. You can start this up again IF the economy improves in the future.

Make an investment in a home safe and put cash, coins and metals in a safe at the primary residence rather than a financial institution. In the event of no electricity, the ATMs will not operate nor will the bank be able to make any deposits or withdrawals. In this economy, banks can easily collapse.

During a short-term disaster, paper and coins would likely still be accepted as currency to purchase and sell goods and services. During medium-term disasters, precious metals (gold and silver) may also serve as currency under specific circumstances. For example, if paper and coins can no longer be used, there may be individuals who would be willing to accept precious metals as payment for goods and services in the hope the financial system and government would again be re-established in the foreseeable future. **However, somewhere along the road of disaster, when the length reaches the three month period of time, the general population may ultimately recognize the severity of the national and financial decline and would no longer be willing to accept even metals or stones as currency. It will be at this point in time the nation would return to the barter system to gather goods and services in order to survive.**

Self-reliant people do not need the government to provide all the services that it tries to give us. Governments that provide too much take away our power and too many people are allowing it. They are willingly giving the government their power. We have become a needy people - who are now enabled by a corrupt government and self-serving bankers and politicians.

BARTER SYSTEM

Bartering is very simple – individuals trade <u>goods</u>, <u>supplies</u> and <u>services</u>. For example, one person has excess apples and another person has excess bananas. The two persons come together and trade apples and bananas. Other examples could be one team is willing to cut and stack a pile of wood (service) in return for getting a case of corn and a box of matches from another team or one team agrees to process a deer in return for receiving needed first aid from another team. The system becomes a win-win scenario – all persons are happy with the outcome and have items and services they need to survive.

As part of the overall emergency plan and anticipating the possibility of bartering during any level of disaster, there are specific items that would be considered as fundamental, essential and crucial to all teams as well as to families and individuals who have <u>not</u> *prepared in advance* for emergencies. Depending on the level of disaster, some items will be in demand sooner as normal supplies are used up and become scarce. The price (or cost) to obtain these commodities will increase – whether bartering goods and services or using some form of currency.

In addition to bartering one supply for another supply, and depending on the length of the disaster, cash could also be used as a bartering instrument. For example, if it is obvious that the length of disaster will last only a few days or even a few months, team members may consider either giving cash or accepting cash for trading goods, supplies and services.

The following list includes items that would be critical or popular supplies. Teams who are proactive in *planning in advance* should consider these items as being valuable bargaining and bartering supplies.

Ammunition	Candles	**Cooking Oil**	Hand Sanitizer	Pens and Pencils	**Tea**
Baby Supplies	**Canning Supplies**	Duct Tape	Lamp Oil Wicks	Plastic Bags	**Toilet Paper**
Batteries	Cards	**Hygiene Supplies**	Lip Balm	Rope	**Tools**
Blankets	**Chocolate**	**Medical Supplies**	**Liquor**	**Salt**	Toothbrush
Bleach	**Cigarettes**	**Food**	Lotion	**Seeds**	Toothpaste
Books	Cloth	**Fuel**	**Matches**	Sewing Kits	Vinegar
Bucket	Clothing	Garbage Bags	**Medications**	Shoe Laces	**Vitamins**
Buttons	**Coffee**	Grains	Paper	**Soap**	**Weapons**

*Those marked in bold are exceptionally critical items and will be anxiously sought by other teams.

CHAPTER FOUR

COMMERCIALIZATION

There are both manmade and natural disasters that can have an adverse impact on the **COMMERCIALIZATION** Element. These commercial markets include public, private and charitable manufacturing, processing, distribution, wholesale and retail companies, markets, businesses, corporations, organizations or systems providing goods and services to a consumer. I am talking about companies, businesses and organizations such as *Proctor and Gamble*, *Johnson & Johnson*, *General Motors*, *Wal-Mart*, *McDonalds*, *Kellogg's*, *Home Depot*, *ConAgra*, *Foster Farms*, *Syscon* and the *Red Cross.*

Commercialization includes small businesses as well including food cooperatives, farmers' markets and family farms who raise produce and animals for market or individuals who make or produce crafts and goods in their homes and sell in some type of market system. Commerce affects every one of us because we all purchase goods and services <u>from</u> others or sell goods and services <u>to</u> others. No person is an island – including those individuals who attempt to become totally self-sufficient. Somewhere in the commercial matrix – everyone is forced to transact with others in gathering or purchasing supplies and services needed to continue everyday living.

The commercial market systems are fragile and extremely vulnerable to crisis events or disasters that can "disrupt or break the chain" of the market. The system becomes so susceptible that a disaster in one part of the world can have a devastating affect on companies and businesses located in another part of the world. The conjoined twins of the **COMMERCIALIZATION** Element are **TRANSPORTATION** and **FINANCIAL INSTITUTION** Elements.

Commercial markets depend on transportation infrastructure, vehicles and operations to transport the supplies, goods and services between locations. The financial institutions are needed in order to actually purchase or sell the goods. A broken link in the chain of transportation or financial institutions will immediately influence commercial markets. This disruption could be caused by various elements including fuel shortages, electrical outages and government instability.

EMERGENCY PREPARATION PRINCIPLES

There are <u>four</u> principles that can be incorporated into the overall emergency plan to prepare for times when commercial markets would be temporarily or permanently closed, depending on the circumstances:

- *Prepare in advance* to gather and purchase necessary resources, supplies and goods for each element used to maintain the health and well-being of team members throughout the duration of the disaster.

- *Prepare in advance* to learn the skills necessary to process meat, render first aid, prepare food from scratch, build a fire, hunt and fish etc.

- Recognize that a disaster (manmade or natural) taking place anywhere in the world could have a *direct* or *indirect* affect on commercial businesses being able to bring goods, supplies, resources and services to market - which in turn, can affect team members from being able to obtain critical items during an emergency situation.

- Even a <u>short-term</u> crisis or disaster lasting a few hours, a few days or a few weeks can affect markets; for example, if for any reason the power goes off for what may be a couple of hours or an extended period of time, stores will immediately escort customers outside and will close their doors until power is restored.

MANMADE DISASTERS

There are countless manmade disasters that can disrupt or destroy the operation of these commercial market chains including rioting, fire (arson), terrorist attacks, pandemics and explosions and more serious and deadly disasters such as nuclear war, terrorist attacks or biological and chemical warfare. Perhaps one of the most likely manmade disasters affecting commercial markets would be the financial collapse of the economy and the inability of the government politicians to manage or control the meltdown.

NATURAL DISASTERS

There are many types of natural disasters that can have serious and deadly impacts and consequences on a specific region, state, country or even the entire world including earthquakes, flooding, cold temperatures, hurricanes and tornadoes. Depending on the level of disaster (1-3), commerce could experience extensive power outages that affect lighting, computer and security systems, equipment and machinery, communications, banking services, cash registers, access to fuel and of course, transportation of goods and services.

Depending on the location(s) of:

- Raw materials (wood, rubber, fruits and vegetables, metals, oil, hides etc.)
- Manufacturing (Proctor and Gamble) and processing (Foster Farms) facilities
- Distribution Sites (Syscon)
- Transportation infrastructure, vehicles and operations (roads, rail, air, water, pipeline etc.)
- Wholesale dealers or retail outlets (Wal-Mart, mom and pop stores, home businesses etc.)

- and where the disaster takes place – the **WEAKEST LINK IN THE CHAIN** could be damaged or destroyed causing the entire chain to shake and tremble.

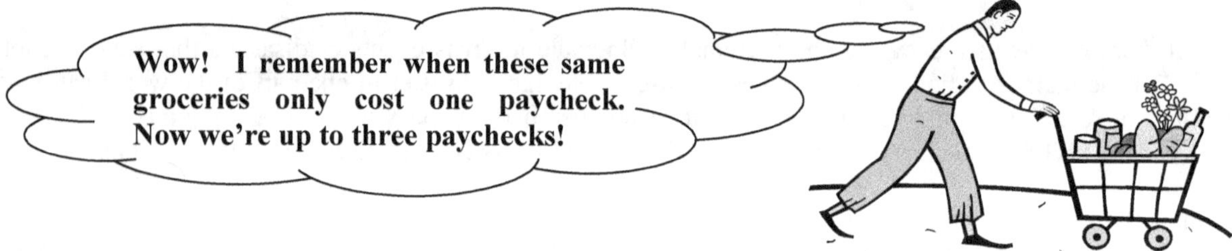

POSSIBLE SCENARIOS

A vital element in emergency preparation is the health of the commercial enterprise. If there is a serious disaster – even for a short period of time or extending into months, a year or even longer, those large and small corporations and businesses throughout the country and around the world that provide us with the many goods, resources and supplies we use every day may temporarily close their doors or be out of business. For example:

- If teams run out of toothpaste, paper cups, light bulbs, diapers or most other supplies - Wal-Mart is closed.

- If teams want a sandwich for lunch – we better have the peanut butter and jelly in our pantry and have the ingredients, equipment and fuel to make the bread – the grocery stores are closed.

- Every time the team prepares a meal, the items must already be in the pantry and will have to be prepared from scratch – McDonalds, Olive Garden and Wolfgang's Steakhouse are closed.

- If teams want to pick up a couple of rib-eye steaks for dinner and have meat on the table – you will have to go out and hunt, kill and process the meat – the local meat market is closed.

- If teams want fruits and vegetables, the items must already be in the pantry and you will have to grow a garden – the produce farms and the local produce market is closed.

- If teams need a new shirt, items must be in the pantry or you will have to make it by hand – and that's providing you have the cloth and sewing materials – the local fabric store is closed.

- If teams need light to read a book, heat to keep warm or gas to cook a meal - alternative light, heat and cooking supplies must be in the emergency pantry - the utility companies are closed.

- If teams have a toothache, headache or injury, illness or disease – the medication must already be in the pantry, you will have to hunt for herbal or other natural remedies, live with the pain or succumb to the illness or disease – the local hospital and pharmacy is closed.

- If teams want to watch a movie or play a video game – the items must already be in the pantry with an alternative source of power or you will have to pull out a deck of cards and a board game – the local video store, the gas station and the utility companies are closed.

- If teams want to travel to a nearby town that is twenty miles away – you will more than likely have to walk – the local gas station is closed.

- If teams want to use the Internet or a cell phone - members may need to resort to writing a hand-written note and delivering it by hand - the Internet and cell phone companies are closed.

- If teams are thirsty and want a cold soda or drink of water, water must already be in the pantry or you will need to find the nearest safe water source– the soft drink and ice companies are closed.

HERE ONE MINUTE - GONE THE NEXT

There have been several reports and studies done listing the top items that instantly vanish from store shelves during a crisis situation.

SUPPLIES THAT ARE HERE ONE MINUTE - AND GONE THE NEXT	
Aluminum Foil	Hydrogen Peroxide
Antacids	Ice
Antibiotics	Lantern Fuel/Oil
Antihistamine	Lantern Wicks/Mantles
Army Knife	Lanterns
Axes	Laundry Detergent
Baby Supplies	Laxatives
Band Saws	Liquor
Bandages	Matches
Batteries	Milk
Bleach	Moisture Wipes
Boots	Mouse Bait
Bouillon Cubes	Mouse Traps
Bug Spray	Nylon Tarps
Butane Igniter	Paper Plates
Camp Stoves	Paper Towels
Can Opener (manual)	Plastic Bags (resealable)
Candles	Plastic Buckets (5-gallon)
Canned Soup	Pocket Knife
Canvas	Portable Toilets
Chain Saws	Powdered Milk
Charcoal/Grill	Prescriptions
Cigarettes	Propane (stoves)
Coffee/Tea	Radios (Hand Crank)
Diarrhea Remedies	Rain Gear
Disinfectant	Rope
Dry Cereal	Rubbing Alcohol
Duct Tape	Salt
Dutch Ovens	Shampoo/Conditioner
Epsom Salts	Shaving Supplies
Feminine Supplies	Soap (Bath)
First-Aid Tape	Solar Panels
Flashlights	Soup Mixes
Flour	Sugar
Food Items	Thermal Underwear
Frying Pan	Toilet Paper

Gas	Toothbrush
Gasoline Containers	Toothpaste
Gauze Pads	Trash Bags
Generators	Vitamins
Gloves (Heavy/Work)	Water
Hand Sanitizer	Water Filters

Remember - during any level of disaster, teams should expect a "run" on the stores – in other words – everyone will be heading for the stores to stock up on supplies. Depending on the circumstances, it won't take long to deplete all the shelves in the store. BE PREPARED - PLAN IN ADVANCE!

APPLE CRISP

6 apples, peeled
½ cup granulated white sugar
2 tablespoons water
4 tablespoons butter *or* margarine
½ cup brown sugar, firmly packed
1 teaspoon grated lemon peel
1 cup rolled oats
½ teaspoon cinnamon
½ cup nuts, chopped (optional)

Slice apples and spread in greased 8x8 inch pan. Sprinkle water and ½ cup sugars onto apples. Mix remaining ingredients and spread over apples. Bake at 350 degrees for 45 minutes or until tender. Serve warm or cold. If desired, top with ice cream or whipped topping.

GRAHAM CRACKERS

1 cup whole wheat flour
½ cup oat flour
a cup *plus* 1 tablespoon granulated white sugar
½ teaspoon baking soda
a cup butter *or* margarine
1 tablespoon honey
1 tablespoon milk

Sift flours, sugar and baking soda into mixing bowl. Heat butter or margarine, honey and milk until melted. Pour into dry ingredients and stir until smooth. Chill 30-45 minutes. Roll out dough to ¼ inch. Cut into squares. Bake in 250 degree oven for 15 minutes. DO NOT OVERBAKE. Prick crackers with fork as they come out of the oven.

CHAPTER FIVE

EMOTION

HUMAN FACTOR

An essential part of any disaster is the *human reaction* to stress, anxiety, fear, confusion, anger and depression so prevalent during a crisis. Human behavior is complex and unpredictable and would certainly escalate during a serious catastrophe that happens rapidly without giving the human mind time to process the events.

With the entire population reacting to the disaster instead of just a few individuals or small groups, the situation could be out of control and dangerous for all citizens. The human mob tends to act irrationally and chaos breeds more chaos. The more frantic the mob, the more difficult it is to contain the population. As human beings – we should not flatter ourselves into thinking that we are exempt from losing control during a crisis.

Reaction to disaster can take place over a considerable period of time and is not just one problem but a series of problems. The real challenge of managing a disaster can actually come from *social disorganization* and not from individual emotional behavior.

A disaster can destroy or damage physical facilities and electricity, fuel, communication, transportation, medication and technological developments associated with it. When these elements are damaged or destroyed, the result is social paralysis and later recovery depends on external assistance such as government agencies, or from historically more stable and honorable religious and charitable organizations.

There are many opinions and theories on how the general population will react to various types of disasters. Based on my research, reaction by the general population will be based on several factors:

The <u>first</u> factor is related to **PAST HISTORY** and **FUTURE EVENTS**.

1. Disaster has <u>happened in the past or can be expected to happen in the future</u>. Although we may not have been personally involved or directly affected by a specific type of disaster, we are aware in the past it has occurred in our area and we understand the possibility of the same type of disaster and consequences happening in the future. For example, a power outage, wild fire, flood, hurricane, tornado, thunderstorm, lightning, landslide, drought, riot, terrorist attack, earthquake, heat wave, extreme cold, tsunami, volcano, or explosion.

   or

2. Disaster has <u>not happened in the past or is thought to be unlikely to happen in the future</u>. Although we may be familiar with these disasters happening in other countries based on what we have viewed on television or read in newspapers or magazines, the probability of this type of disaster occurring in our area – or in our country – is <u>believed</u> to be a remote possibility. For example, biological or chemical warfare or nuclear war.

Although not everyone has experienced *all* disasters, we are at least somewhat familiar with most of them. For example, individuals in New York City on 11 September can fully appreciate a terrorist attack but through the media, the rest of the nation was also able to be a part of the crises and experience the destruction, devastation and death. And over the years, the nation has watched the recovery of ground zero. In essence, as a nation, we are now familiar with a terrorist attack and have more or less worked through the healing process.

Our country has <u>not</u> experienced biological or chemical warfare, a nuclear attack or an enemy ground invasion on our soil, and as individuals, we may not have personally experienced a riot, landslide, wild fire, flood, hurricane, tornado or earthquake, but we know people who have gone through these disasters and we have watched the crisis being aired on television and read about the event in the newspapers. At some level – we are familiar with these disasters as well.

As a nation, we are more likely to react in a *constructive* way to disasters we have experienced in the past or are familiar with by watching the news media. That is not to say we would not feel the negative emotions that come with any disaster, but we would be able to cope with the consequences and work towards returning to a normal lifestyle and standard of living. However, a disaster that is uncommon and in our opinion, unlikely, serves to escalate a negative reaction resulting in accelerated stress, apprehension, fear, anger, confusion, resentment, anxiety and sadness.

The _second_ factor is related to the **AMOUNT OF TIME** one has to prepare *prior* to the disaster.

1. Disaster occurs immediately and there is no time to prepare for the consequences. We are caught off-guard and we must take the necessary time to process the event. For example, we are at work and the office building begins to shake and rumble from a 9.2 earthquake; we are driving on the freeway and a truck slides off the road and dumps toxic chemicals; we are at home and the power station explodes across the street; or we are walking down Broadway in New York City and a plane flies into the World Trade Center.

   or

2. Disaster is not immediate and we have a longer period of time to prepare for the consequences. We have been given warning time to prepare *prior* to the disaster and are able to focus in advance on survival techniques. In some cases, we may have less than an hour to prepare and in other cases, we may have months or even years to prepare for a disaster. For example, we have been informed a hurricane or tornado is heading towards our city and should be in our area within an hour; heavy snowfall from winter storms is anticipated to bring flooding to the valleys in the spring; a wild fire burning on the hill and prevailing winds suggest damage to surrounding structures; or continued dry spells throughout the country taking a toll on wheat, fruit and vegetable crops.

Depending on an immediate or extended time for a disaster, each person will have to deal with the emotional and psychological fallout in their own way. Remember that although your team may have *prepared in advance* for future disasters – others will not. Team members must be prepared to deal with those who are not prepared and their reactions and behaviors that will ensue during and after the crisis.

The _third_ factor is related to the **DURATION** of the disaster and of the **CONSEQUENCES** - a short time or an extended length of time.

1. Disaster and consequences last a short amount of time – generally one hour to a month. The actual disaster generally lasts for only a short period of time, for example, an earthquake only shakes the earth for a few seconds or a hurricane moves rapidly through an area. Although we may experience stress, fear, anxiety or panic during the disaster, once the calamity is over, we are relieved and able to evaluate any consequences. The consequences could be nothing more than an inconvenience or annoyance to our daily schedules. For example, as a result of a wind storm, electrical power could go out for several hours or even an entire day or night; or a riot in the city requires stores and markets to close for a few days in order to repair damage and restock supplies.

   or

2. Disaster and consequences last an extended length of time – generally one month to one year and even up to five years. The actual disaster and consequences alter our life style, our standard of living and our ability to survive each day. As the length of time increases, the ability for the human psychic to cope and function rationally becomes strained. For example, a heat wave involving extreme temperatures overcome a region over an entire season, an extended famine reduces or eliminates many of the food sources in the area or a world-wide nuclear war, solar flare and EMP could involve every country on the planet.

If the disaster is short-lived, most human beings can process the event and focus on how to manage the aftermath of consequences. However, a long-term disaster has a tendency to wear down our ability to battle the dragons and we may lose the will to fight and confidence we can overcome the odds we perceive are stacked against us. I believe this is where the "God Factor" becomes important – we would be able to cope with the consequences and hopefully survive the overall disaster.

The _fourth_ factor is related to the **SEVERITY** of the disaster and of the **CONSEQUENCES**.

1. Disaster and consequences are mild to medium in nature. As a result, the consequences will more than likely also be mild or medium in inconvenience, damage or destruction. For example, a wind storm passing through the area uproots only a few trees; a wildfire is quickly contained causing no structural damage or loss of life; an

earthquake registering only 3.1 on the Richter Scale with very minor damage to structures; or a river overruns the bank where there is no damage to natural resources, humans or wildlife.

or

2. Disaster and consequences are <u>severe</u> in nature. As a result, the consequences will likely result in severe damage, destruction and devastation. For example, a comet could literally strike the earth causing a complete and catastrophic environmental change to our entire planet; a world war lasting for years; a volcano could erupt destroying entire villages; a hurricane could be so severe as to cause wide-spread flooding in cities and vital agricultural areas; or a drought, famine or pestilence could be so relentless and brutal as to wipe out entire civilizations, states and nations.

The severity of the disaster will have a direct impact on how the human population will react during the crisis. During a severe disaster, the ability to avoid stress and use our logic, common sense, judgment and reason will be stretched to the limit. There will be many persons who will become overwhelmed with anxiety, fear, confusion and anger over the circumstances. The ability to avoid panic will be difficult and challenging.

There are other factors that become prevalent *before*, *during* and *after* a disaster. For example, there are specific <u>elements</u> that are fundamental to survival for all living creatures. The **OPERATIONS** Element includes many sources needed for life, namely shelter and water. Without shelter from environmental (heat, cold, wet, dry) and man-made (ammunition, biological and chemical warfare, nuclear attack, bombs) elements, a living creature will be susceptible to death in a short period of time.

A healthy human being can survive without drinking water for three or five days. The question one must ask is how long do you believe it would take before <u>you</u> took drastic action to get these fundamental survival items for you and the team members and more importantly, how long do you think others will wait?

For many centuries, societies have managed to live productive and successful lives without the use of cell phones, automobiles, computers, toilets, aspirin, McDonalds and Wal-Mart – but these advancements provide conveniences to our society we take for granted and have learned to depend on for our day-to-day living. These man-made "toys" are engrained in our lives and to be denied could result in severe and vicious withdrawal and our ability to cope with the disaster could be a problem.

The unconditional need for shelter, water and food and the desire for perceived luxuries could easily drive many human beings to behave, respond and act "as necessary" to get supplies for their ultimate survival during any disaster. The factors listed above will ultimately determine the thinking process, physical reaction and behavior of a human being in dealing with disaster scenarios and the ability of society to maintain social order.

EMOTION PHASES

There are several factors that influence the <u>reaction</u> we have to fear, anxiety and stress and some factors that are generally beyond our influence:

- the disaster type, intensity and duration

- the duration of time between receiving a warning and the disaster event

- the time of day and the season of the year

Other factors are susceptible to our influence including:

- education, preparation and training a person takes prior to disaster situations

- government knowledge, competency and preparation of disaster events and what civil defense preparation has on the population

- actual location of team members *before*, *during* and *after* the disaster

A disaster generally has five phases that are part of the human ability to deal with the consequences. The mind first issues a <u>warning</u> to the body that a disaster is coming or in process. The disaster is then met with <u>crash</u>, followed by <u>alarm</u>, then a <u>retreat</u> phase and finally a <u>healing</u> phase.

Warning

It is important for team members to heed the counsel of religious leaders, scientists, government and other knowledgeable agencies about the possibility of disaster and prepare and practice a definite plan of action *in advance* of an anticipated disaster scenario. Lack of preparation causes anxiety - especially if there is knowledge that a disaster is a possibility.

If the population is apathetic to danger or lacks practice and experience of warning, it fails to recognize the nearness of danger and to react in a reasonable manner. In preparing the overall emergency plan, and as a team, there should be no doubt as to the action to be taken during a disaster scenario. The plan of action for each scenario should be well understood and well rehearsed by all team members.

During any serious disaster, a large number of people will be stunned or dazed. There would be no professional, psychiatric or medical care because all physicians would be engaged in life saving treatment. The other agencies such as police, fire, military and civil defense volunteers would be assigned to re-establishing vital functions, services, systems and facilities to the nation.

As a team *prepared in advance* for disaster – members will be more likely to survive the ordeal with less mental, emotional, psychological and physical repercussions than those in the population who chose not to heed the warning and are unprepared to face the crises.

Crash

Once the disaster happens, crash is the time period (generally lasting a few minutes to an hour) when the population reacts to the situation. The reaction to the impact by the population can be divided into three groups (1) the cool and collected (these people are effective), (2) the stunned, dazed or bewildered (most of the population), and (3) the confused, bewildered and anxious including those who exhibit hysterical crying (these persons are ineffective and unable to look after themselves).

Social disorganization occurs immediately at the time of crash and will be extensive throughout the population. The behavior of individuals may appear confused to the outside observer and lack of uniformity in action looks like "panic" but it is really a symptom of social disorganization.

During a serious disaster, there will be few individuals, if any, who exhibit a cool and collected demeanor. Those who do have their wits about them will more than likely be religious leaders and perhaps some community leaders. The individuals who are stunned, dazed or bewildered are typical of normal people and at some point, the stunned response will be replaced by irritability, difficulty in making up the mind, sadness or resentment of authority, muscular tension or freezing of action, sweating, rapid heart rate, rapid breathing, giddiness, nausea or even vomiting. These are normal bodily functions in preparation for fight or flight.

Team members should understand *before, during* and *after* a disaster, there will be a reaction to the disaster and consequences (including even rioting and general chaos) will occur as a result of the crises. By *planning in advance*, the team will be better equipped to successfully cope with these consequences unlike the population who exhibits confusing and anxious reactions.

Alarm

Flight does not mean alarm or panic because when danger is recognized, the population rightfully seeks safety by purposeful flight. Terror means <u>blind</u> flight and is based on the perception of danger and the impression that all escape routes are blocked. Some studies even conclude that wide scale panic is <u>not</u> a common finding even in large-scale disasters. I disagree.

During an actual emergency situation, orderly flight would be the only rational choice if one is to survive. For example, if a large group of people are in a burning building, it would be logical to assume that if individuals exit the building in an orderly fashion, it is more likely that everyone will be able to get out of the building. On the other hand, if everyone rushes to the exit, there are going to be people who fall and get trampled or pushed and shoved aside while other frantic persons attempt to make their escape.

Unfortunately, the human species is <u>not</u> known for being logical – especially during a crisis situation. It is more probable that during an actual serious disaster, there will be **MAJOR PANIC** by most of the population affected by the disaster. If an individual truly believes they are facing imminent death - calmness, good manners and compassion for others may not be at the top of their priority list.

During some types of disaster, an immediate large-scale exodus could no doubt take place and after a momentary escape, may be followed by return and purposeless activity. Team members must recognize that during an actual emergency, although they may be able to deal effectively with the crisis – others will not – and these are the individuals that team members must deal with when managing their own safety and security – and more importantly – their overall health.

Retreat

Retreat usually lasts several hours to several days as survivors achieve more awareness of what has happened. Disaster tends to lead towards dependency feelings and survivors may move toward each other for mutual protection and emotional support and begin to depend on one another for survival. The need to be with others becomes so strong that social barriers can disappear and results in a dramatic increase of social solidarity. There could be an outpouring of love, generosity and self-sacrifice in those who have experienced the disaster.

However, it is not as marked in people outside the disaster area, that is, among people who will be called upon to share home and food with disaster victims. For psychological first aid, an important healing component will be the need to ventilate and express oneself in talking through the ordeal with other team members and teams. The management of this phase may be of crucial significance to the subsequent overall health of all survivors.

After the disaster, survivors will spontaneously select their leaders. In general, the group will look to the "cool and collected" persons for leadership. These leaders would more than likely be known religious leaders or prominent community leaders whose role will be to foster morale, lead their groups into constructive activity and provide an atmosphere of confidence and reassurance to those individuals assigned to the group. Depending on the severity, duration, and consequences of the disaster, and the status of government, politicians and workers may or may not be available or even accepted by survivor groups.

Healing

The healing process extends from a few days after collision and after the danger has passed and may cover the rest of a person's life. The environment is no longer threatening but is somewhat predictable. The first full awareness occurs now – an awareness of what the disaster has "meant" in terms of loss and possessions, home and loved ones. The reactions can include anxiety, fatigue, depression and hysteria. It is important to allow team members to talk out the experiences and perform useful activity.

EVALUATING EMOTIONAL HEALTH

As part of *planning in advance*, it is important for *all* mature team members to evaluate their own level of *emotional, mental* and *psychological* stability and ponder various disaster scenarios. Determine how you believe you *would* realistically react to the circumstances at the time AND how you *should* react to those same circumstances as an individual with a strong conviction of what would be needed in order to survive the consequences of the entire disaster.

During this evaluation, don't be intimidated, embarrassed or surprised to learn that you may not be as strong, brave or competent as you think you would be during a disaster OR how others may perceive you would react during a crisis. This is an important learning process - it is critical to be honest with yourself in evaluating your personality traits and ability to react in a competent and effective manner when dealing with a disaster situation.

As part of your evaluation, if you recognize specific phobias or fears you have that may inhibit a competent performance in dealing with emergency situations, now is the time - *before* the disaster - to take steps in solving the issues. At the same time, evaluate your strengths to see how these traits can help you and others during a disaster. For example, for many years, I have interviewed countless individuals to determine what each perceives to be their own personal strengths and weaknesses they would be dealing with in a disaster. As part of the interviews, we discussed countless scenarios and made numerous assumptions in figuring out how each person would react and be able to cope with different disaster situations. During this excruciating process, here were *some* of the comments individuals discovered about themselves:

- I have a severe phobia about being in enclosed places. I would have a complete nervous breakdown if I was to be tightly confined in rubble from a fallen structure. I am very uncomfortable being in a large crowd and surrounded by countless numbers of people - especially in an elevator or even a room. I would also not do well living in a cave, underground tunnel, parking structure or even a basement.

- I have a severe phobia of heights. It would not be in my best interest - or anyone around me - to be caught in a high rise building, at the edge of a cliff or in an airplane during a disaster. Bad for me. Bad for them.

- I have a severe phobia of sharp objects. I am petrified of needles, knives, blades, swords or other pointed paraphernalia. I would more than likely find myself paralyzed if someone tried to attack me with a sharp object in order to take away my emergency supplies.

- I have a strong phobia of letting others be in charge. I have to really trust and believe in the competence, intellect and capability of someone else before I would be willing to follow their instruction and direction. I must also believe they are looking out for my best interest as well as their own.

- I do not like being afraid or stressed out because it inhibits me from being in control and taking competent and effective steps in meeting a goal or working through a challenge. I also don't like others to be afraid or stressed out who are around me.

- I am a control freak. I strive to plan and prepare in advance as I look down the road to the future. I want to be in charge of my own destiny.

- I tend to react to a specific event based on my current mood and physical well-being at the time. If I am in a good mood and feel physically well, I am more likely to work well with others, be a team player and support the overall team objective. On the other hand, if I am in a bad mood or not feeling physically well, I am more likely to be irritable, bad-tempered and judgmental of others.

- I do not like to be inconvenienced. I am not going to appreciate being without electricity, being too hot or too cold, or not being able to get in the car and drive to my favorite restaurant for a great meal.

- I admire strength and detest weakness - both in myself and in others. During a disaster, I would do better if those around me are strong. If I experience weakness in either myself or others, I will have a hard time dealing with the tasks that need to be done during disaster.

- I am goal oriented. I tend not to be worried about the means needed to reach the goal as long as I believe the goal is attainable and more importantly - important to the well being of myself and those around me. Therefore, if someone else has to be insulted, upset or offended so a critical goal can be reached to help the team survive the disaster - so be it.

- I have a strong faith in my religion and believe in God. It is through His will I will survive any disaster.

So - you get the idea. Dig deep. Dig hard. Dig long. Find out who you are and more importantly, find out who you are not. Recognize your strengths. Accept your weaknesses. Make sure as part of your analysis, you also evaluate other team members, friends, neighbors and others who will be close by during a disaster. Recognize not everyone will react the same way to different circumstances. Some will be passive. Some will be aggressive. Some will be weak. Some will be strong. Some will be smart. Some will be stupid. Some will want to share. Others will simply take what they need and not worry about anyone else. How will you deal with your own emotional, mental and psychological makeup and how will you deal with the emotional, mental and psychological makeup of others. Figure it out now - <u>in advance</u>!

CHAPTER SIX

OPERATION

One of the most important components in an emergency preparation plan is to ensure *operational* needs and concerns are addressed <u>prior to any emergency</u> to reduce overall problems in obtaining shelter, electricity, light, heat, clothing, tools and water during a disaster situation.

EMERGENCY PREPARATION PRINCIPLES

There are <u>six</u> principles that can be incorporated into the overall emergency plan to prepare for and in some cases eliminate *operational* issues that can become prevalent during an emergency situation. For example:

- Purchases for the **OPERATION** Element are a high priority – we are dealing with ultimate survival – shelter, electricity, light, heat, clothing and water.

- Know your operations inventory and where it is stored. Know how much you have of all resources, supplies and items associated with the **OPERATION** Element. Supplies should be readily available and logistically located for easy access and transport.

- A shelter-in-place is a vital component for emergency preparation. Obtain all necessary supplies and store in the designated room.

- A place of refuge is essential in the event of evacuation from the primary residence. This location could be a family-owned trailer house, motor home, trailer, camper or summer home. It could also be a public shelter, church, school or even a location in the mountains or desert. Scout out the area and make sure all members are familiar with the surroundings and a plan is in place for survival at these locations.

- Investigate all alternative shelter, electrical, heat, light and water natural resources in the area for use during a disaster.

- When creating your emergency operations plan, use methods that include *alternatives* or *layers* of sources and items so if one fails or is not available or realistic to use, another item or source may be used instead.

SHELTER

During a disaster, there are several scenarios that could happen with regards to shelter. For example:

1. A disaster has occurred but you still have the primary residence for protection and all or some utilities and other important facilities, equipment, machinery and/or tools.

2. A disaster has occurred and the primary residence is damaged or destroyed, all or part of the utilities is damaged and other arrangements must be made to provide shelter.

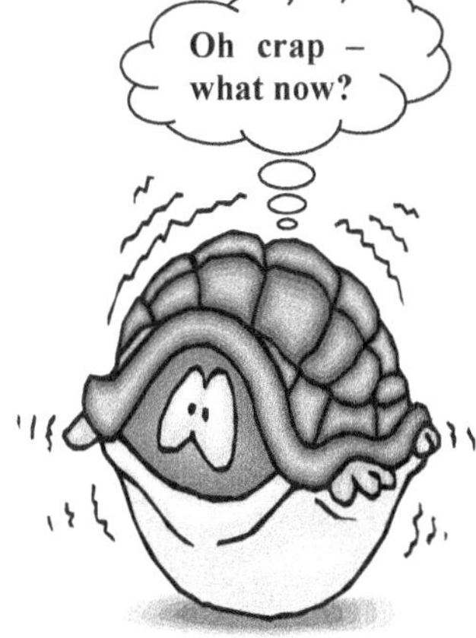

SHELTERING IN PLACE

Depending on the type of emergency, and assuming your primary residence is alright and utilities are working, "sheltering in place" may be a proper first response to guarantee survival. A shelter-in-place can be used for several scenarios: (1) a disaster or emergency has occurred that makes residing in the <u>entire</u> residence impossible or impractical and (2) a disaster has occurred that requires team members to locate in the primary residence *and* an enclosed area. And once again – planning ahead for this possibility will eliminate stress and possible loss of life.

A common emergency that merits the use of a shelter-in-place room is a broken furnace in the middle of winter (with below freezing temperatures) and it's going to take several days to get the part *or* a power outage in an area that could mean no heat from the furnace and no water in the taps. Until the furnace has been repaired or electricity is restored and the power comes back on - the shelter-in-place room would be a logical location to "set up camp".

Other possible disasters that could initiate this type of shelter may be a biological or chemical attack or even a chemical spill where the main security measure will be to avoid breathing in the contaminated air. In such a circumstance, you would either witness the disaster first-hand and/or be directed by the Emergency Alert System through the media to immediately take shelter and provide as much protection for the team as possible. Team members who reside in regions that may be susceptible to biological or chemical spills should take special precautions.

In the event of biological or chemical disasters, retreat to a room as far from outside air as possible and seal your team into it by covering window and door openings, air ducts and heater vents with plastic sheeting, and sealing the edges securely with tape. This room should be on an <u>upper</u> floor since chemical and biological agents are heavier than air and will settle to the lowest point. When selecting the room at the primary residence to serve as a "shelter-in-place" – consider using a room with little or no outside windows and doorways.

If possible, use a room with direct access to water and/or bathroom facilities. Sinks and toilet drain traps should have water in them which acts as a seal. You can use the toilet but you should **NOT** drink water from the sink or bathtub tap. More than likely, electrical power could be available and appliances requiring electricity in your room could be used providing you seal the electric plug and/or the electrical outlet being used by the appliance to avoid air from the outlet coming into the room. The team would most likely not be in the shelter for more than a few hours; however, you should plan for a minimum of three days. Listen to the media announcements indicating it is safe to leave your shelter.

The following items should be readily available in this designated room:

- Food - ready to eat
- Water (one gallon of water per person or pet per day in plastic bottles)
- First Aid Kit / Medications
- Bedding / Sleeping bag
- Books (Spiritual and Entertainment)
- Flashlight / Lantern (<u>solar</u>)
- Radio (crank-handle or solar-powered)
- Duct Tape
- Scissors (<u>to plan ahead</u> - have plastic pre-cut)
- Towels
- Plastic sheeting (heavy duty)
- Stapler and staples (heavy duty)
- Telephone
- Heater (if cold weather)
- Weapon/Ammo

Once the decision has been made to shelter-in-place, use the following steps:

1. Release the livestock from enclosures and pens – give them a chance to run and survive
2. Get inside the house as quickly as possible (**DON'T FORGET THE PETS**)
3. Shut and lock all outside doors and windows
4. Turn off the air conditioner, furnace and all fans
5. Go into your designated shelter-in-place room and shut the door (<u>take pets with you</u>)
6. Close all outside windows in the room
7. Shut fireplace flue and tape heavy-duty plastic over the opening of the fireplace (chemical/biological)
8. Tape heavy-duty plastic over the windows in the room
9. Use duct tape around the windows, doors and vents and make an unbroken seal
10. Seal any electrical outlets or other openings
11. Turn on television and/or radio for instructions

<u>**Loss of Electrical Power**</u>

A situation may occur in many areas where the electrical power is off for an extended period of time during the winter (cold) months. When electrical power is lost, the inconvenience is much greater than not being able to turn on the lights. For most households, the furnace heating the home requires electrical power. Households using underground wells for water also require electrical power to run the pump that brings water from underground into the home.

During a power outage lasting for an extended period of time, and depending on the season, weather conditions or outside temperature, <u>the main focus will be to maintain heat and warmth for the team and to ensure that water pipes are not frozen</u>.

Again, a modified "shelter-in-place" plan can be used during this type of emergency situation. Select a room that is adjacent to an alternate heat source that has water and bath facilities if possible.

1.   Using your heavy duty plastic sheeting and duct tape, seal off any outside windows and doors and construct a barrier (that allows for individuals to come in and out of the room but still keeps the heat in the room) on the inside door connecting this room with the rest of the house

2.   If an alternative heat source is available in this "shelter-in-place" room, i.e., fireplace, wood-burning   stove), make sure adequate fuel is available

3.   Gather bedding and sleeping bags (if necessary) and put in this room – this room is where the entire survival team (and pets) can sleep for the duration of the emergency

4.   Gather warm clothing for all team members to wear during the emergency, i.e. warm pants, shirts, coats, hats, gloves, socks, shoes, underwear, house slippers, robe and sleepwear

<u>To drain water out of water pipes in the house and to keep them from freezing and breaking</u>:

5.   Although the electricity is off, turn off the main electrical breaker switch to the house (usually located in the garage or utility room). If using an underground well for water, this will guarantee that the electric pump in the well will not operate to bring any water from the well into the house.

6.   Turn off the main valve bringing water into the house so no additional water gains access into the water pipes of the home.

7.   Drain the hot water heater (do not turn on the electric breaker controlling the hot water heater while the water heater is empty - it will cause serious damage to the heater).

8.   Open all taps (kitchen, sink, utility room) and allow water to drain out (you may wish to catch this water in a container for use). <u>Leave the taps open</u>.

Once the emergency is over and electrical power has been restored, (1) turn on the main electrical breaker switch, (2) turn <u>off</u> the breaker that controls the hot water heater, (3) close all open taps, (4) open the main water valve, (5) fill the hot water heater, and (6) turn <u>on</u> the breaker that controls the hot water heater. Depending on the conditions, you may wish to say in the "shelter-in-place" room until the furnace can regenerate adequate heat throughout the house.

PLACE OF REFUGE

A healthy human can survive for several weeks without food and several days without water. However, without proper shelter from the environment - especially during cold winter months, inclement weather, heat waves etc., chances of survival could be reduced to several hours. That is why it is important to *prepare in advance* for alternative shelter facilities and if necessary, know how to build an emergency survival shelter – or have a place of refuge in the event the team must evacuate the primary residence and find other facilities. This place of refuge would be designated as the "new primary residence" and would be considered as the location where team members could then focus on survival through the course of the emergency. In some cases, teams may elect to designate a location other than the primary residence as the principal place of refuge where team members will go at the very onset of the disaster (regardless of the condition of the homes where team members reside) and would remain at this location throughout the crisis.

If the main household of residence or designated primary residence is damaged or destroyed, there are many *layers* or *alternatives* that could be used for short-term, medium-term and long-term shelter purposes including:

- **Second Residence, i.e., cabin or summer home (stocked)**
- **Bomb Shelter (stocked)**
- **Motor Home (stocked)**
- **Travel Trailer (stocked)**
- **Camper (stocked)**
- **Houseboat (stocked)**
- **Public Shelter**
- Tent
- Sandbags
- Shed
- Barn
- Vacant Lot
- Horse Trailer
- Van/Car
- Abandoned buildings, structures or cars
- Friend or Relative
- Neighbor
- School
- Post Office (always open)
- Hotel/Motel
- Apartment/Condo
- Public Shelter
- Underground Bunker
- Igloo (during winter months)
- Caves
- Tree House
- Lean-To Structures (Tarps, Ropes, Knife)

> **Depending on the circumstances, team members should have <u>advanced permission</u> to access and reside in buildings and/or structures they do not legally own. Owners tend to become cranky when "squatters" set up house on their property.**
>
> **Although United States Post Office buildings are always open, this should <u>not</u> be considered as an open invitation to set up a permanent household. The post office would be only a very short-term (one night) solution until more permanent arrangements could be made for the team.**

An important factor to <u>consider</u> is the physical location of the place of refuge. As a general rule, if the place of refuge is a motor home, travel trailer or camper located on the property of the primary residence, make sure it is located as far away as possible from the primary residence - that way, if the primary residence is damaged or destroyed, there is a likelihood your alternative place of refuge may still be available. If it is to be a cabin or summer house, the location should <u>not</u> be any more than 5-10 miles from the primary residence. It may be possible for the team to walk a longer distance but it may not be advantageous to make the journey. For example, the canyon access to a cabin could be impassable, the roads leading to the summer house could be destroyed, or there could be mobs or gangs canvassing the vicinity creating unsafe travel conditions.

Unless the place of refuge is a government or church building, the structure should be a location where at least one team member has legal ownership or authority to occupy the physical premises or property. Unless circumstances require immediate action, all vacant buildings or structures should be avoided as a place of refuge – property owners generally do not take kindly to perceived "squatters" occupying their property - even during disasters.

If a cabin, summer house, motor home, travel trailer or camper are to be used as the place of refuge, try to stock it *in advance* with all basic emergency supplies needed for the duration of a disaster. During an actual disaster is <u>not</u> the time to begin stocking these places of refuge with emergency supplies.

PUBLIC SHELTERS AND RECEPTION CENTERS

<u>The first preference is to remain in our homes and/or primary residence during the course of a disaster.</u> But as we have learned, that may not always be possible and alternatives may have to be made by team members. Some teams may choose to head for the mountains or desert and others will have access to recreational vehicles. However, many teams will not have the luxury of these amenities, including most college students, citizens and illegal aliens living off government assistance, the homeless, the elderly, newlyweds, or individuals living in apartments, condominiums or

trailer courts. At some point in time during the course of an extended disaster, most citizens may have to rely on public shelters to offer shelter (in the event their home and/or primary residence is damaged or destroyed) as well as food, water, clothing, sanitation and first aid supplies once their own supplies have been used up.

There are other structures that may be designated as *reception centers*. In many cases, these structures include local churches (although many churches will plan to serve as actual shelters for their congregations) or even city or county buildings. The role of a reception center is to register refugees, perform triage (determine extent of injuries), provide *basic* first aid and advise city and/or county emergency personnel of any serious medical or transportation requirements. Government officials, in turn, would attempt to make arrangements for medical and/or transportation for individuals requiring additional care. In most cases, neither the county nor city would provide any food, water, clothing, sanitation or other emergency supplies to these reception centers. Individuals would be required to provide their own emergency supplies.

The federal government has given authority to the American Red Cross to scrutinize and designate government buildings and other public facilities that can be used as public shelters, if necessary, during an emergency. These buildings must meet stringent criteria, i.e., number of toilets, kitchen facilities and square footage, in order to be approved as being a public shelter facility. After a disaster has occurred, local emergency officials would contact the American Red Cross assigned to their region, and based on the severity and location of the disaster, the American Red Cross would approve specific structures that would serve as public shelters during the course of the emergency. The local officials would then provide this information to local citizens using communication media available in the area. As part of this plan, the Red Cross **IF POSSIBLE** would contract with local services to provide food, water, sanitation and medical support for the occupants in the public shelter. In many cases, recreation centers, stadiums, convention centers and local schools are designated as public shelters.

It is important to recognize a few significant points about both public shelters and reception centers:

- Individuals who are housed in either a public shelter or reception center would be required to register.

- Both public shelters and reception centers will become more crowded as the length of the disaster increases, both with families who loose the use of their home or primary residence and when families and individuals run out of food, water and other emergency supplies.

- Due to safety reasons, fire and fuel of any kind would not be allowed in any public shelter or reception area. Any cooking (if allowed) would be done outside of the building.

- There would be individuals who would insist on smoking, drinking and playing loud music.

- There will be a significant diversity of people from different races, wealth, ethnic backgrounds, creeds, cultures, customs, traditions, morals and religions - count on the fact that not everyone is not going to behave in the same way that you do - get ready for some possible confrontations.

- Most refugees would be frightened, angry, confused, frustrated, stressed and discouraged - which many times will lead to quick-tempered outbursts and the inability to tolerate the behaviors of others.

- There would be a large number of children whose parents are unable or unwilling to control their children's behavior and actions. Insist on parents controlling their children.

- Privacy and space for each team and/or individual would be limited.

- Count on long lines at available and/or working restrooms and food lines.

- It is possible that hardened criminals, pick-pockets, child molesters, thieves, drug dealers, addicts and gang members may also choose to take shelter in these public shelters or reception centers.

- Not everyone will consider using trash receptacles and toilets - prepare for probable garbage, trash, urine and feces in and around the facility.

- Prepare for bad smells - smells from unusual or rotten food, possible sewer backups, trash and garbage, urine and feces and lack of personal hygiene including individuals who are not *able* or *willing* to shower, brush their teeth, use deodorant or wash their clothes. This may even include you.

- Prepare for continual loud noises, screaming, talking and shouting. Not everyone will maintain the same sleep schedule.

- Prepare for interrupted, reduced or no utilities, including electricity, heat, air conditioning, lights, etc.

- Depending on the severity and the duration of the disaster, food, water, sanitation and medical supplies may or may not be available - even in public shelters.

Special care and precautions should be taken by team members at all times while staying in any type of public shelter or reception center - watch children carefully and enforce their good behavior and guard your supplies. On the other hand, the simple fact that there are a large number of people in the shelter would generally discourage thugs and gang members from challenging any one individual - there really is strength in numbers.

As part of *preparing in advance*, contact the local officials in your city, county and state and find out about the emergency plan in your area, where the public shelters and reception centers will be located, the process to be used to notify the public about availability, use, and rules and guidelines that will be enforced at the facility.

HEAT (WARMTH)

If living in a region that experiences cold temperatures, and depending on the time of year when an emergency happens, team members must have adequate heating sources. As part of *planning in advance*, make sure the primary residence and all homes where team members reside have ample insulation in the attic and walls of the structure. Various forms of insulation are also available for water pipes (under the sinks) and for flues attached to the furnace. Make sure all windows and doors are caulked. Make sure you have an outside thermometer to read temperatures.

Based on the severity of the disaster, it is probable utilities including electricity, natural gas and/or propane would be disrupted. For most households, the furnace heating the home requires electrical power. During a power outage lasting for an extended period of time and depending on the season, weather conditions or outside temperature, <u>a critical factor will be to maintain heat and warmth for the team – and the pets</u>! Again, a modified "shelter-in-place" plan could be used during this type of emergency situation.

It is important to have several *alternatives* or *layers* of heat (warmth) available such as:

- **Fireplace** (wood-burning)
- **Wood Burning Stove**
- **Wood** (for fireplace and stove)
- **Axe** (for cutting wood)
- **Coal** (for fireplace and stove)
- **Generator and Fuel** (preferably a <u>solar</u> powered generator)
- Space Heaters (electric and/or butane)
- Catalytic Heaters
- Barbeque and Briquettes – outside only (for heating hot water for hot water bottle, drinks etc.)
- **WARM CLOTHING** (coats, shirts, pants, socks, shoes, hats, gloves, robe, sleepwear, slippers)
- **Rain Gear**
- **Thermal Underwear**
- Chemical Hand and Feet Warmers
- Hot Water Bottle
- Heating Pad
- **BEDDING** (quilts and blankets)
- **SLEEPING BAGS** (tested for cold weather)
- **Plastic** (Heavy-Duty) - place over windows/doorways
- **Stapler and Staples** (Heavy-Duty)

- Campfire
- **Matches**
- Flint Fire Starter Tool
- Fire Extinguisher
- Fire Alarm (battery operated)
- Carbon Monoxide Detector (battery operated)
- Tent (pop tent that does not require staking)
- Card Table (for making a tent)

> It is easier to heat a small space than a large space. Consider setting up a freestanding pop tent inside the room where you plan to sleep. The tent would trap and conserve heat – even if it's only body heat. Another way to set up a tent is to use a card table and spread a large blanket or quilt over the top and sides. Either way, the idea is to contain all the heat you can in a small space. This concept can also be used to house and shelter pets during cold temperatures.

BLANKETS AND BEDDING

There are many types of blankets on the market today. Assuming the primary residence is intact and you live there during the emergency, you may require alternative heat sources. These blankets would be <u>located</u> at the primary residence, would <u>stay</u> at the primary residence and would be <u>used</u> at the primary residence.

CLOTHING

Depending on the level of disaster (1-3), all manufacturing, wholesale and local retail clothing outlets could be damaged or destroyed within a short period of time. There are specific types of clothing that should be part of all team members' emergency pantries depending on the time of year, season, temperature and weather conditions. The clothing for THIS event should be manufactured for every-day use and for the work environment. Clothing articles do not need to be new items, <u>but should be well made and in good condition</u>. There are many places where used clothing can be purchased including charitable organizations, garage sales, second-hand stores, or even from relatives, friends and neighbors.

Consider the likelihood of growth and expansion for most team members – infants, children and teenagers will more than likely grow taller and adults tend to grow wider - - - sigh. When selecting clothing for emergency pantries –spring, summer, fall or winter seasons – hot and cold temperatures – dry and wet weather - use common sense and select items that are durable, resilient, hard-wearing, long-lasting and flexible. Choose fabrics that are "wash and wear" – easy wash – quick dry – no iron! Clothing articles should be distributed over the primary residence, place of refuse, automobile, evacuation and work pantries. If applicable, the emphasis should be placed on <u>warm</u> clothing during cold and wet seasons. <u>In cold regions, it could be warm bedding and warm clothing that will provide the warmth we need to survive.</u> <u>Prepare yourselves.</u>

BABY SUPPLIES

If the team currently has or plans to have a baby in the future, planning and preparation must be made for clothing and supplies. If this is the first baby to the household, purchase a baby book providing detailed information on raising a baby. There may be an ample supply of used clothing and supplies worn and used by older children in the closet that can certainly be passed down to this new or future arrival of the household.

If there is <u>any</u> possibility of a new baby in the foreseeable future, be very cautious about donating current supplies of clothing – keep them! If this clothing is not actually used by a new arrival – the clothing can be used as a bartering tool for other items needed by the team during a disaster. Baby clothes and supplies are expensive. Check out garage sales, discount stores and charitable outlets in addition to department store sales. During disaster situations, teams could set up a swap meet with other teams to exchange and/or share baby supplies.

Most families with children in diapers cannot afford to purchase sufficient disposable diapers to support lengthy disasters - it is unrealistic. If you have a baby in the home, you may find a diaper problem under emergency conditions. It is best to keep an ample supply of disposable *and* <u>cloth</u> diapers on hand for emergency use. In addition, any moisture resistant material can be cut and folded to diaper size and lined with absorbent material. Most families with children in diapers, however, cannot afford to purchase sufficient diapers to support lengthy disasters. <u>During a disaster lasting for an extended period of time, parents may be forced to consider unpopular decisions on how often a diaper will be changed.</u> Get Ready!

TOOLS

Due to the critical nature of including tools, hardware and parts in the emergency supply pantries, I have provided a list of tools that should be considered by team members during any disaster. These tools will be used across most every element and can and will make the difference in surviving any level of disaster.

CONSTRUCTION/REPAIR/MAINTENANCE		GARDENING & YARD TOOLS
Bars	Paintbrush	AXE
Bolt Cutter	Planers	HATCHET
Bolts / Nuts	**PLIERS**	HOE
Cement Trials	Punch	**LAWN MOWER** (Manual)
Chisels	Putty	Lopper
Clamps	**RATCHETS/SOCKETS**	PICK
Crimpers	Sand Paper	PITCH FORK
Duct Tape	Sander	PLOW
Files	**SAWS**	PRUNER
Glass Cutter	Scrapers	PRUNING SAW
Glue	**SCREWDRIVERS**	RAKES
HAMMERS	**Screws**	SHEARS
KNIFE (putty, utility)	**SLEDGE HAMMER**	SHOVEL
KNIFE SHARPENER	Snips	Spades
LADDERS	Spikes	Weeder
Level	Squares	
Lumber	Tape Measure	**MAKE SURE ALL TOOLS AND PARTS ARE IN THEIR PROPER PLACE – ORGANIZED – EASILY ACCESSIBLE!**
Mallet (rubber)	Vise	
Miter Box with Saw	**Washers**	
Nails	**WEDGE**	
Nut Drivers	**WRENCHES**	

ELECTRICITY

Electricity is <u>extremely vulnerable</u> to most disaster types. With few exceptions, the power grid is susceptible to earthquakes, explosions, extreme cold, fire, floods, heat waves, hurricanes, landslides, lightning storms, nuclear attacks, riots, terrorist attacks, thunderstorms, tornados, tsunamis, volcanoes, war, wind and winter storms. There is no manmade resource that can totally and completely bring down an entire civilization, their standard of living, their ability to survive and their will to live like the "power" of electricity. The ultimate "power" of electricity is the ability to <u>control</u> the power of the other elements!

When the power is out, gasoline pumps cease to function, computers are inoperable, cash registers shut down, garage doors will not open, television stations and household televisions are quiet, light bulbs are cold and dark, x-ray machines are lifeless, restaurants and fast food outlets are closed, banks are unable to handle funds, furnaces and air conditioners are silent, water taps are dry, household appliances are unresponsive, government agencies are scrambling to find data that is now inaccessible and the utility companies are frantic to restore the life-blood back into our lives.

ONE OF THE MOST IMPORTANT CONTINGENCIES TO BE MADE FOR ADVANCED PLANNING IN EMERGENCY PREPARATION IS THE ABILITY TO SECURE ELECTRICAL POWER TO BE UTILIZED ON A DAILY BASIS USING A RELIABLE AND NATURAL SOURCE TO GENERATE THE ELECTRICITY. The obvious answer is **<u>solar power</u>** using the sun as the natural source to generate the electricity. With *solar panels* or a *solar powered generator*, many of your electrical appliances may be able to be used during the emergency when the standard electrical grid is out.

Another positive argument for a solar power is that households relying on electrical power for running the furnace (electricity is required to run the motor), turning on all or some of the lights, running the electrical pump in an underground well used to bring water to the surface, and running medical equipment (oxygen) - will quickly discover that a solar power can provide this vital source of electricity during a disaster.

Solar power can also provide power for small electric heaters to heat individual rooms in the home and a small electric hot plate for cooking meals. Furthermore, for emergency supplies requiring batteries, unless the team has a solar powered battery charger and there is an ample supply of batteries – at some point in time, the batteries are going to expire or will need to be recharged – using – electricity.

Even with the use of a solar power source and when preparing for a disaster across all elements, every effort should still be made to purchase and store sources, items and supplies that does <u>not</u> directly or indirectly require electrical power. Be prepared for a challenge. Many items requiring manual operation are hard to find and alternatives to electrical power can be extremely expensive for the middle-class household.

If possible, it is important to have several *layers* or *alternatives* of electrical power available such as:

- **GENERATOR - SOLAR POWERED (SHORT, MIDDLE, LONG-TERM)**
- **SOLAR PANELS (SHORT, MIDDLE, LONG-TERM)**
- Wind Turbine (long-term)
- Generator and Fuel (short-term)
- **SOLAR POWERED BATTERY CHARGER/BATTERIES (SHORT TO LONG-TERM)**

LIGHT

One of the elements largely affected by electric power disruption is providing light for our households or shelters during an emergency. It is important to have several *alternatives* or *layers* of light available such as:

- Candles
- Flashlights (solar/hand crank)
- Lamps
- Lanterns (solar/battery/fuel)

- Light Bulbs
- Light Sticks
- Matches
- Mirror *

- Oil Lamps
- Solar Battery Charger
- Solar Garden Lights
- Sun

*place behind oil lamp or candle to make the light brighter!

WATER

REMEMBER - THERE IS NO SUBSTITUTE FOR WATER. Having an ample supply of clean <u>drinking</u> water is a top priority in any emergency. A normally active person should drink at least two quarts (half gallon) of water each day. Individuals living in hot environments, children, nursing mothers, and sick people require even more water. Teams should store at least one gallon of drinking water per person/pet per day and consider storing at least a two-week supply of drinking water for each team member and pet. If supplies run low, minimize the amount of water the body needs by reducing activity and staying cool. The most common signs and symptoms of dehydration are:

- Dark and sunken eyes
- Dark urine with a very strong odor and low input
- Delayed capillary refill in fingernail beds
- Emotional instability
- Fatigue
- Loss of elasticity in the skin
- Thirst - you are already two percent dehydrated by the time the body craves fluids
- Trench line down center of tongue

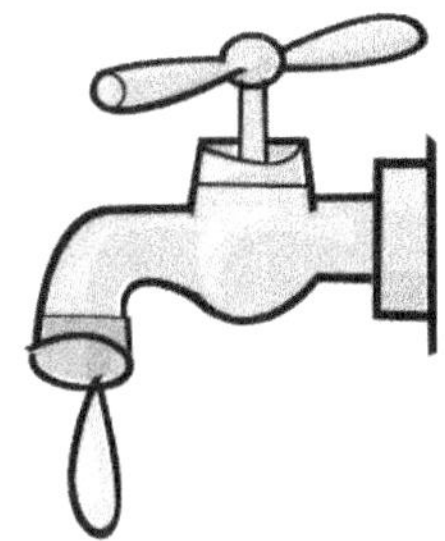

The body also looses electrolytes (body salts) with the loss of water. Our diet can generally keep up with these losses but in a disaster, additional sources are needed. <u>A mixture of ¼ teaspoon of salt to one quart of water will provide a concentration the body can absorb</u>.

During an emergency, team members should drink water when eating since it is used as part of digestion and can lead to dehydration if not enough water is consumed. If necessary, ration water until a suitable source is found. A daily intake of ½ quart of a sugar-water mixture (2 teaspoons sugar per quart of water) will suffice to prevent severe dehydration for at least a week provided you keep water losses to a minimum by limiting activity and heat gain or loss. Limit sweat producing activities but continue to drink water.

As part of emergency preparation planning, the need of water for certain individuals and circumstances could require a larger amount of water being stored than just the minimum requirement. For example:

- **Activities** – increased physical activities and work could result in the need for additional water.

- **Babies** - consider how much water is needed for preparing formula, baby food and personal hygiene.

- **Foods** – depending on the type of food storage in emergency pantries, i.e., freeze-dried or dehydrated rather than canned and ready to eat, you will need additional water to prepare them.

- **Habit** – many people drink a lot of water as part of an overall health regiment and to dramatically cut back on this regiment, especially during a disaster, could result in physical complications.

- **Heat** – if living in an area with extreme heat during the summer months and if the crisis was to occur during this time, additional water would be required to meet minimal needs.

- **Invalids** – consider their need for increased water to take medications or for personal care.

- **Pets** – family pets and livestock will also need to have a fresh and ample supply of water.

- **Teenagers** – generally have more energy than adults and need more of water. As part of *planning in advance*, conduct serious discussions with teens on what the allowable water rations will be during a disaster and the necessary containment of activities that will be required.

WATER TYPES

Based on the severity of the disaster, it is likely water lines will be damaged or destroyed. There are several types of water sources that should be available for team members including (1) drinking, (2) cooking, (3) personal hygiene i.e. bathing, brushing teeth, washing hair, (4) laundry, (5) cleaning and disinfecting, i.e., cleaning counters and appliances and washing dishes, (6) toilet, and (7) water for pets, livestock and plants.

Since the most vital water is used for drinking and depending on the <u>level</u> (1-3) of the disaster, you may be able to stay at the primary residence or the team may be forced to evacuate and seek alternative shelter. This alternative shelter may or may not have water sources available. Regardless of the level of disaster or whether the team members will be at the primary residence or located in another area, it is important to have *alternatives* or *layers* of drinking and other water available such as:

White Water

White water used for *drinking, cooking, brushing teeth* and *washing dishes* comes from several <u>safe</u> and <u>uncontaminated</u> sources including:

- **Wells** - safe water that comes from underground rivers or aqueducts and is pumped up to the surface of the ground by electric pumps and then forced into the home using water pipes. Water from wells service most individuals living in a country setting as well as many city residents.

- **Reservoirs** - safe water flowing along natural or manmade pathways into natural or manmade depositories that hold water used by citizens living in the nearby area.

- **Springs** - safe water from underground rivers or aqueducts that naturally comes to the surface of the ground.

- **Toilet Tank** - safe water that flows *into* the toilet <u>tank</u>.

- **Creeks and Streams** - safe water coming from either melting snow high in the mountains or from springs that have naturally come to the surface of the ground and now <u>rapidly</u> flow downhill. In order for this water to be safe for drinking, the water must flow swiftly enough to prohibit any animals or fish from being able to live, swim, walk, drink, defecate or urinate in the water.

- **Rain** - safe water that falls <u>directly</u> into a sanitized water-safe container.

- **Bottled** - safe water that is commercially available in plastic containers.

- **Drums** - safe water *previously* stored in large drums (55-gallon) or containers and contains bleach based on the size of the drum.

- **Tankers** - safe water *previously* stored in large 275+ gallon water tankers and contains bleach based on the size of the tanker.

- **Hot Water Heater** - safe water stored in hot water heater.

- **Juices** - from vegetable and fruit cans and bottles.

- **Radiator** - safe water stored in the radiator.

- **Hot Water Boiler** - safe water stored in a hot water boiler.

- **Snow** - fresh and clean snow must be melted - avoid the yellow stuff!

- **Underground Still** - safe water vapor in the air that condenses into water in an underground still.

It is highly probable safe <u>white</u> water will be scarce. However, if there is **no doubt** there will be an adequate supply of white water available for the entire length of the disaster, then this water can and should be utilized; however, if there is **any doubt** whatsoever that white water is or will become scarce, <u>white</u> water that is *clean*, *sanitary* and *uncontaminated* should be used for only four (4) major tasks as follows:

- **Drinking*** - water used for human drinking
- **Teeth** - water used for brushing teeth and cleaning dentures
- **Eating** - water used for cooking food, making ice cubes or is required in the recipe
- **Dishes** - water used for washing and rinsing dishes

If white water is plentiful, there are three (3) additional tasks that can be included as follows:

- **Drinking** - water used for drinking by animals, pets and livestock
- **Cleaning**** - water used for general cleaning purposes including counters, spills etc.
- **Personal Hygiene**** - water used for showering, bathing and washing hair

*If necessary, water from natural resources such as lakes, rivers and streams could be used for drinking and cooking by humans provided water is correctly boiled, chlorinated or distilled.

**Although it is preferred to use white water for showering, bathing, washing hair and cleaning - it will more than likely be necessary to use gray water since safe white water may be scarce.

<u>**Gray Water**</u>

The water has previously been used for specific purposes **and/or** contains some contaminates that may be harmful if ingested. Gray water comes from several sources as follows:

<u>**Previously Used**</u>

- **Dishes** - water that was previously used for washing and rinsing the dishes
- **Laundry** - water that was previously used for washing clothes
- **Bath or Shower** - water that was previously used for taking a bath or shower
- **Water Bed** - water from a water bed treated with chemicals including bleach
- **Swimming Pool** - water from a swimming pool treated with chemicals
- **Hot Tub** - water from a hot tub treated with chemicals

Depending on the level and type of contamination or chemicals in the water, this previously used gray water could be used again for:

- **Personal Hygiene** - shower or bath - avoid water containing bleach or strong chemicals
- **Washing Hair** - washing hair - avoid water containing bleach or strong chemicals
- **Shaving** - shaving face/arms/legs - avoid water containing bleach or strong chemicals
- **Garden** (outdoor and indoor) - fruits and vegetables (avoid water containing bleach or strong chemicals)
- **Trees, shrubs and vines** - avoid water containing bleach or strong chemicals
- **Cleaning** - wiping floors, counters*, appliances*, spills*, garbage cans, toilet*
- **Toilet** - manual flushing
  *use disinfectant (if possible) after wiping

<u>**Contains Some Contaminates**</u>

- **Natural Sources** - water coming from dams, lakes, rivers, canals, ponds and streams
- **Rain** - water that falls on the roof of the house and then flows directly into a sanitized container
- **Toilet Bowl** - water from tank into <u>bowl</u> *with no urine, feces or bodily fluids*

Depending on the level and type of contamination or chemicals in the water, this semi safe water can be used for:

- **Drinking** - water for animals, pets and livestock
- **Personal Hygiene** - shower or bath
- **Washing Hair** - water used for washing hair
- **Shaving** - water used for shaving the face, underarms or legs
- **Laundry** - water used for laundry
- **Plants** (outdoor and indoor) - watering fruits, vegetables, trees, shrubs, vines, grass
- **Cleaning** - wiping floors, counters*, appliances*, spills*, trash cans, toilet*
- **Toilet** - manual flushing
  *use disinfectant (if possible) after wiping

NOTE: Safe water coming *into* the toilet tank is considered <u>white</u> water. Once the water leaves the tank and flows into the bowl, it is considered <u>gray</u> water even though the water may contain no urine, feces or bodily fluids. The toilet bowl itself is unsanitary and contains countless bacteria and germs as well as other chemicals used to actually keep the toilet bowl clean. Once the bowl contains urine, feces or other bodily fluids, it is really not safe for any human/pet use.

<u>**Black Water**</u>

The water has previously been used for specific purposes **and/or** due to a natural phenomenon, now contains contaminates that are unsafe for any human or animal use. Black water can come from several unsafe sources as follows:

- **Toilet Bowl** - water that flowed from the tank into the toilet bowl and now contains urine, feces, bodily fluids or other icky stuff

- **Rain** - water known to be *acid* rain

- **Ponds** - *standing* water containing debris, trash, large amounts of dirt, dead humans and animals, feces, urine

- **Natural/Manmade Sources** - contaminated water with dangerous chemicals and/or toxins from manufacturing plants, or littered with debris, trash, dead humans or animals, feces, urine and other substances deposited by humans into lakes, rivers, canals, ponds and streams

- **Salt Water Sources** - contains salt including oceans, seas and lakes

During an emergency, and when water sources become scarce, there will be confrontations taking place between individuals and groups on rights to the water and being able to take water from a source. As part of *planning in advance*, know where <u>all</u> water sources are located in your area. For example, dams, lakes, rivers, creeks, streams and springs are obvious sources of water. Keep in mind that during a water shortage, many people will be lined up at these particular sources to get water. Locate other less obvious sources (natural springs or small creeks) adjacent to the primary residence and/or evacuation location.

<u>**Hidden Water at the Residence**</u>

There are safe drinking water sources in the primary residence including water in the hot-water tank, pipes and even ice cubes. Team members should protect water sources already in the primary residence from contamination if there are broken water or sewage lines, and if local officials advise you of a problem. To shut off incoming water, locate the main valve and turn it to the closed position. Be sure all <u>adult</u> team members know *in advance* how to perform this important procedure.

After shutting off the main value and to use the water in the pipes, let air into the plumbing by turning on the faucet in the home at the *highest* level. A small amount of water will trickle out. Now get water flowing out of the *lowest* faucet in the home. To use the water in the hot-water tank, make sure electricity or gas is off and open the drain at the bottom of the tank. Start the water flowing by turning off the water intake valve at the tank and turning on a hot-water faucet. Refill the tank before turning electricity or gas back on. If the *natural* gas is turned off, a professional will be needed to turn it back on and reinstate gas service to the house.

> Make sure you KNOW <u>in</u> <u>advance</u> where water from *natural* sources and especially flowing springs are located. During a serious disaster, a person's claim of owning the rights to the water will become insignificant. Make sure you have the tools and equipment needed to transport the water.

There are several sources of water <u>not acceptable</u> as a water source for *drinking*. These include *alcoholic beverages* that dehydrate the body. *Urine* contains harmful body wastes and an excessive amount of salt. *Sea water* contains over four percent salt and takes over two gallons of body fluids to rid the body of waste from one gallon of sea water. By drinking sea water, you deplete the water supply in your body resulting in death. Finally, *blood* is salty, requires additional body fluids to digest and can transmit deadly diseases.

<u>**Taste and Appearance**</u>

Stored water tastes "flat" (as does boiled water) because it has no air in it. It does not harm the water in any way. Pouring it back and forth between two containers can add oxygen back into the water and make it taste better. Refrigeration, if available, also helps the taste. There are also taste-neutralizer tablets and commercial carbon filters on the market that will remove chemical odors and tastes.

TREATING WATER

If using bottled water, make sure the seal is not broken. Otherwise, water should be boiled or treated before use. Boiling water kills harmful bacteria and parasites and by bringing water to a rolling boil for one minute will kill most organisms. If you cannot boil water, treat water with chlorine tablets, iodine tablets or unscented household chlorine bleach (5.25% sodium hypochlorite).

If using chlorine tablets or iodine tablets, follow the directions that come with the tablets. If using household chlorine bleach, add **1/8 teaspoon of bleach per gallon** of water if the water is clear. For cloudy water, add ¼ teaspoon of bleach per gallon. Mix the solution thoroughly and let stand for thirty minutes before using it. Treating water with chlorine tablets, iodine tablets or liquid bleach will not kill many parasite organisms. <u>Boiling is the best way to kill these organisms</u>. In addition to having a bad odor and taste, contaminated water can contain microorganisms (germs, bacteria, and viruses) that cause disease such as dysentery, typhoid and hepatitis. You should treat all water of uncertain quality before using it for drinking, food preparation or personal hygiene.

There are many methods to treat water and often the best solution is a combination of methods. For example, boiling or chlorination will kill most microorganisms but will not remove other contaminants such as heavy metals, salts and most other chemicals. Before treating, allow any suspended particles to settle at the bottom, or strain them through layers of paper towel, clean cloth or a coffee filter. The instructions below are for treating water of <u>uncertain</u> quality in emergency situations when no other reliable clean water source is available.

Boiling	In a large pot or kettle, bring water to a rolling boil for one full minute, keeping in mind that some water will evaporate. Let water cool before drinking. Boiled water will taste better if you replace oxygen by pouring the water back and forth between two clean containers. This will also improve the taste of stored water.
Chlorination	Use newly opened regular household liquid bleach containing 5.25 to 6.0 percent sodium hypochlorite. Do <u>not</u> use scented bleaches, color safe bleaches, or bleaches with added cleaners. Add 16 drops (1/8 teaspoon) of bleach per gallon of water, stir and let stand for thirty minutes. The water should have a slight bleach odor. If not, repeat the dosage and let stand another fifteen minutes. If the water still does not smell of bleach, discard it and find another source of water. Iodine or water treatment products (sold in camping or surplus stores) that do not contain 5.25 to 6.0 percent sodium hypochlorite as the only active ingredient should not be used.
Distillation	Distillation will remove microorganisms and heavy metals, salts, and other chemicals. Distillation is boiling water and collecting the vapor that condenses back to water. The condensed vapor will not include salt or other impurities. Fill a pot halfway full with water. Tie a cup to the handle on the pot's lid so that the cup will hang right-side-up when the lid is upside-down (make sure the cup is not dangling into the water), and boil the water for twenty minutes. The water that drips from the lid into the cup is distilled.

SOURCE: Federal Emergency Management Administration/United States Army

<u>**Rain Barrel**</u>

A good item to include in emergency supplies is a rain barrel. When water is scarce and at premium prices, a rain barrel full of water can give the team a valuable and important water resource. A rain barrel can be above or below the ground. The concept of a rain barrel is to collect rain water from the roof or directly from the clouds and into a barrel. Even a brief summer shower will quickly fill a rain barrel. A quarter-inch of rain falling on a 14' by 25' roof area will provide almost fifty gallons of water. This rain water can then used to water the garden, take showers, and other non-drinking uses. Another use for a rain barrel is to collect rain water to be used for <u>drinking</u> purposes. In this case, the rain is directed into the barrel *before* it falls to the ground. Rain barrels are available for purchase through commercial outlets and come with features that make saving water easy and convenient.

SHELF LIFE OF WATER

Water can be stored for long periods of time - up to ten years or more, if it does not react with the container or its components. Drinkable water stored in glass or polyethylene containers will remain safe, but may change in taste or odor. Although some of these qualities may be undesirable, they are not harmful. Check stored water every year to determine whether the containers have leaked or if any undesirable characteristics have developed.

TRANSPORTING WATER

As a guideline, consider that <u>one gallon of water weighs eight pounds</u> – govern yourself accordingly. How much water you <u>should</u> carry is going to realistically be superseded by how much you <u>can</u> carry. As part of our focus on *planning in advance* for an emergency, fill some jugs or bottles with water and practice carrying them to your car, down the stairs or across the street. Even better, walk to your nearest natural source of water (river, lake, spring, well) with your bucket, fill the bucket with water, and carry the bucket filled with water back to your home. It may seem absurd now but during an emergency situation, team members do not want to learn how heavy a container of water can be or how it seems to increase in weight the further it is carried.

> Another method to carry water is to use a heavy-duty polyethylene trash bag and place it <u>inside</u> of a pillowcase. The trash bag serves as a water proof liner! Slick!

SHUTTING OFF UTILITIES

<u>Gas and Propane</u>

For households using *natural* gas, an automatic valve (Earthquake Command System) is commercially available that turns the gas off in the event of an earthquake. After an emergency situation and especially an earthquake, do <u>not</u> use matches, lighters, appliances, or operate light switches unless certain there are no gas or propane leaks. Sparks from electrical switches can ignite gas or propane causing an explosion.

If you smell the odor of gas or propane or notice a large consumption of gas being registered on the gas meter, shut off the gas or propane immediately by finding the main shut-off valve, generally located on a pipe next to the gas meter (if using natural gas) and located on the top of the propane tank (if using propane). Use an adjustable wrench to turn the valve to the "off" position. Whether using natural gas or propane, *prepare in advance* <u>by tying an adjustable wrench to the gas meter or propane valve</u>. That way, you will not have to waste valuable time looking for a wrench when the gas needs to be turned off.

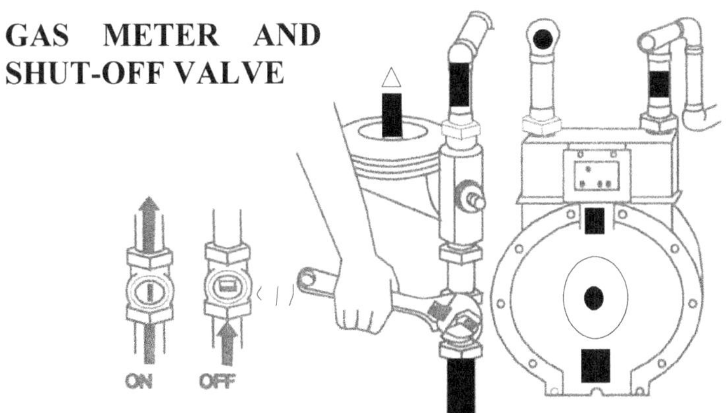

> **Before turning off natural gas, make sure that it is essential to do so to avoid an explosion. <u>Once turned off, only a professional from the gas company can turn it back on.</u>**

The <u>natural</u> gas meter shutoff diagram shows the shutoff valve location on the pipe coming out of the ground. To turn off the valve, use a wrench to turn the valve clockwise one-quarter turn.

<u>**Electricity**</u>

After a major disaster, shut off the electricity. Sparks from electrical switches can create a shock or fire hazard. Carefully turn off electricity using the main breaker switch on the electrical panel in your home.

<u>**Water**</u>

For individuals using city water, water can generally be turned off at two locations: (1) the main meter, which controls water flow to the entire property, and (2) the water main leading into the home. Shutting off the water main retains the water supply in your water heater. For individuals using well water, water is turned off at the main valve located somewhere inside the house. Depending on your water source, make sure water valves are marked and easily identified as **INSIDE** and **OUTSIDE**. <u>Attach a wrench to the water line and/or valves.</u>

PUMPKIN COOKIES

½ cup shortening *or* butter
1 ½ cups granulated white sugar
1 egg
1 cup pumpkin
½ cup chopped nuts
1 cup raisins *and/or* chocolate chips
1 ½ cups white flour
1 teaspoon vanilla
1 teaspoon cinnamon
1 teaspoon nutmeg
1 teaspoon baking powder
1 teaspoon baking soda
½ teaspoon salt

Mix all ingredients together. Drop by spoonful on cookie sheet. Bake at 375 degrees for 10 minutes.

OATMEAL COOKIES

2 cups white flour
1 teaspoon salt
1 teaspoon baking soda
4 ½ cups rolled oats
½ cup vegetable oil
1 teaspoon vanilla
¾ cup honey
3 eggs
½ cup raisins, soaked in 3-4 tablespoons water

Stir together flour, salt, baking soda and oats. Add vegetable oil, vanilla, honey, eggs and raisins. Mix together and drop by spoonful on greased baking sheet. Bake at 350 degrees for about 8 minutes.

WHOLE WHEAT BROWNIES

1 cup shortening, melted
5 tablespoons cocoa
4 eggs, beaten
2 cups whole wheat flour
1 cup granulated white sugar

Beat together all ingredients and spread in greased and floured 9x13 inch pan. Bake at 350 degrees for 25 minutes. Brownies will set up after being taken out of oven.

CHAPTER SEVEN

MEDICATION

A critical component in an emergency preparation plan is to have <u>current</u> medical, medication and immunization needs fully addressed <u>prior to any emergency</u> to reduce overall medical needs that may arise during a disaster. *I cannot stress enough the importance of being proactive in getting treatment for any type of medical ailment or injury in a <u>timely</u> manner and stocking any products or supplies used to treat body malfunctions! During a serious disaster, due to contaminated water and food sources and sewage backups, there will be plenty of medical ailments and serious injuries without worrying and dealing with a painful toothache, dry skin, chapped lips or a headache.*

After a major disaster, we must assume most first responders, clinics, hospitals, pharmacies and other medical institutions in the area would be out of action and/or overwhelmed. In fact, it is likely outside assistance may not be available for days, weeks or even months after the disaster. Depending on the severity of <u>current</u> medical conditions and specific medications taken by team members – life-saving medical treatment or prescription medications may not be available. <u>Remember, during many disasters, there will be casualties due to injuries and lack of available medical and pharmaceutical treatments</u>. During serious or long-term disasters, there will also be suicides. Prepare mentally and psychologically for these casualties.

It could be legitimately argued that physicians who practiced medicine fifty to one hundred years ago would be better able to serve patients in an emergency than those who practice today. During a serious and long-term disaster, medical services may be compromised because of the inability of physicians to practice medicine without advanced technology.

EMERGENCY PREPARATION GUIDELINES

There are several guidelines that can be incorporated into an overall emergency plan to prepare for and in some cases eliminate medical issues that could become prevalent during an emergency situation. For example:

- Sign up for CPR, FIRST AID or CERT training courses and learn the procedures for basic lifesaving techniques including mouth-to-mouth resuscitation and the Heimlich maneuver.

- Learn alternative methods for treating wounds, burns, infections, blisters, diarrhea, constipation and nausea.

- Study and learn alternative methods for using herbs and other natural sources to heal the body and keep the body healthy.

- All supplies in the first aid kits should be freshly stocked, not expired and in good working condition.

- A "word of wisdom" to everyone – maintain a healthy weight, eat nutritious food, exercise, avoid tobacco, alcohol, and illegal drug use and abuse of prescription and over-the-counter drugs.

- Know the exact location of nearby hospitals and medical treatment centers and have a list of phone numbers for your physician, dentist and other medical personnel in a convenient and safe place in the home, car and work (consider laminating the list).

- Keep all medical equipment (wheelchairs, crutches) in good working condition.

- Keep all <u>electronic</u> medical equipment and supplies (diabetic) in good working condition.

- Ensure that all prescription and over-the-counter medicines have not expired (and if so, replace them).

- Keep all <u>prescriptions</u> filled and attempt to keep at least a three-month supply.

- Everyone should schedule a yearly overall <u>medical and dental</u> examination.

- Anyone with <u>vision</u> problems should have regular examinations and up-to-date prescriptions for glasses and contacts and have an extra pair of glasses including sunglasses.

- Maintain a list of all medications in wallet or purse including drug name, strength, dosage, and schedule.

- Wear a medical-alert bracelet or necklace at all times and/or keep any other medical information device up-to-date and readily available.

- Any medications used to stabilize an existing medical condition or keep a condition from worsening (medications for asthma, seizures, cardiovascular disorders, diabetes, psychiatric conditions, HIV, and thyroid disorders) should be carried with you, if possible, in a purse or briefcase in labeled containers.

- Do not store medications in areas susceptible to extremes in heat, cold, and humidity (e.g., car, kitchen or bathroom) as this could decrease the effectiveness of the medication.

- If children or pets are in the home, use child-resistant containers, and secure all medicine cabinets, purse, wallet and briefcase.

- Rotate medications whenever prescriptions are refilled to use them before the expiration date.

- Refill prescriptions while still having a 5-7 day supply of medication. Keep in mind that some sources, such as mail-order pharmacies, have a longer refill lead time.

- If your child takes medications, talk to the school and learn their emergency preparedness plans.

- If being treated with a complex medication regimen, talk to your physician or pharmacist to create appropriate emergency preparation plans. Such regimens include injectable medications, including those delivered by pumps (e.g., insulin, analgesics, chemotherapy), medications delivered by a nebulizer (e.g., antibiotics, bronchodilators) and dialysis.

MEDICAL INFORMATION FOR RESPONDERS

Recalling details of medications, diseases or disabilities does not come easily during a medical emergency and especially during a serious disaster. Emergencies happen when we least expect it, so it is important to prepare ahead of time. Here are some products and services designed to assist in preparing for an emergency. Regardless of which one you use, <u>be sure to *regularly* update medical information</u>. Outdated information may be *more* dangerous than none at all.

E-HealthKEY from MedicAlert Foundation International (www.medicalert.org)

The E-HealthKEY is from MedicAlert that keeps all personal medical information available on a portable USB device attached to a key ring. The device is supported by a database at MedicAlert headquarters. Medical information is made available using any PC with an Internet connection. A computer not connected online can access the emergency section in the device. The cost is approximately $40.00. *Problem:* Some ambulances do not have computers.

Medic Tag USB Device

Medic Tag is a Windows PC compatible USB device (portable flash drive) that does not use the Internet to access personal medical information. They are easy to use with nothing to install and has preloaded software. Most devices have 256 megabytes of memory to store medical information and contact lists. Over 95% of emergency responders will check for a bracelet, necklace or key chain for medical information. A first responder can easily view and print out the list. The cost is approximately $30.00. *Problem:* Some ambulances are not equipped with portable computers to access these devices.

Personal Medical Jewelry

Medical bracelets or necklaces have basic personal medical information engraved on the back of the jewelry and emergency workers can immediately see important conditions or allergies. Jewelry may also be used to address end-of-life decisions. Some jewelry is supported with databases that can be accessed by emergency workers. The cost is approximately $10.00. *Problem:* You have to wear it!

Wallet Cards

A simple <u>laminated</u> personal medical information card for first responders can be carried in the wallet or purse. It does not need to be detailed, but should cover basic information:

- ***Name / Birthdate***
- ***Drug or food allergies***
- ***Prescription Medications***
- ***Medical Conditions***
- ***Emergency Contacts***

Whether you print the information on a card with a computer or by hand, <u>make sure it is legible</u>. *Problem:* Ambulance personnel may not look in your purse or wallet. The card will be found at the hospital.

Cell Phone on ICE (icesticker.com) or 1425 Market Blvd, Suite 330-155, Roswell, GA 30076

ICE stands for "In Case of Emergency." Putting "ICE" next to a number in the cell phone's contact list will tell medical or law enforcement personnel which number to call in an emergency. A sticker on the outside of the phone will alert emergency workers that there is an emergency contact identified in the contact section of the phone. By accessing the website, you can purchase the stickers. Prices range from $2.00 for one sticker, $7.50 for 5 stickers, $10.00 for 10 stickers, $25.00 for 50 stickers and $60.75 for 250 stickers. *Problem:* Ambulance personnel may not look in your phone. They will take the phone to the hospital where workers may find it and can call the emergency contact.

Vial of Life (www.vialoflife.com) – (888) 724-1200

The *Vial of Life Project* is free to use and provides a decal and form to fill out with medical information. Fill out the Vial of Life form and answer all or any pertinent questions. Make blank copies of the form to keep information current or go to the website to maintain and store updated information. Attach a decal to the front of a heavy-duty plastic baggie. You may also consider placing a copy of an EKG, living will or equivalent, DNR (Do Not Resuscitate) and a recent photo of yourself. Securely tape the plastic baggie at eye level to the front of the refrigerator door. Place a second decal on the front door or window for easy visibility by anyone responding to a medical emergency.

The Vial of Life system can work in the automobile and at work. In the automobile, place a decal in a secure location <u>inside</u> of the car, e.g., windshield or visor. Then place the baggie (with a decal on the front) in the glove compartment. At work, the baggie can be placed in a conspicuous location in your office area and/or given to a trustworthy and responsible individual in the office. *Problem*: **None - good choice**!

Scroll Identification

The scroll is a keychain device with a small scroll inside for personal medical information. It carries the same type of personal medical information as a wallet card. One method to draw attention to the keychain is to identify the outside of the container as a medical information device using some type of medical sticker. Identification issues are eliminated by putting the owner's picture on the scroll. The cost is approximately $5.00. *Problem:* This product is not as well known and rescuers may not recognize this object as a medical information device.

DISEASES AND INJURIES OF DISASTER

During peaceful times, the "diseases of disaster" may be rare in this country, but a disaster carries with it increased sanitation issues which will activate many dormant diseases that normally would not affect the general population. In other cases, disease is simply spread from one person to another through close contact with others. For example, strains of flu can quickly become epidemic and then travel throughout other areas where citizens tend to congregate in large numbers. A buffet of injuries can also occur due to falling objects, falling down or being careless when cleaning up. Depending on the severity of the disaster, there could be countless injuries, diseases and even deaths due to lack of vaccines, medical facilities or treatment options. The Centers for Disease Control (CDC) provide a list of <u>some</u> of the diseases and injuries that can become prevalent and deadly during a disaster including:

Influenza

According to the Centers for Disease Control, a pandemic or worldwide outbreak of a new influenza virus could overwhelm the health and medical capabilities of this country. The CDC further states the next pandemic is likely to come in waves, each lasting months and pass through communities of all sizes across the nation and world. In a worst case scenario, the general public would stay in their homes with no work, school or shopping for up to three months. To reduce the spread of flu, get a flu shot every year and be prepared to follow public health recommendations that may include limiting attendance at public gatherings and travel for several days, weeks or even months.

Cholera

Cholera is an acute, diarrheal illness caused by a bacterial infection in the intestine. The infection is often mild or without symptoms but can sometimes be severe. Approximately five percent of infected persons will have profuse watery diarrhea, vomiting and leg cramps. In these people, rapid loss of body fluids leads to dehydration and shock and without treatment, death can occur within hours.

The cholera bacteria are <u>usually found in water or food sources that have been contaminated by feces</u> from a person infected with cholera. Cholera is most likely found and spread in places with <u>inadequate water treatment, poor sanitation and poor hygiene</u>. The cholera bacteria may also live in brackish rivers and coastal waters.

Cholera can be successfully treated by immediate replacement of fluid and salts lost through diarrhea using an oral rehydration solution - a prepackaged mixture of sugar and salts mixed with water and drunk in large amounts. All persons (visitors or residents) in areas where cholera is occurring or has occurred should observe the following recommendations:

- Drink only bottled, boiled, or chemically treated water and bottled or canned carbonated beverages. When using bottled drinks, make sure the seal is not broken. Avoid tap water, fountain drinks and ice cubes.

- To disinfect your own water: boil for one minute or filter the water and add two drops of household bleach or ½ iodine tablet per quart of water.

Dysentery

Dysentery is an inflammatory disorder of the intestine and colon and is usually caused by a bacterial or protozoan infection or infestation of parasitic worms, but can also be caused by a chemical irritant or viral infection. If left untreated, dysentery can be fatal.

In developed countries, dysentery is generally a mild illness with symptoms consisting of mild stomach pains and frequent passage of feces. Symptoms appear after one to three days and are usually no longer present after a week. The frequency of urges to defecate, the volume of feces passed, and the presence of mucus and/or blood depends on the pathogen causing the disease. Vomiting blood, severe abdominal pain, fever, shock and delirium can also be symptoms.

To reduce the risk of contracting dysentery during a disaster, the following precautions are suggested:

- Wash hands with soap and water *prior* to handling, cooking and eating food, handling babies, feeding young or elderly people, using the toilet or coming in contact with an infected person

- Avoid contact with someone known to have the disease

- Wash laundry using the hottest water possible (may not be possible)

- Avoid sharing personal items such as towels and face cloths

- *Dispose of feces and urine in a sanitary manner to prevent contamination of water and food sources*

- Use bottled, boiled, or chemically treated water to drink, wash dishes, brush teeth, wash and prepare food or make ice

- Eat foods that are packaged or freshly cooked and served hot and do <u>not</u> eat raw and undercooked meats or seafood and unpeeled fruits and vegetables

<u>Sexually Transmitted Diseases</u>

There is one very simple method to avoid sexually transmitted diseases and that is to avoid sex – but it is not a realistic choice. Did you know that during disasters, the sexual activity of individuals living in the area actually increases and sure enough, nine months later, the hospitals are inundated with pregnant women? Make careful and smart choices with regards to your sexual activity. Married couples should honor their vows and remain monogamous to one another and single persons should behave responsibly and use protection to avoid contracting these diseases. By avoiding a sexually transmitted disease – it is one less obstacle to address during serious disasters. **BEHAVE YOURSELF!**

<u>Infection</u>

Due to increased medical emergencies during a disaster, infection becomes widespread. Any breach in the skin provides the opportunity for infection and due to sanitation problems, superficial abrasions or deep and large wounds could easily become infected. There are several signs that occur when a wound is infected, including:

- Chills and fever
- Increased pain and swelling
- Limited movement
- Persistent and elevated temperature
- Pus draining directly from the wound or collecting in an abscess or boil under the skin
- Redness surrounding or spreading from the wound
- Swollen lymph nodes

As part of your overall emergency preparation planning, *learn in advance* what steps to take to treat infection caused by wounds or other injuries.

<u>Burns</u>

Burns will be a very common injury during a disaster. There are three classifications of burns, including:

- *First Degree* – burn appears on outer layer or epidermis of the skin. The skin appears mildly red, swollen and painful. There are no blisters. An example of a first degree burn is *sunburn*.

- *Second Degree* – burn passes through epidermis and extends into the dermis or secondary layer of the skin. The pain and swelling is moderate and blisters are present.

- *Third Degree* – burn reaches into the underlying fat and muscle tissue of the body. The skin appears charred and leathery and is numb to the touch.

Burns to the face, neck, hands, feet, genitalia and buttocks are serious. Facial burns can result in serious damage to the respiratory tract and cause breathing problems. Burns that completely encircle the body can have a tourniquet effect on the victim. A person experiencing serious or third degree burns has damaged capillaries that allow blood serum to leak into the burned tissue. This fluid loss reduces the blood volume of the body and rapidly causes shock. People with severe burns require massive amounts of intravenous fluids in order to survive.

<u>Diarrhea</u>

During an emergency, a common problem is diarrhea caused by a number of variables including stress, intestinal infections from contaminated water, food poisoning from eating spoiled food and allergies. There are two types of diarrhea, including:

- ***Traveler's diarrhea*** generally caused by the E.coli bacteria with an incubation period of twelve to forty-eight hours and will last between two and five days. Symptoms include abdominal stress, cramps and watery stools. This type of diarrhea can generally be treated with Pepto-Bismol or Imodium AD.

- ***Bacterial diarrhea*** includes additional symptoms of chills and fever, and blood, pus or mucous in the stool. This type of diarrhea is very serious and would be treated with anti-microbial medication and NOT Pepto-Bismol or Imodium AD as these medications will prolong the illness.

Severe diarrhea (ten bowel movements per day) and the resulting severe dehydration can kill young, old or weaker team members. The replacement of fluids and electrolytes (sodium and potassium) is vital for all victims of diarrhea. Remember that fruit juices and sodas make diarrhea worse. Most adult dehydration caused by diarrhea, vomiting or fever can be improved by drinking plain water.

In an emergency, this homemade oral rehydration solution can be used for those who may need more than simply water to rehydrate a sick body:

- **½ teaspoon salt**
- **½ teaspoon baking soda**
- **3 tablespoons sugar**
- **1 quart of room temperature drinking water**

> **Make sure to accurately measure the ingredients.**

Mix the above ingredients in the quart of water and drink the entire contents.

Affected people under three years old, over sixty five years old, who are pregnant or who have had severe diarrhea for more than 48 to 72 hours with abdominal tenderness should seek medical care as soon as possible.

Constipation

The normal length of time between bowel movements ranges widely with some people having bowel movements three times a day while others only one or two times a week. Going longer than three days without a bowel movement makes the stool or feces harder and more difficult to pass. Constipation is usually caused by a disorder of bowel function rather than a structural problem.

Many of the causes of constipation occurring during a disaster include:

- Antacid medicines containing calcium or aluminum
- Depression
- Disruption of regular diet or routine
- Inadequate activity, exercise or immobility
- Inadequate fiber in the diet
- Inadequate intake of water
- Medicines (especially strong pain medicines)
- Overuse of laxatives (stool softeners)
- **STRESS**

Chronic constipation - at least two of the following for at least three months:

- Hard stools more than 25% of the time
- Incomplete evacuation more than 25% of the time
- Straining during a bowel movement more than 25% of the time
- Swollen abdomen or abdominal pain
- Two or fewer bowel movements in a week
- Vomiting

> **Did you know that the only time you apply a tourniquet is as a very last resort? You have tried everything else, and the victim is going to die soon because you can't stop the bleeding. Using a tourniquet will cause the victim to lose their limb below the point of the tourniquet. If they lose a limb but save their life, it may be worth it. But if their life was not ever in question, using a tourniquet consigns them to living the rest of their life as an amputee for no reason. One paramedic of thirteen years said he had never needed to use a tourniquet.**

If constipated, consider the following treatments:

- Eat prunes, dates and figs
- Exercise on a regular basis
- Use a very mild stool softener or laxative
- Avoid caffeine and soft drinks
- Add fruits, vegetables, legumes, whole grains and bran to the diet
- Drink two to four extra glasses of water every day (unless fluid restricted)
- Drink warm liquids - especially in the morning (coffee helps many people)

Blisters

During a disaster, transportation may present a problem and team members may be required to walk from place to place. As part of *planning in advance*, all survival team members should have good and sturdy walking shoes in order to avoid blisters on the feet. A ruptured blister is an invitation to infection so the instant a blister appears on the foot – **stop** – take off your shoes – dry out your socks – and apply a bandage or tape (first aid or duct tape) over the hot spot.

Upon discovery of a small blister - do not open it because an intact blister is safe from infection. Apply padding material around the blister to relieve pressure and reduce friction. If a blister bursts, clean and dress it daily and pad around it. Leave a large blister intact. Once the blister is cleaned, run a sterilized needle and thread through the blister, detach the needle, and leave both ends of the thread hanging out of the blister. The thread will absorb the liquid inside which reduces the size of the hole and ensures the hole does not close up. Pad around the blister.

Bee and Wasp Stings

If stung by a bee or wasp, remove the stinger and venom sac by scraping with a fingernail or a knife blade. Do not squeeze or grasp the stinger or venom sac since squeezing will force more venom into the wound. Wash the sting site with soap and water to lessen the chance of a secondary infection. If allergic to insect stings, always carry an insect sting kit with you. Relieve itching caused by insect bites by applying one of the following treatments:

- **Cold Compresses**
- **Mud and Ashes**
- **Coconut Meat**
- **Garlic Cloves (crushed)**
- **Dandelion Sap**
- **Onions**

Rash

To treat rashes, use the following guidelines: ***If it is moist, keep it dry - If it is dry, keep it moist - Do not scratch it***

To treat a skin rash - learn what is causing it. Use a compress of vinegar or tannic acid (derived from tea, or boiling acorns or the bark of a hardwood tree) to weeping rashes. Keep dry rashes moist by rubbing a small amount of rendered animal fat or grease on the affected area. Treat rashes as open wounds and clean and dress them daily.

Wounds

There are many "natural" treatments available for use as antiseptics for wounds (including a rash):

- *Baking Soda*: Prepare a paste of baking soda and water
- *Bee Honey*: Use it straight or dissolved in water
- *Garlic*: Rub on a wound or boil to extract the oils and use the water to rinse area
- *Iodine Tablets*: Use five to fifteen tablets in a gallon of water to produce a good rinse
- *Salt Water*: Use two or three tablespoons per gallon of water to kill bacteria
- *Sphagnum Moss*: Found in boggy areas, it is a natural source of iodine and used as a dressing

Intestinal Parasites

Ugh!! To avoid worm infestations and other intestinal parasites, take preventive measures and never go barefoot! The most effective way to prevent intestinal parasites is to avoid uncooked meat and raw vegetables contaminated by raw sewage or human waste used as a fertilizer. There are home remedies that work on the principle of changing the environment in the gastrointestinal tract that kills the parasite - but none are fun choices.

- ***Kerosene*** - drink two tablespoons of kerosene *but no more*. If necessary, repeat this treatment in twenty-four to forty-eight hours. Do not inhale the fumes and by all means, do not smoke! The kerosene may cause lung irritation. (Try not to blow yourself up) ☹

- ***Nicotine*** - eat one to one-and-a-half cigarettes. The nicotine in the cigarette will kill or stun the worms long enough for your system to pass them. If the infestation is severe, repeat the treatment in twenty-four to forty-eight hours *but no sooner*. ☹

- ***Peppers*** - *spicy* peppers are effective only if they are a steady part of the diet. You can eat them raw or put them in soups or rice and meat dishes. They create an environment that prohibits parasitic attachment. ☹

- ***Salt Water*** - dissolve 4 tablespoons of salt in 1 quart of water and drink. Do <u>not</u> repeat this treatment. ☺

STORAGE

Emergency medical supplies should be stored in a location providing easy access and protection from outside elements, i.e., water, sun, cold, humidity, fire and structural damage. Remember: **COOL - DARK - DRY**. <u>The container should be clearly marked and identifiable as the first aid kit.</u> The medical supplies for the car and work should be stored in a compact container and also clearly marked and identifiable as the first aid kit. Inspect supplies in the home, car and work regularly and keep them freshly stocked. Important medical information and most prescriptions can be stored in the refrigerator that also provides excellent protection from fires.

BIRTH CONTROL

Many parents believe that a child is a blessing from God – but a child is also a <u>responsibility</u> for both the mother and father. When considering the role of birth control in emergency planning – team members should recognize that a child born in the middle of a serious and long-term disaster will <u>command the right</u> to be sheltered, fed, clothed and cared for by the <u>parents</u> through infancy, childhood and up to adulthood. It is <u>not</u> the responsibility of others to provide emergency rations for you and your children. **Be <u>responsible</u> and <u>accountable</u> for sexual and reproductive decisions.**

MEDICAL SUPPLIES

When asked my opinion about first aid kits for the primary residence, place of refuge, work, auto and evacuation pantries, I offer the following advice:

> *"The primary residence should have a larger assortment of first aid items available for the team members. Depending on how many members are on the team will determine the amount of first aid supplies to include in the kit. Include <u>basic</u> first aid supplies in your place of refuge, work, auto and evacuation kits."*

Here is a list of emergency medical supplies to consider for first aid kits for the primary residence, place of refuge, evacuation, auto and work kit:

BANDAGES

- Adhesive tape rolls
- Bandages - elastic
- Bandages – strips (various sizes)
- Bandages – triangular (various sizes)
- Bandages – fingertip (various sizes)
- Bandages – butterfly (various sizes)
- Bandages - knuckle
- Brace - Ankle

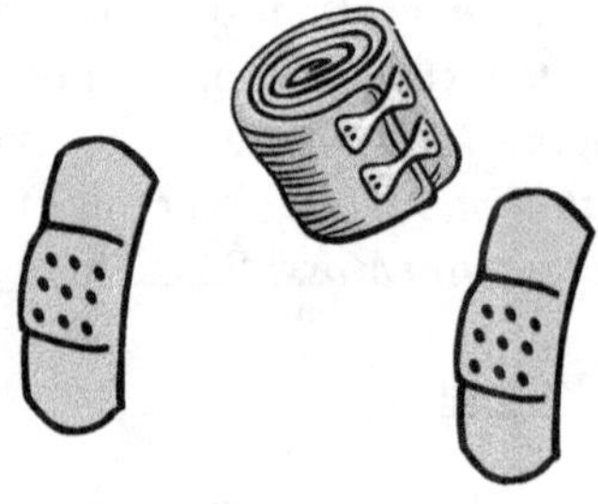

- Brace – knee
- Brace – wrist
- Compress (hot and cold)
- Dressings – burn (various sizes)
- Gauze – rolled (various sizes)
- Gauze – squares (various sizes)
- Gauze sponges (various sizes)
- Pads – abdominal (various sizes)
- Pads – eye
- Pads – non-adherent (various sizes)
- Splints (various sizes)
- Wound Closures – butterfly (medium/large)

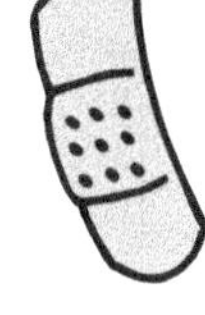

MEDICATIONS AND MISCELLANEOUS

- *Antibiotics*
- *Activated Charcoal* - for poisoning (Kaopectate)
- *Analgesics* - aspirin, acetaminophen (Tylenol), Ibuprofen (Advil or Excedrin)
- *Antacid* (Rolaids, Alka Seltzer, Prilosec, Nexium)
- *Antihistamine* (Benadryl)
- *Antiseptics and Topicals*
    - Calamine Lotion
    - Hydrocortisone Cream
    - Hand Sanitizer (antiseptic)
    - Hydrogen Peroxide
    - Liquid Soap (Dial)
    - Minor Burn Cream
    - Rubbing Alcohol (bottle and wipes)
    - Triple Antibiotic Ointment (Neosporin)
    - Wipes (antiseptic/individually wrapped)

- *Birth Control* (pill or device)
- *Cough Suppressants and Throat Lozenges*
- *Diarrhea* (Imodium or Pepto-Bismol)
- *Eye Drops* and/or *Eyewash Solution*
- *Laxative* (Milk of Magnesia)
- *Toothache Remedies* (Eugenol or Anbesol)

TOOLS AND OTHER ITEMS

- Baby Supplies
- Blanket and Pillow
- Cold Pack
- Compression Socks/Stockings
- Cotton Balls and Swabs
- CPR Microshield
- Dust Masks
- Epson Salts
- Eye Glass Repair Kit
- Feminine Supplies
- First Aid Manual
- Gloves (latex)
- Heat Pack
- Heating Pad
- Hot Water Bottle
- Ice Pack
- Matches (for sterilization)
- Medicine Dropper/Spoon
- Nail Clippers
- Needles/Thread
- Noxzema
- Paper Cups
- Petroleum Jelly
- Plastic Bags - Small
- Pocket Knife
- Rubber Syringe
- Safety Pins
- Scissors
- Shampoo – (lice killing)
- Sunscreen
- Suppositories
- Swabs - alcohol
- Swabs - cotton-tipped
- Swabs - insect bite
- Thermometer
- Tissues
- Tongue Blades
- Tweezers
- Vapor Rub (Vicks)

HERBAL REMEDIES

During serious and long-term disasters, it may be necessary to utilize various methods or remedies used for healing purposes. It is wise to prepare *alternatives* that could be used for eliminating or reducing diseases and symptoms. One of these methods is using herbs for treating ailments. Depending on the circumstances, physicians, drugs and standard medical facilities may not be available. As part of *preparing in advance*, consider purchasing an herbal remedies guide at your local bookstore.

Consider combining forces when buying first aid supplies! Contact other teams and share the load. For example, each team may only want to purchase ten finger bandages but they come in a box of fifty if purchased at a wholesale medical supply outlet. Split the cost of one box with five other teams and divide up the bandages – each team gets ten finger bandages to be stored at the respective five primary residences. The same approach can be taken with prescription and over-the-counter drugs.

OATMEAL PANCAKES

½ cup whole wheat flour
2 teaspoons baking powder
¼ teaspoon salt
2 tablespoons granulated white sugar
⅓ cup dry non-fat milk powder
2 eggs, separated
3 tablespoons vegetable oil
1 cup rolled oats
1 cup water

In medium bowl, combine flour, baking powder, salt, granulated white sugar and dry milk powder. Stir until well blended. In small bowl, beat egg whites until stiff and set aside. In large mixing bowl, combine egg yolks, water, oil and oats. Beat slightly and allow to stand 5 minutes. Beat again until blended. Mix in dry ingredients and fold in beaten egg whites. Drop 2 tablespoons batter onto griddle for small pancakes or pour ¼ cup if larger pancakes are desired. Bake on griddle until cakes are full of bubbles on top and undersides are lightly browned. Turn with spatula and brown other side. Serve with applesauce, jam, butter or syrup. Makes 8-10 pancakes.

CHAPTER EIGHT

IMMUNIZATION

Depending on the level of the disaster (1-3), there could be a severe breakdown of medical facilities and supplies in this country. There could be increased injuries, contaminated food and water and other factors that can awaken dormant diseases in a matter of days. Remember – the main goal and objective in preparing for an emergency is to safeguard and maintain our HEALTH. NOW is the time to make sure team members have all necessary immunizations. KEEP THEM UP TO DATE. BE PREPARED!

The table below lists <u>some</u> diseases that can be contracted by persons who are <u>not</u> vaccinated. During a serious and long-term disaster, these disasters will show up throughout the general population. All team members must *plan in advance* to avoid these diseases – get immunized <u>now</u>!

DISEASE	AFFECTS	CAUSE	SPREAD	SYMPTOMS/AFFECTS
Diphtheria	Throat Lungs Heart Nerves	Bacteria	Person to person by breathing, sneezing, coughing and talking	Causes thick covering in back of throat, breathing problems, paralysis, heart failure, nerve damage, death
Hepatitis A	Liver	Hepatitis A Virus (HAV)	Found in the stool of infected persons and easily spread to hands and objects. Contracted through close personal contact and by eating contaminated food or drinking water.	Mild flu-like illness, jaundice, severe stomach pains, diarrhea, liver damage, death
Hepatitis B	Liver	Hepatitis B Virus (HBV)	Contact with blood or body fluids of infected person	Loss of appetite, diarrhea, vomiting, jaundice, muscle pain, liver damage, death
Human Papillomavirus	Genitals Throat Cervix	Virus	Sexual contact	Warts in genital area or throat. Attributed to cervical cancer in women
Influenza	Lungs Throat Ears Stomach Bowels	Virus	Person to person by breathing, sneezing, coughing and talking	Fever, sore throat, headache, cough, muscle aches, loss of appetite, tiredness, ear infections, stomach ache, vomiting, diarrhea
Measles	Skin	Virus	Person to person by breathing, sneezing, coughing and talking	Rash, cough, runny nose, eye irritation, fever, ear infection, pneumonia, seizures, brain damage, death
Meningococcal (Meningitis)	Brain Spinal Cord	Bacteria	Person to person by breathing, sneezing, and coughing. Can also be spread through direct contact with infected persons.	Infection brain and spinal cord fluid as well as blood infections, pneumonia
Mumps	Ears Glands Genitals	Virus	Spread through the air by sneezing, coughing or breathing infected droplets. Can also be spread through direct contact with infected droplets or saliva.	Fever, headache, earache, tenderness under the jaw, swollen glands, deafness, meningitis, painful swelling of testicles or ovaries, death
Pertussis (Whooping Cough)	Lungs Brain	Bacteria	Spread through the air by coughing, sneezing and breathing infected droplets.	Coughing spells, vomiting, disturbed sleep, pneumonia, seizures, weight loss, incontinence, rib fractures, brain damage, death

DISEASE	AFFECTS	CAUSE	SPREAD	SYMPTOMS/AFFECTS
Pneumococcal (Pneumonia)	Lungs	Bacteria	Transmitted directly from person to person through close respiratory droplets contact.	Fever, cough, chest pain, blood-tinged sputum, headache, shortness of breath
Polio	Muscles	Virus	Enters body through the mouth	Paralysis and death
Rubella (German Measles)	Skin	Virus	Person to person by breathing, sneezing, coughing and talking	Rash, fever, arthritis, impaired eyesight
Tetanus (Lockjaw)	Muscles Mouth	Bacteria	Enters the body through cuts, scratches or wounds	Painful tightening of muscles all over the body. Lockjaw – victim can not open mouth or swallow Leads to death in two out of ten cases.
Typhoid	Blood Intestines	Bacteria	Bacteria lives only in humans. Disease is spread by eating food or drinking beverages that have been handled by a person who is shedding bacteria or if sewage contaminated with bacteria gets into the water used for drinking or washing food.	Fever, weakness, stomach pains, headache, loss of appetite, rash
Varicella (Chickenpox)	Skin	Virus	Spread from person to person through the air (breathing, coughing, talking, sneezing) or by contact with fluid from chickenpox blisters	Rash, itching, fever, tiredness, skin infection, pneumonia, scars, brain damage, death
Zoster (Shingles)	Skin	Virus	Only someone who has had chickenpox can get shingles. You cannot catch shingles from another person who has shingles.	Skin rash with blisters, fever, headache, chills, upset stomach, blindness, hearing problems, pneumonia, brain inflammation, death

SOURCE: United States Department of Health / Centers for Disease Control

The recommended immunization schedules for adults, young adults and children for 2017 are listed below. **Be sure to check with your physician before getting *any* type of vaccination or immunization**. The cost of immunization varies and in many cases, medical insurance will cover all or part of the cost. In addition to receiving the vaccinations from your physician, most states offer these vaccines through their respective health departments and in many cases, will directly bill your insurance company.

The list of recommended immunizations (2017) for <u>adults</u> is listed below:

VACCINE	DOSES	SCHEDULE	DURATION
Hepatitis A*	2 doses	1 - 2	Life
Hepatitis B*	3 doses	1 - 2 - 6	Life
Human Papillomavirus**	3 doses	1- 2 - 6	Life
Influenza	1 dose	One time	1 year
Measles/Mumps/Rubella	2 doses	1 - 2	Life
Meningococcal (Meningitis)	1 dose	One time	Life
Pneumococcal (Pneumonia)	1 to 2 doses	1 - 2	Life
Polio	1 dose	One time	Life

VACCINE	DOSES	SCHEDULE	DURATION
Tetanus, Diphtheria and Pertussis (Whooping Cough)	1 dose	One time	10 years
Typhoid***	1 dose	One time	5 years
Varicella (Chickenpox)	2 doses	1 - 2	Life
Zoster (Shingles)	1 dose	One time	Life

SOURCE: UNITED STATES DEPARTMENT OF HEALTH - CENTERS FOR DISEASE CONTROL

*   There is a combination vaccine for Hepatitis A and B with three doses required – Month 1 - Month 2 – Month 6.

**   There is a vaccine for males to protect women from contracting cervical cancer (Human Papillomavirus)

***   Although a Typhoid vaccination is not included on the list approved by the ACIP, it is highly recommended you get this immunization.

The recommended immunization schedule for persons aged <u>7 through 18 years</u> – United States 2017 approved by the Advisory Committee on Immunization Practices, is as follows:

VACCINE	7-10 YEARS	11-12 YEARS	13-18 YEARS
Hepatitis A			
Hepatitis B			
Human Papillomavirus			
Influenza			
Measles/Mumps/Rubella			
Meningococcal (Meningitis)			
Pneumococcal (Pneumonia)			
Polio			
Tetanus, Diphtheria and Pertussis (Whooping Cough)			
Typhoid			
Varicella (Chickenpox)			

Range of recommended ages for all children

Range of recommended ages for certain high risk groups

Range of recommended ages for catch-up- immunization

The recommended immunization schedule for persons aged <u>0 through 6 years</u> – United States 2017 approved by the Advisory Committee on Immunization Practices, the American Academy of Pediatrics, and the American Academy of Family Physicians is as follows:

VACCINE	BIRTH	1 Month	2 Months	4 Months	6 Months	12 Months	15 Months	18 Months	19-23 Months	2-3 Years	4-6 Years
Hepatitis A						HEP A (2 doses)				HEP A Series	
Hepatitis B	HEP B	HEP B				HEP B					
Rotavirus			RV	RV	RV						
Influenza						Influenza (Yearly)					
Measles Mumps Rubella						MMR					MMR
Meningococcal (Meningitis)										MCV4	
Pneumococcal (Pneumonia)			PCV	PCV	PCV	PCV					
Polio			IPV	IPV	IPV						IPV
Diphtheria Tetanus Pertussis			DTaP	DTap	DTaP	DTaP					DTaP
Typhoid										ViCP S	ViCP S
Varicella (Chickenpox)						VAR					VAR
Haemophilus Influenza			Hib		Hib						

Range of recommended ages for all children

Range of recommended ages for certain high risk groups

DUTCH APPLE PIE

1 pie crust, uncooked
2 cups dried apples, firmly packed
2 cups boiling water
a cup granulated white sugar
½ teaspoon cinnamon
2 tablespoons *plus* ½ cup white flour
1 tablespoon *plus* ¼ cup butter
a cup brown sugar, firmly packed

In saucepan, place apples. Pour boiling water over apples and let stand for five minutes. Mix together white sugar, cinnamon and 2 tablespoons flour. Add to apple mix and continue cooking until thick, stirring constantly to prevent scorching. Pour mixture into pie shell and dot with 1 tablespoon butter. Place brown sugar, ¼ cup butter and ½ cup flour in bowl and cut into each other until crumbly. Sprinkle over apple mixture and bake in 350 degree oven for 55 minutes.

CHAPTER NINE

NUTRITION

Food storage is essential – but the priority for food during an emergency is <u>not</u> the first item on your agenda. During short-term disasters, it is more important to obtain *shelter*, *heat*, *light* and *water* <u>prior</u> to worrying about food. In fact, a *healthy* human being can survive <u>without</u> food for up to three weeks before succumbing to serious organ failure and death. During a Level One (1 hour to 7 days) emergency, although the availability of food is certainly a desired convenience – it should <u>not</u> be considered an absolute necessity for healthy individuals. The true significance of having adequate food pantries lies with the probability that an emergency could quickly become a Level Two or Level Three disaster. It then becomes obvious that the **NUTRITION** Element is paramount to survival.

EMERGENCY PREPARATION PRINCIPLES

Remember the **NUMBER ONE PRIORITY** for every individual during an emergency is to maintain <u>health</u>. An important component in an emergency preparation plan is to guarantee that *nutritional* needs and concerns are addressed <u>prior to any emergency</u> to reduce problems in obtaining food sources during a disaster situation. Since food production in this country and around the world is vulnerable to manmade and natural disasters, an important part of the **NUTRITION** Element is to guarantee that the food items we purchase, process and store provide the nutrition we need to maintain our health.

There are several principles that can be incorporated into the overall emergency plan to prepare for and in some cases eliminate nutrition issues that could become prevalent during an emergency situation.

- **Buy on sale and buy in bulk** whenever possible.

- **Know your food inventory** and where it is stored. Know how much food is in your emergency pantries and make sure the food is readily available and logistically located for easy access, use and transport.

- **Practice alternative methods to <u>obtain</u> food** including growing a garden, orchard, bushes and vines and indoor methods including sprouting and garden boxes. Consider constructing a chicken coop and learn how to hunt and fish.

- **Learn where alternative food sources are available** that grow <u>wild</u> in your area including *edible* plants, flowers, roots, berries – and yes, *edible* insects.

- **Practice alternative methods to <u>store</u> and package food** i.e., greenhouses, root cellars and large capacity storage bins. Use the proper type of storage unit, package like items together and label container contents.

- **Plan alternative methods to <u>prepare</u> food** including the use of <u>manual</u> equipment i.e., a good quality grain mill, oat roller, juicers and canning and bottling equipment and supplies.

- **Prepare for alternative methods to <u>cook</u> food** i.e., a wood burning stove, solar oven and propane stoves.

- **Study nutrition** and learn what foods and combinations of foods are good to support healthy eating habits and survival during a disaster.

- **Begin to accustom your body** to eating the basic food staples <u>before</u> you are forced to eat them during a disaster. Include grains, beans and other whole foods in <u>current</u> meal plans. Learn *now* how to cook *when*!

- During a disaster situation, picky eaters, <u>including children</u> must learn that this event is <u>not</u> Burger King and they don't get it their way. Everyone must recognize that **food choices may be different and not as appetizing**. All team members must understand they will eat the food items set out before them - and no whining.

- Special attention must be given to ensure that adequate **protein** is included in the diet, which during an emergency situation, usually combines a grain and a legume that creates the protein we need in our bodies.

- Meal planning should be kept **simple** and **uncomplicated** to avoid unnecessary time and effort being expended on daily meal preparation.

- When purchasing food resources, **equal consideration** should be placed on (1) what team members **like** to eat (2) **vitamins** and **minerals** contained in specific foods essential for health (3) food items that **store easily** and offer an **extended shelf life** and (4) food items that are **easy** and **quick** to prepare.

- **Analyze** and **drill down** when purchasing food items to determine if all **ingredients** and **equipment** are available to create desired recipes, and an alternative **cooking source** has been stored that does not require electricity or fuel.

- Include **vitamin** and **mineral supplements** in food pantries located at the primary residence and/or place of refuge.

VITAMINS AND MINERALS

It is important to know the vitamins and minerals our body needs in order to maintain <u>health</u> – the Number One priority during a disaster. As part of emergency planning efforts to gather food staples, <u>the critical need for vitamins and minerals must be considered when purchasing, gathering, processing and storing food supplies.</u>

Listed below is a list of vitamins and minerals required by our bodies to maintain health. The table also provides data on what the element provides for our body and some examples of good food sources containing the mineral or vitamin.

ELEMENT	*PURPOSE*	FOOD SOURCES
Calcium	*Essential for bone growth and strength, blood clotting, muscle contraction and of nerve signal transmission*	Milk, yogurt, hard cheeses, fortified cereals, spinach, sardines, salmon, broccoli, dandelion greens, soy flour, collards, tofu, kale
Choline (Vitamin B Complex)	*Plays a key role in the production of cells and neurotransmitters*	Milk, liver, eggs, peanuts
Chromium	*Helps control blood sugar levels*	Meats, poultry, fish, some cereals, potatoes, fresh vegetables, cheese, chicken legs
Copper	*Important in the metabolism of iron*	Seafood, nuts, seeds, wheat bran cereals, whole grains
Fiber	*Helps with digestion and maintenance of blood sugar levels; reduces heart disease risk*	Bran cereal, peas, lentils, black beans, fruits, vegetables
Fluoride	*Prevents the formation of tooth cavities and stimulates bone growth*	Fluoridated water, sea fish, toothpaste, mouth rinses
Folic Acid (Folate)	*Development of cells, protein metabolism and heart health, helps prevent birth defects*	Dark leafy vegetables, whole grain breads; fortified cereals
Iodine	*Important in production of thyroid hormones*	Processed foods and iodized salt
Iron	*Key component of red blood cells and many enzymes*	Fortified cereals, beans, lentils, eggs, beef, lima beans, sunflower seeds, raisins, brewer's yeast, turkey, chicken, fish, peas, apricots
Magnesium	*Helps with heart rhythm, muscle and nerve function, bone strength*	Green leafy vegetables, nuts, soybeans, halibut, quinoa, soy flour, buckwheat flour, tofu, kidney beans, lima beans, bananas, avocadoes, peanut butter, oatmeal

ELEMENT	*PURPOSE*	FOOD SOURCES
Manganese	*Formation of bones and some enzymes*	Nuts, beans, legumes, tea, whole grains
Molybdenum	*Key in the production of some enzymes*	Legumes, grains, nuts
Phosphorus	*Allows cells to function normally, helps body produce energy, bone growth*	Milk, dairy products, peas, meat, eggs, some cereals and breads
Potassium	*Maintains normal fluid balance, controls blood pressure, reduces risk of kidney stones, helps nerves transmit messages, aids digestive enzymes, guides normal growth and ensures proper functioning of muscles – most notably the heart muscle.*	Sweet potatoes, orange juice, squash, apricots, peaches, bananas, raisins, yogurt, soybeans, avocadoes, tomatoes, sardines, milk, tuna, flounder, salmon, beef liver, haddock, pork, lamb, turkey, chicken
Selenium	*Protects cells from damage; regulates thyroid hormone*	Organ meats, seafood, some plants (if grown in soil with selenium) Brazil nuts
Sodium	*Important for fluid balance*	Salted meats, nuts, butter, processed foods
Vitamin A	*Necessary for normal vision, immune function, reproduction*	Sweet potatoes with peel, carrots, spinach, fortified cereals, beef liver, cantaloupe, kale, broccoli, squash, apricots, watermelon, endive, lettuce, asparagus, peas, green beans, corn, parsley, eggs
Vitamin B$_1$ (Thiamin)	*Process carbohydrates and some protein.*	Whole grains, breads, cereals
Vitamin B$_2$ (Riboflavin)	*Key in metabolism and conversion of food into energy; helps produce red blood cells*	Milk, bread products, fortified cereals
Vitamin B$_3$ (Niacin)	*Assists in digestion and conversion of food into energy, important in production of cholesterol*	Meat, fish, poultry, enriched and whole grain breads, fortified cereals
Vitamin B$_5$ (Pantothenic Acid)	*Important in fatty acid metabolism*	Chicken, beef, potatoes, oats, cereals, tomatoes
Vitamin B$_6$	*Important for nervous system, helps body metabolize proteins and sugar*	Fortified cereals, fortified soy products, organ meats
Vitamin B$_7$ (Biotin)	*Helps synthesis of fats, glycogen and amino acids*	Liver, fruits, meats
Vitamin B$_{12}$	*Important in production of red blood cells*	Fish, poultry, meat, fortified cereals
Vitamin C	*Antioxidant that protects against cell damage, boosts immune system, forms collagen in the body*	Red and green peppers, kiwis, oranges, strawberries, broccoli, grapefruit, papaya, Brussels sprouts, cantaloupe, turnip greens, potatoes, cabbage, blackberries, spinach, blueberries, cherries, mung bean sprouts
Vitamin D	*Crucial in metabolizing calcium for healthy bones*	Fish liver oils, halibut, herring, mackerel, salmon, tuna, fortified milk products, fortified cereals, sunlight
Vitamin E	*Antioxidant that protects cells against damage*	Fortified cereals, sunflower seeds, almonds, peanut butter, vegetable oils, pecans, hazelnuts, peanuts, lobster, salmon
Vitamin K	*Important in blood clotting and bone health*	Green vegetables, spinach, collards, broccoli, Brussels sprouts, cabbage
Zinc	*Supports the body's immunity and nerve function; important in reproduction*	Red meats, seafood, fortified cereals, cheese, cashews, rolled oats, peas, lentils, beef, chicken liver, sunflower seeds, Brazil nuts

SOURCE: Utah Department of Health

PH LEVEL

In chemistry, the pH measures how *acidic*, *alkaline* or *neutral* a substance is - and pH levels range from 0 to 14 on the pH scale. A pH level of 7.0 is considered neutral, a pH *below* 7.0 is acidic and a pH *above* 7.0 is alkaline. The teams who are familiar with gardening know that depending on the plant, a specific range of pH level in the soil is required for the plant to grow. It may be surprising to learn that humans *also* require a specific pH level in order to grow – and survive. The human blood pH level should be slightly alkaline (7.35 - 7.45). Below or above this range will result in symptoms and disease.

An *acidic* pH level in the body occurs from an acid forming diet, emotional stress (common in a disaster environment), toxic overload, immune reactions or any process that deprives cells of oxygen and other nutrients. This acidic level will decrease the body's ability to absorb minerals and other nutrients, decrease energy production in cells, decrease the ability to repair damaged cells, decrease the ability to detoxify heavy metals, increase the possibility of tumor cells and make the body more susceptible to fatigue and illness. A blood pH of 6.9, which is only slightly acidic, can induce coma and death.

In the United States, acidic pH levels are common due to the typical American diet far too high in acid producing animal products such as meat, fish, poultry, eggs and dairy and processed foods such as white flour, sugar, coffee and soft drinks. Our diets are far too low in alkaline producing foods such as fresh vegetables. As a society, we use WAY too many drugs (which are acid forming) and artificial sweeteners.

The best way to correct an overly acid body is to modify the diet and lifestyle. To maintain health, the diet should consist of 60% alkaline forming foods and 40% acid forming foods. To restore health, the diet should consist of 80% alkaline forming foods and 20% acid forming foods. Alkaline forming foods include most fruits, green vegetables, peas, beans, lentils, spices, herbs, seasonings, seeds and nuts.

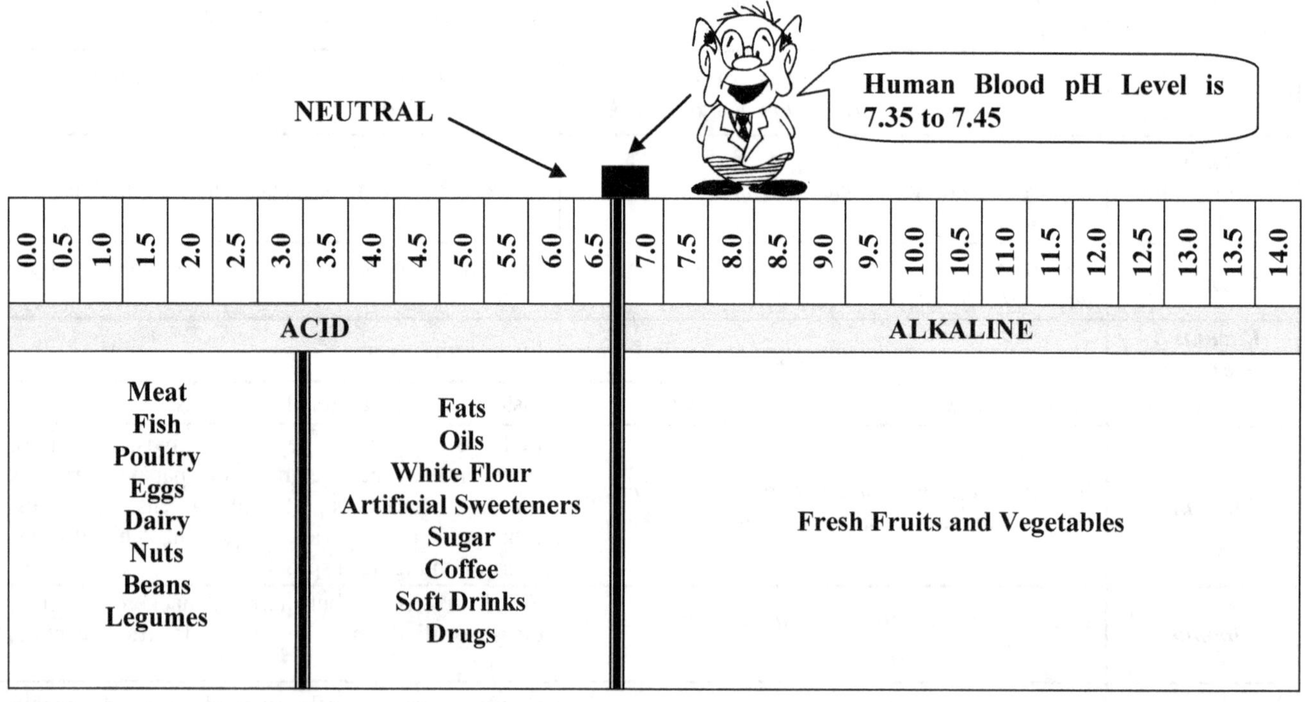

The United States Department of Health provides a list of foods that are high in acid and foods that provide a more alkaline pH level as follows:

ACID FOODS		ALKALINE FOODS	
VEGETABLES Corn Lentils Olives Squash (Winter) **FRUITS** Blueberries Cranberries Currants Plums Prunes **GRAINS** Amaranth Barley Bran (Oat and Wheat) Bread Cornstarch Crackers (Soda) Flour (White/Wheat) Kamut Macaroni Noodles Oatmeal Oats (rolled) Quinoa Rice Rye Spaghetti Spelt Wheat **BEANS/LEGUMES** Black Beans Chick Peas Green Peas Kidney Beans Lentils Pinto Beans Red Beans Soy Beans Soy Milk White Beans **DAIRY** Cheese Ice Cream **NUTS** Cashews Peanut Butter Peanuts Pecans Walnuts **ANIMAL PROTEIN** Bacon Beef Carp Clams Cod	**ANIMAL PROTEIN** Corned Beef Fish Haddock Lamb Lobster Mussels Organ Meats Oysters Pike Pork Rabbit Salmon Sardines Sausage Scallops Shellfish Shrimp Tuna Turkey Veal Venison **FATS AND OILS** Butter Canola Oil Corn Oil Flax Oil Hemp Seed Oil Lard Olive Oil Safflower Oil Sesame Oil Sunflower Oil **SWEETENERS** Carob Corn Syrup Sugar **ALCOHOL** Beer Hard Liquor Spirits Wine **MISCELLANEOUS** Catsup Cocoa Coffee Mustard Pepper Soft Drinks Vinegar **DRUGS/CHEMICALS** Aspirin Chemicals Drugs Herbicides Pesticides Tobacco	**VEGETABLES** Alfalfa Barley Grass Beets Broccoli Cabbage Carrots Cauliflower Celery Chard Greens Collard Greens Cucumber Dandelions Eggplant Garlic Green Beans Green Peas Kale Kohlrabi Lettuce Mushrooms Mustard Greens Onions Parsnips Peas Peppers Pumpkin Radishes Spinach Sprouts Sweet Potatoes Tomatoes Watercress Wheat Grass **FRUITS** Apples Apricots Avocadoes Bananas Berries Blackberries Cantaloupe Cherries Coconut (fresh) Currants Dates and Figs (dried) Grapes Grapefruit Honeydew Melon Lemons Limes Nectarines Oranges Peaches Pears **FRUITS** Pineapples Raisins Raspberries Rhubarb Strawberries	**FRUITS** Tangerines Tomatoes Watermelon **PROTEIN** Almonds Chestnuts Millet Tofu Whey Protein Powder **SWEETENERS** Stevia **SPICES/SEASONINGS** Chili Pepper Cinnamon Curry Ginger Herbs (all) Mustard Sea Salt Tamari **MISCELLANEOUS** Apple Cider Vinegar Bee Pollen Fresh Fruit Juice Mineral Water Molasses Soured Dairy Products Vegetable Juices

Although it may appear that citrus fruits would have an acidifying effect on the body, the citric acid contained in the fruit actually has an alkalinizing effect in the system.

A food's acid or alkaline forming tendency in the body has nothing to do with the actual pH of the food itself. For example, a lemon is very acidic but the end products they produce after digestion and assimilation into the body are very alkaline and as a result, lemons are alkaline forming in the body. On the other hand, meat will test alkaline before digestion but leaves a very acidic residue in the body. As a result, most animal products are very acid forming.

VARIETY IS THE SPICE OF LIFE

In order to guarantee that team members receive the best balanced nutrition during a disaster, it is important to store a variety of food items. During any level of disaster, *variety* is a key for maintaining health and wellness but during a long-term disaster, food items that store well for long periods of time will be important.

Some of these food items include wheat, dry milk, sugar and salt, but if these are the only food items stored in emergency pantries, the diet will not only be deficient in important nutrients, but frankly, it will really be crappy to come to the table for dinner. When storing grains, make sure you include not just wheat, but also oats, barley, rice and legumes in the pantry. By adding dehydrated carrots or dried apples, the diet becomes not only healthy but is more palatable during extended disaster situations.

> **WHEN *PLANNING IN ADVANCE* FOR EMERGENCY FOOD STORAGE - A VARIETY OF FOOD CHOICES AND THE MORE DIVERSE WAYS THE FOOD IS PROCESSED AND PACKAGED PROVIDES BETTER MEALS AND MENUS THAT CAN BE CREATED DURING THE LENGTH OF THE DISASTER.**

FOOD BASICS

As you begin purchasing, gathering, processing and storing food items – there are specific foods considered to be basic staples that should be included in emergency pantries. The emphasis is on the following items:

- **Grains (Wheat, Oats, Barley, Rice, Corn)**
- **Legumes (Beans, Lentils, Peas)**
- **Salt**
- **Vinegar**
- **Sugar or Honey**
- **Fats and Oils**
- **Pasta**
- **Dry Milk**
- **Supplementary Items (Spices, Seasonings, Bouillon, Soup Base, Yeast, Baking Powder, Baking Soda)**

> **If storing whole grains, don't forget a good quality manual wheat grinder and oat roller as part of the emergency preparation pantry.**

During a devastating famine or other serious disaster when food is not available, these foods would keep team members alive. Are these basic food items as fun to eat as a nice juicy cheeseburger or gourmet chocolates? No.

> **REMEMBER! During a long-term disaster and when relying on just food storage, and using only the basic food staples, Vitamin C would be lacking which causes *scurvy*. A common multi-vitamin tablet could eliminate stress or problems with diseases.**

These basic items are fairly economical (although becoming more and more expensive every month), require minimal storage space, have a long shelf life (when stored properly) and provide the calories to sustain life. Balancing these staples with economy and sound nutrition is vital to a program where team members are prepared for a *worst case scenario*.

Some additional points to consider:

- <u>**Include more than just four or five items from the basic food staple list**</u>. When storing grains, store <u>multiple types</u> of grains including wheat, barley, oats and rice. When storing legumes, store <u>multiple types</u> of legumes including pinto beans, navy beans, white beans, lima beans, red beans, black beans, pink beans, split peas and lentils. When storing pasta, store <u>multiple types</u> of pasta including spaghetti and macaroni.

- <u>**Accustom the team members to eating these foods** *before* **they are 'forced' to eat them**</u>. This is especially important for children and teenagers who would be more resistant to a restricted and limited diet. Begin now by preparing and eating whole grains and beans into current meal plans.

- <u>**Include other items**</u> in the emergency pantries to make the basics more adaptable and edible.

PROTEIN

A major problem when filling emergency food pantries is making sure there are adequate *protein* food sources. We generally get our protein requirements from eating meat, poultry, fish and eggs, but during a medium to long-term disaster, these food sources may not be as readily available. A **legume** is a source of protein but doesn't supply all of the essential amino acids. BUT - if you mix and match beans with **grain**, the grain fills in the missing amino acids and the combination of the two provides a complete protein! When planning disaster menus, if you combine grain and legumes together, the combination will result in a high-quality protein.

DRILLING DOWN

As I review emergency strategies of teams, families and individuals over the years, I have discovered a glaring flaw in their foolproof plans - especially when it comes to stocking the food pantries. The problem? They make plans based on a *normal* environment instead of a *disaster* environment and forget the methods used in a disaster environment to *prepare*, *process* and *cook* food would be radically different than when preparing those same meals under normal circumstances. For one thing - the plan must recognize the **LACK OF ELECTRICITY**, and in many cases - the **LACK OF AN AVAILABLE FUEL SOURCE** i.e. natural gas or propane, etc.

For example, a team may decide to purchase a supply of whole wheat - which is a very good idea. Whole wheat has a much longer shelf life than flour. When stored properly, whole wheat will last as long as 25-30 years whereas flour will last about 7-10 years. When the hull is cracked on whole wheat, the nutrient level rapidly diminishes so only the amount of wheat needed should be ground for the meal. Once the team decides to buy whole wheat, the members must analyze (and drill down) into other factors that will be involved in *using*, *storing*, *preparing*, *processing*, and *cooking* the wheat as part of meal preparation **in a disaster environment**.

The following questions are then asked and answered and appropriate action taken:

TASK	QUESTION	ANSWER	SOLUTION/ACTION
Using	What will the wheat be used for in meal preparation?	Bread and Rolls	Purchase of **whole wheat** to support team members (preferably a one year supply)
Storing	How will the wheat be stored?	Stored in heavy duty plastic containers with a tight seal. Moisture proof, insect proof, etc. Stored in a *cool*, *dark* and *dry* environment	Purchase of appropriate **storage containers** to store the wheat in a *cool*, *dark* and *dry* environment
Preparing	How will we grind the wheat into flour?	Will use a high quality and heavy duty wheat grinder	Purchase of a **wheat grinder**
Processing	What process will we use to make the bread and rolls? What recipes? What are the other ingredients in the recipes and how will they be stored?	We will mix the ingredients together by hand. Additional ingredients include baking powder, baking soda, salt, yeast, oil, sugar etc. These ingredients will be stored in airtight, moisture proof and insect proof containers in a *cool*, *dark* and *dry* environment	Store necessary **mixing bowl**, **measuring cups** and **spoons**, and **baking pans**. Select **recipes** to be used in making bread and rolls. Purchase **recipe ingredients** and **storage containers**.
Cooking	How will we bake the bread and rolls **without electricity**? What other alternative cooking equipment and required fuel could we use to bake the bread and rolls?	We will bake the bread and rolls using a solar oven that does not require electricity or fuel. As an alternative, we will use a wood-burning cooking stove that has an oven for baking.	Purchase **solar oven**, **wood-burning cooking stove** and adequate **fuel** (wood and coal) for stove.

Based on the above analysis, in order to make bread and rolls using whole wheat ***during a disaster environment***, the team would have to make available the following supplies:

- Whole Wheat
- Wheat Grinder
- Storage Containers (for whole wheat and the other ingredients needed in the recipes)
- Mixing Bowl
- Measuring Cups
- Measuring Spoons
- Mixing Spoon
- Baking Pans (if using solar oven, baking pans must be a dark color)
- Recipes
- Recipe Ingredients (baking powder, baking soda, yeast, oil, honey/sugar, salt, etc.)
- Solar Oven
- Wood-Burning Cooking Stove
- Wood (for wood-burning cooking stove)
- Coal (for wood-burning cooking stove)

As you can quickly see from this exercise, there is <u>much more involved</u> than just buying whole wheat. Obviously, there are many alternatives that could be used when electing to include whole wheat in the food pantry including the use of alternative cooking equipment. For example, if the team had an alternative power source such as solar panels or a solar-powered generator, an electric oven could serve as the means to bake the bread. Another possibility could be a propane-powered oven providing adequate propane was stored to support meal preparation. Remember! For all food items included in the food pantries, team members must **DRILL DOWN** and make sure <u>all</u> of the bases are covered for using a specific food item in a **disaster environment** - <u>without</u> **ELECTRICITY** and possibly without 'normal' fuel sources such as **NATURAL GAS** or **PROPANE**. In most cases, **COOKING** or **BAKING** the food will be the biggest challenge because in a normal environment, we use the microwave oven or the cooking stove - both requiring electricity and/or natural gas.

FOOLPROOF WHOLE WHEAT BREAD
Using a SOLAR OVEN

2 tablespoons dry yeast
5 cups hot water
2/3 cup oil
12 cups whole wheat flour (or 7 cups whole wheat flour and 5 cups white flour)
½ cup warm water
2 tablespoons salt
2/3 cup honey or sugar

Sprinkle yeast into ½ cup warm water. Let stand 10-15 minutes. Add 1 tablespoons sugar. Combine the remaining 4 ½ cups hot water with 7 cups whole wheat flour in a large bowl. Add salt, oil and honey or sugar. Continue mixing until well blending. Add 1 cup flour to mixture. Add prepared yeast to mixture and blend thoroughly. Add 3 to 4 more cups of flour. Knead for 10 minutes or until there is a consistency like cookie dough. A stickier dough will result in a moister bread.

Oil hands and divide dough into four parts. Mold into loaves on oiled counter. Place in oiled pans. Oil top of loaves if soft crust is desired. Cover loaves with damp cloth and let rise 1/3 in bulk.

Place loaf pans in dark pans with lids or invert an empty loaf pan on top of each loaf of dough. Cover. Place in <u>solar oven</u> by 11:00 AM. Bake 1 ½ hours.

No one knows for sure – that is the correct answer. There are several organizations who have attempted to determine how much is really enough when preparing for the **NUTRITION ELEMENT** during a disaster. Utah State University has actually provided some clarification as to how much food storage would be recommended.

> # ONE POUND OF DRY MATTER PER PERSON PER DAY SERVES AS THE BASIS FOR A FOOD STORAGE PROGRAM. THIS IS A VERY <u>MINIMAL</u> DAILY AMOUNT – 1600 CALORIES IS A CALORIE-RESTRICTED DIET FOR MOST PEOPLE EVEN IN GOOD TIMES, BUT IT WOULD KEEP YOU ALIVE. ONE POUND OF DRY MATTER PER DAY IS 365 POUNDS FOR A YEAR.

REMEMBER! <u>Variety</u> is the key factor so vary the items within groups according to the needs and tastes of team members while at the same time, sticking fairly close to the general category amounts.

Do <u>not</u> reduce the amounts for small children or young adults. Remember that as time passes, that small child or teenager will one day be taller than you – stronger than you – and will demand to eat the same amount of food as you. Count EVERYONE on the team as an adult and always round the amounts up – and not down. DON'T FORGET PETS!

The following chart provides important information on food storage and the recommended amounts of basic food staples each person should store for three months, six months, one year (our goal) and even five years. These amounts are for an average adult male – an average adult female would require a little less.

RECOMMENDED AMOUNTS OF BASIC FOOD STAPLES
(ONE PERSON)

ITEM	3 MONTHS	6 MONTHS	1 YEAR	5 YEARS
Grains	100 lbs	200 lbs	400 lbs	2000 lbs
• Wheat	45 lbs	90 lbs	175 lbs	375 lbs
• Flour	5 lbs	10 lbs	20 lbs	100 lbs
• Corn	12 ½ lbs	25 lbs	50 lbs	250 lbs
• Oats	12 ½ lbs	25 lbs	50 lbs	250 lbs
• Rice	20 lbs	40 lbs	80 lbs	400 lbs
• Barley	1 ¼ lbs	2 ½ lbs	5 lbs	25 lbs
• Pasta	10 lbs	20 lbs	40 lbs	200 lbs
Legumes	15 lbs	30 lbs	60 lbs	300 lbs
• Dry Beans	11 ¼ lbs	22 ½ lbs	45 lbs	225 lbs
• Dry Lima Beans	½ lb	1 lb	2 lbs	10 lbs
• Dry Soy Beans	½ lb	1 lb	2 lbs	10 lbs
• Dry Split Peas	½ lb	1 lb	2 lbs	10 lbs
• Dry Lentils	½ lb	1 lb	2 lbs	10 lbs
• Dry Soup Mix	1 ¾ lbs	3 ½ lbs	7 lbs	35 lbs
Fats and Oils	2.5 qts	5 qts	10 qts	50 qts
• Cooking Oil	1 qt	2 qts	4 qts	24 qts
• Shortening	½ qt	1 qt	2 qts	10 qts
• Mayonnaise	¼ qt	½ qt	1 qt	5 qts
• Salad Dressing	¼ qt	½ qt	1 qt	5 qts
• Peanut Butter	¼ qt	½ qt	1 qt	5 qts
• Butter/Margarine	¼ qt	½ qt	1 qt	1 qt
Milk	4 lbs	8 lbs	16 lbs	80 lbs
• Nonfat Dry Milk	3 ½ lbs	7 lbs	14 lbs	70 lbs
• Evaporated Milk	3 cans	6 cans	12 cans	60 cans
Sugars	15 lbs	30 lbs	60 lbs	300 lbs
• Granulated Sugar	10 lbs	20 lbs	40 lbs	80 lbs
• Brown Sugar	¾ lb	1 ½ lbs	3 lbs	15 lbs
• Molasses	¼ lb	½ lb	1 lb	5 lbs
• Honey	¾ lb	1 ½ lb	3 lb	15 lbs
• Corn Syrup	¾ lb	1 ½ lb	3 lb	15 lbs
• Jams/Preserves	1 ¼ lbs	2 ½ lbs	5 lb	15 lbs
• Powdered Fruit Drink	1 ½ lbs	3 lbs	6 lb	30 lbs
• Flavored Gelatin	¼ lb	½ lb	1 lb	5 lbs
Miscellaneous				
• Salt	2 ½ lbs	5 lbs	10 lbs	50 lbs
• Dry Yeast	2 oz	4 oz	½ lb	2 ½ lbs
• Baking Soda	¼ lb	½ lb	1 lb	5 lbs
• Baking Powder	¼ lb	½ lb	1 lb	5 lbs
• Vinegar	½ qt	1 qt	2 qt	10 qt

SOURCE: Utah State University, Extension Service

NOTE: Fruits, vegetables, meats, eggs and complements would enhance the nutritional value of this diet.

<u>**Grains**</u>

Although whole grains used to be affordable – they are becoming more and more expensive. If purchased in bulk, it is more feasible for teams to afford this product. <u>Consider combining forces with other teams to purchase and divide grains among the respective teams.</u> Whole grains are adaptable as well as wholesome and versatile. Wheat is one of the most common grains and is considered important due to its gluten content (bread making qualities). Wheat will also grind into flour that makes bread, muffins or raised dough on its own. In addition to storing wheat, there are other grains that offer variety, nutrition and versatility including rice, barley, millet, cornmeal and oats.

The basic cooking instructions for grains are simple. Presoaking hard grains such as whole wheat is optional but will reduce the actual cooking time. Soak the hard grains for six to eight hours and cook them in the soaking water. For the softer grains such as rice or pearled barley, they can be cooked without soaking. To boil grain, bring the water to a boil, add the grain and return to a boil. Reduce the heat and simmer (covered) until done. The grain will be done when the water is absorbed and the grain is softened. Most grains will still be slightly chewy when cooked. When the grain is cooked, remove from the heat and fluff with a fork. Cover and allow to sit for ten minutes.

> **Flour also serves a medical purpose. If burned, place the burned body part in a bowl of flour for about fifteen minutes. The pain should be eliminated or reduced.**

There is a difference between *hard* wheat and *soft* wheat. Soft wheat has a lower nutritive value (protein) than hard winter wheat. Although they are both categorized as hard grains, the hard wheat varieties store better than the soft wheat (thirty or more years for hard wheat versus fifteen to twenty years for soft wheat). There are two major varieties of hard winter wheat – hard *red* wheat and hard *white* wheat. The hard red or white winter wheat is better for home food storage programs.

The hard wheat generally contains smaller kernels and is harder than soft wheat kernels. Hard wheat contains high protein and gluten levels primarily designed for making bread flours, but depending on the variety and growing conditions, hard wheat also has vastly different protein levels. The hard varieties of wheat can have protein levels up to fifteen percent. For bread making, wheat should have a minimum of twelve percent protein. Most bread makers prefer the hard red wheat for a more robust flavor and a more traditional textured loaf of bread.

GRAIN TO WATER RATIO FOR COOKING GRAINS	
GRAIN	**GRAIN/WATER RATIO**
Amaranth	1:2
Bulger	1:3
Kamut	1:3
Millet	1:3
Oats (rolled)	1:3
Pearl Barley	1:3
Quinoa	1:2
Spelt	1:3
Wheat (whole)	1:3
Wheat (cracked)	1:3

SOURCE: Utah State University Extension Service

> **As part of the emergency preparation plan, make sure you have a heavy-duty <u>manual</u> wheat grinder. Grains should be purchased as whole grains and then ground into flour as small batches. Once wheat is cracked or ground, the nutritive value drops dramatically. The shelf life of whole grains is 25-30 years (depending on storage conditions) compared to flour which is only 7-10 years (depending on storage conditions).**

<u>**Rice**</u>

There are over 6,500 varieties of rice! Although the price of rice continues to increase, it is still economical if purchased in bulk. Rice can be used in main dishes, casseroles and desserts. Some of the more common varieties of rice include Basmati (white and brown), brown (medium, short and sweet), Jasmine (brown and white), long grain, short grain, Texmati (brown and white), Whani and wild rice.

The basic cooking instructions for cooking rice are simple. Do <u>not</u> rinse rice prior to cooking. Place the rice and water in a saucepan and add ¼ teaspoon of salt to the mixture. Bring to a boil and reduce the heat to low. Cover and simmer (thirty minutes for regular white rice and forty minutes for brown rice) until the water has been absorbed. Remove from heat and fluff with fork. Let stand - covered for ten additional minutes.

GRAIN TO WATER RATIO FOR COOKING RICE	
GRAIN	**GRAIN/WATER RATIO**
Basmati (white)	1:2
Basmati (brown)	1:2
Brown (medium)	1:2
Brown (short)	1:2
Brown (sweet)	1:2
Jasmine (brown)	1:2
Jasmine (white)	1:2
Long Grain	1:2
Short Grain	1:2
Texmati (brown)	1:2
Texmati (white)	1:2
Whani or Red	1:2
Wild and Brown Mix	1:3
Wild	1:3

SOURCE: Utah State University Extension Service

<table>
<tr><td>

Pets must be considered as part of emergency preparedness planning. If no longer able to purchase or obtain regular pet food, rice can be used as an alternative. During difficult times, it would be important for their well-being if they are already acclimated to eating rice. <u>Prepare in advance</u>, by slowly adding rice to their diet a little at a time. Remember that pets are part of the family and should be considered as part of the team.

</td></tr>
</table>

Corn

Corn is a valuable food source to store but not as versatile as wheat nor does it have as long of shelf-life. The shelf life for whole corn is eight to twelve years (depending on storage conditions) and cracked or ground corn is eighteen to thirty-six months.

Corn should be purchased as whole kernels and ground into cornmeal as small batches. Similar to wheat, once the kernel is cracked, the inner germ is exposed and decreases the storage life and nutritive value by over eighty percent. Using the coarse setting on a mill, you can make cracked corn quickly and a finer setting will make cornmeal. Corn can store well *if* the moisture content is <u>low</u>. Check out the moisture content – mold loves moisture! <u>Never</u> eat moldy corn – it can cause death.

Popcorn can be in the basic food staples and provides a morale boost and good nutrition during a lengthy disaster. Store popcorn in an airtight container. Consider purchasing a manual popper that can be used over the fireplace coals.

<table>
<tr><td>

For old popcorn that has lost its "pop" – it is most likely due to lack of moisture. Place two to three cups of unpopped popcorn into a quart jar and add one tablespoon of water. Put the lid on and shake the bottle to distribute the water throughout the corn. Set aside for several days so the water can be absorbed.

</td></tr>
</table>

Flour

Grain can be made into flour and flour can then be made into many meals including bread, pancakes, cupcakes, cookies and pizza crust (providing you also have the other ingredients). The reason grain is considered a basic food staple instead of flour is because of the difference in shelf life. Grains (if properly stored) will last for years but shelf life of flour is somewhat limited, depending on how it is stored. As a general rule, flour may be stored for up seven to ten years before it could go rancid. Again, if using whole grain, make sure you have a good manual grain mill as part of the emergency pantry to grind grain into flour.

Legumes

Legumes are considered a basic food staple because they can be *substituted for animal protein*. When combining grains and other beans, we have a legitimate source for protein. If oil supplies are low and you are unable to replace them, pureed beans can be substituted for some of the oil in baked goods. Up to half of the required oil can be replaced with pureed beans and still have a successful end product. When selecting beans, look for smooth skins and bright colors. Any beans that are cracked, split, dull or have wrinkled skins should be thrown out because they are <u>dried</u> out.

To cook dry beans, remove any shriveled beans and rinse in cold water. In a heavy pot, boil the beans in water for three minutes. Cover and set aside for an hour. Drain, discard the water, rinse the beans, add fresh water to the pot and proceed to cook the beans based on the chart below. Do <u>not</u> add salt or any acidic flavoring (tomatoes or lemon) until the beans are fully cooked.

BEAN	COOKING HOURS
Adzuki	2
Black Turtle	1 ½
Black-eyed Peas	1 to 2
Chickpeas/Garbanzo	3
Great Northern	2
Green Lentils	1
Baby Lima	1 ½
Navy	2 ½
Red Kidney	1 ½
Red Lentils*	20-30 minutes
Soy	3
Split Peas*	1 to 1 ½

***Do Not Presoak**

SOURCE: USU Extension Service

Pasta

Pasta is a processed form of wheat flour, comes in a wide variety of forms and flavors, is easy to prepare, and makes delicious recipes. The white pasta is made from durum wheat that is refined and ground into semolina flour. This type of flour creates pasta that can be cooked soft enough to eat but firm enough to hold its shape. Pasta is considered as a long shelf-life food providing it is properly stored. Include various types of pasta in the emergency preparation pantry at the primary residence and/or place of refuge such as macaroni, spaghetti, noodles, etc.

Dry Milk

When moisture has been removed from milk, the result is powdered milk having a long shelf life. Depending on processing, dry milk may or may not be fortified with Vitamins A and D. This type of milk never tastes quite as good as the real thing. There are several types of powdered milk including regular nonfat dry milk and instant milk. There is no difference in food value and storability. Dry milk is excellent for cooking. For maximum shelf life, purchase or repackage dry milk into airtight metal cans or sturdy plastic containers. Dry milk must be kept in a *cool, dry* and *dark* environment. If properly stored, dry milk can last for years.

NONFAT DRY MILK	+	WATER	=	RECONSTITUTED MILK
1 ½ teaspoons	+	¼ cup	=	¼ cup
3 tablespoons	+	½ cup	=	½ cup
1/3 cup	+	1 cup	=	1 cup
1 1/3 cups	+	1 quart	=	1 quart
5 1/3 cups	+	1 gallon	=	1 gallon

SOURCE: Utah State University Extension Service

Buttermilk or Sour Milk

Another alternative to regular dry milk is buttermilk or sour milk. Many recipes use these ingredients. Dried buttermilk is commercially available in the supermarkets. To make buttermilk or sour milk from dry milk, use the following recipe:

- **1 tablespoon vinegar or lemon juice**
- **1 cup reconstituted milk**

Stir gently and let sit for five minutes.

Cooking Oil – Fats – Shortening

Although fat should be used sparingly, it is essential for good health and our bodies require fat in order to function properly. Most energy needed by the human body is provided by fat. There are vitamins and nutrients that are fat soluble and can only be carried throughout the body in the presence of fat. When cooking, there are many recipes requiring fat and particularly in baked goods. The fat provides flavor and texture to baking products and is chemically necessary to achieve proper consistency in cooking and baking. As an alternative, <u>it is possible to purchase powdered butter, margarine and shortening in the supermarket – make sure you have these items in the food storage pantries.</u>

> It has been reported that during World War II, <u>cooking oil</u> was the one food item considered to be the most valuable – not only for its nutritional qualities but because it could actually be traded for other items. One quart of oil could be traded for several bushels of apples or several hundred pounds of potatoes. During a Level 3 disaster, team members would discover the value of cooking oil as a bartering tool.

Vinegar

Did you know that one bottle of white distilled vinegar contains an entire shelf worth of specialized cleaners? During World War I, vinegar was used to treat wounds and in the treatment of rashes, bites and other minor ailments. Many of the recipes we use also include vinegar – especially during canning and bottling season. There are many types of vinegar – each one used for different purposes. As part of the overall emergency preparation pantry at the primary residence and the place of refuge, have plenty of vinegar in storage. The basic types of vinegar could include white and red wine vinegars, cider vinegar, balsamic and rice vinegars.

> To make homemade mayonnaise, put 1 egg yolk with salt and pepper in a bowl. Add 2/3 cup olive oil (drop by drop) beating all the time. As it thickens, keep adding oil and add 1-2 teaspoons of cider/white wine vinegar. Mix thoroughly.

Sugars and Honey

During a long term disaster, it is important to include sugar and honey in food pantries. Sugar provides sweetness – this is true. But sugar also plays a critical role in cooking by blending and balancing flavors. For example, when cooking spaghetti sauce, chili, barbeque sauce and other tomato-based recipes, sugar softens the acidity of the tomatoes and blends the flavors. In baked goods, sugar reacts with yeast in a process called fermentation that is vital to bread rising and baking. It is needed in the creaming process that puts air into batters – the sugar crystals help create air pockets that contribute to the pleasing texture in breads, cakes and other baked goods.

Granulated sugar must be kept dry and stored in airtight containers. If stored properly, granulated sugar can be indefinitely stored. **Brown sugar** is made by adding molasses back into refined white sugar. The amount of molasses added during processing determines the color of the sugar. To make homemade brown sugar, mix two tablespoons of molasses with one cup of white sugar. Because of the moisture content in brown sugar, it must be stored in an airtight container. Another type of sugar is **powdered sugar**. Powdered sugar is a staple ingredient in many recipes – especially for baked goods. Store powdered sugar in an airtight container.

Honey has a distinctive flavor and is sweeter than regular sugar. Honey produces moist and dense baked goods. Properly processed, packaged and stored - honey will retain its quality for a long time – even decades. Honey should be stored in a *cool*, *dry* and *dark* environment and should always be stored in air-tight containers. Storing honey in a high temperature environment will shorten the shelf life. Honey will crystallize, darken in color and the flavor will become stronger with age. To remove crystals, warm (not cook) the honey. If exposed to air, mold can invade a large container of honey. Honey is now available as honey powder and can be purchased in local supermarkets.

LEAVENINGS

The most common leavening agents are *yeast*, *baking powder* and *baking soda*. When mixed with liquid, a carbon dioxide gas is produced causing the batter or dough to rise when heated. All three of these leavening agents have a reasonably long shelf life. In recipes, baking powder and baking soda are <u>not</u> interchangeable.

Yeast

Yeast (dry) must be stored in an airtight container and in a *cool* environment with no threat of moisture. Dry yeast comes in three forms. Active dry yeast is sold in the familiar packets in the baking section of the supermarket. It can also be purchased in larger jars that are better for long-term storage. For storage purposes, select the foil brick package for quick-rise yeast and instant dried yeast. One pound of yeast contains about three billion yeast cells. This organism lies dormant until activated by a combination of sugar, moisture, warmth and air. If properly stored, shelf life is five and ten years.

TEST

To test any type of dry yeast for viability, mix one teaspoon of yeast with 1/3 teaspoon of sugar into ¼ cup of warm water (110-120 degrees F). Wait for about five to ten minutes. If the yeast mixture bubbles, it is still alive and can be used. If there are no bubbles at all – the yeast is dead and should be discarded.

Baking Powder

Baking *powder* is a blend of baking <u>soda</u> and <u>cream of tartar</u>. It is known as a double-acting leavening because it begins to release carbon dioxide when moistened and again when heated in the oven.

To make <u>single-acting</u> baking powder, mix ½ teaspoon of cream of tartar with ¼ teaspoon of baking soda. This recipe will replace one teaspoon of baking <u>powder</u> in a recipe. Because it is single-acting, it will create carbon dioxide only when moistened, so batter must be cooked quickly or it will go flat. Since the chemical reaction begins as soon as it comes into contact with water, be sure to thoroughly mix baking powder with other dry ingredients before adding any liquid. If stored in a *cool*, *dry* and *dark* environment, shelf life can be between five and ten years.

TEST

To test baking powder, stir it around in the can to see if there are any lumps which are an indication that it has picked up moisture – rendering it useless. Mix one teaspoon of baking powder into a glass of warm water and see if it fizzes. If it does – it is still good. If is doesn't – throw it out.

Baking Soda

Baking soda reacts immediately when combined with water and should be mixed thoroughly with dry ingredients before adding liquids to ensure even leavening. When using baking soda, any items baked with it should be put into the oven as quickly as possible.

TEST

To see if baking soda is still active, pour a few tablespoons of white vinegar into a small cup and add one teaspoon of baking soda. If it froths – even a little – it is still good.

Since baking soda is an alkaline, any product made with baking soda will require an acid product such as sour milk, molasses, lemon juice, applesauce, buttermilk, honey, brown sugar, cream of tartar, chocolate, cocoa powder, orange and other citrus juices, pineapple or vinegar to cause the chemical reaction or it will not rise at all. Baking soda has a long shelf life and should be stored in an airtight container in a *cool*, *dry* and *dark* environment.

Salt

Salt is a mineral and is essential for good health. Every single cell in our body contains salt and this mineral plays a crucial role in our bodies. In fact, too much or too little salt in our diet can cause severe and even fatal neurological problems. Table salt has been refined and contains ninety-five percent of pure sodium chloride. When purchasing salt in the supermarket, it is generally iodized - small amounts of potassium iodide have been added to the salt which has eliminated iodine deficiency disorders in our country.

Salt has a very important role in food preparation. It brings out natural flavors, retards growth of microorganisms that spoil food and helps to develop proper texture in the food. Salt has an indefinite shelf life providing it is stored in a *dry* and *clean* environment. A large amount of salt should be included in the primary residence emergency pantry – in addition to using salt for cooking, it will become a valuable bartering tool during long-term disasters.

Bouillons, Soup Bases, Sauce Mixes

Bouillon cubes are compressed and flavor-concentrated cubes of dehydrated meat, poultry or vegetable stock and spices, and serves as a valuable food source in the emergency pantry. Instant bouillon granules are the loose and granular form of the concentrate product. Salt is listed as the first ingredient on both types of bouillon so when using bouillon, cut back or eliminate additional salt in the recipe. Bouillon is often used as a clear broth for soups and stews. It should be dissolved in boiling water according to package instructions. Bouillons can be purchased in cans at the supermarket and should be stored in a *cool*, *dark* and *dry* environment.

Soup base is generally processed as a paste in a jar or as a granular concentrate. A soup mix prepared commercially will generally be a mixture of vegetables, grains or beans, small pasta and possibly textured vegetable protein. Providing these products are properly stored, they have a shelf life of many years. The soup mixes found in foil or cardboard packaging needs to be stored in an air-tight container in a *cool*, *dark* and *dry* environment.

Sauce mixes are found in the supermarket and generally have a higher fat content that shortens shelf life. These packets should be stored in air-tight containers in a *cool*, *dark* and *dry* environment. The variety of sauce mixes are incredible – consider storing gravy mixes, sauce mixes for rice and pastas, ethnic sauces and seasoning mixes, oriental beef and broccoli mix and cheese sauces.

Seasonings

Although spices, herbs and seasonings may have minimal nutritional value, they are still very important – especially during a long-term disaster. They are added to food to appeal to the senses and to dramatically reduce the "crappy" factor. As part of the overall food storage, spices, herbs and seasonings MUST be included! Not only should the selection be familiar to team members but select ones that go the longest distance in making the greatest number of simple recipes. All seasonings should be stored in airtight containers in a *cool*, *dark* and *dry* environment. In the supermarket, seasonings can be expensive so check out the "dollar stores" and discount bread outlets – many times seasonings are available for a reasonable price. The shelf life of seasonings is generally one or two years although if stored properly, they can last for a much longer period of time. Whole herbs/spices last longer than ground counterparts.

COMPLEMENTS

When considering the possible scenario of eating only basic food staples for a long period of time, it becomes even more urgent to *plan in advance* so food pantries contain other food sources that can reduce, diminish or even eliminate a diet of only basic foods – a huge "☹" factor. A majority of food complements have an extended shelf life and by adding all or some of these food complements to emergency food pantries, the diet for team members during an extended disaster can be made bearable and even somewhat enjoyable during hard times.

EGGS

The delectable egg provides protein but also serves as food and a functioning ingredient in recipes. One egg contains about one tablespoon of egg yolk and two tablespoons of egg white and weighs about two ounces without the shell.

As part of *planning in advance*, the team may consider constructing a chicken coop and raising chickens to guarantee a plentiful supply of fresh eggs. In addition to fresh eggs, you can purchase dried whole eggs, dried egg whites, dried egg yolks and dried egg mix in air tight canisters.

- The **dried whole egg powder** is one hundred percent eggs. When blended with water, the powder will produce liquid eggs that are used just like a fresh egg. The dried whole egg powder has the same nutritional value as a fresh egg. One pound of dried whole egg powder equals three dozen eggs.

- The **dried egg white** and **dried egg yolk** powder provide convenient methods to use either part without the problem of separation.

- The **dried egg mix** is generally a blend of dried whole eggs, nonfat dry milk, corn oil, color, salt and lecithin or whey.

These products can be purchased in most supermarkets and are stored in metal airtight containers. Store these containers in a *cool*, *dark* and *dry* environment for an extended shelf life. A chicken coop with laying hens is a great way to include fresh eggs in the diet for team members, but egg mix should also be included in the pantries in the event the hens are unable to produce or provide eggs.

There are several substitutions that can be used in recipes if eggs are not available, including the following:

- **Banana** – for each egg needed in a recipe, use 1/2 mashed ripe banana and 1/4 teaspoon of baking powder.

- **Flax Meal** – for each egg needed in a recipe, use two tablespoons of flax meal, 1/8 teaspoon of baking powder and three tablespoons of water.

- **Gelatin** - for each egg needed in a recipe, dissolve one tablespoon of unflavored gelatin in one tablespoon of cold water and add two tablespoons of boiling water. Beat vigorously until frothy.

- **Cornstarch** – for each egg needed in a recipe, substitute one tablespoon of cornstarch plus three tablespoons of water.

- **Mayonnaise** – for each egg needed in a recipe, substitute three tablespoons of mayonnaise.

DEHYDRATED VERSUS FREEZE DRIED FOODS

Both dehydrated and freeze-fried foods provide an important addition to emergency food pantries. Due to superior processing techniques, these foods have the advantage of a long-term shelf life (between fifteen to twenty years if stored in a *cool*, *dark* and *dry* environment), low weight and volume and the ability to accent and supplement menus that use basic food staples.

Dehydration

Dehydrated food takes only twenty percent of the storage space of wet packed foods. For example, thirty tomatoes can fit into a pint-sized jar; ten pounds of carrots will fit into a quart-size jar; and twenty-seven cans of peas fits into a No. 10 canister. Dehydrated foods contain multiple ingredients used to make a complete meal without adding anything else. Shelf life is fifteen to twenty years if stored in a *cool*, *dark* and *dry* environment.

Freeze Drying

The freeze-drying process results in the food looking more like the original product when rehydrated. Freeze drying also preserves virtually all the fresh taste, color, aroma and nutritional contents. Freeze dried products are more expensive and take up more space to store than a dehydrated cousin. The shelf life for freeze-dried products is twenty to thirty years for items commercially dried in metal cans with oxygen removed. Again, the cans should be stored in a *cool*, *dark*, and *dry* environment.

There are substantial differences between dehydrated and freeze-dried food products as follows:

DIFFERENCE	FREEZE DRIED	DEHYDRATED
Taste	Requires cooking, seasonings and other items, i.e. rice, meat, potatoes, salt, pepper, hot sauce, garlic, etc.	Pre-seasoned, pre-cooked and pre-mixed with other ingredients. Generally tastes better.
Cooking	Cooking time is short - 10 to 15 minutes	Cooking time is short - 10 to 15 minutes
Seasoning	Should be seasoned	Does not require additional seasoning
Ingredient	Usually single ingredients that can be mixed with other dehydrated foods or food items	Do not require additional ingredients to make a complete meal. Add hot water and cook for about 10 minutes.
Best Value	Costs less	More expensive
Number of Servings	Highly concentrated compared to canned, bottled or frozen foods	
Opened Containers	Container should be sealed with lid to keep out humidity, moisture and insects. Should be stored in a *cool*, *dark* and *dry* environment.	
Shelf Life	When stored property, shelf life is 15-30 years. This type of food storage must be stored in a *dry*, *cold* (or cool) *dark* place out of direct sunlight, preferably at a constant temperature. You can double, triple or even quadruple the shelf life by lowering the temperature proportionally. **The basic rule of thumb is to store freeze-dried and dehydrated foods in as low of temperature as possible to increase shelf life and retain nutritional value**.	

FRUITS AND VEGETABLES

During a medium to long term disaster – fruits and vegetables will not only be mandatory – but welcome - and from a health and taste perspective – vegetables and fruits should be a high priority for the primary residence food pantry. In addition to fresh fruits and vegetables from the garden, most fruits and vegetables are commercially available in dehydrated or freeze-dried canisters as well as in cans.

In many areas, there are religious organizations that provide canning operations. Members can purchase and can a variety of freeze-dried and dehydrated foods including onion and potato flakes, chopped carrots, peppers and mushrooms or sliced apples and bananas. The local supermarkets also stock a wide variety of fruits and vegetables in No. 10 canisters. These sources are expensive – be sure to wait for the case lot sales – many of these emergency preparation items are on sale during that time. There are numerous selections from which to choose – make sure you have ample supplies included in the food storage plan. Attempt to select choices that appeal to all team members, are flexible enough to be included in a large variety of menus but still provide the needed vitamins and minerals.

Proper storage is the key for canned goods as well dehydrated, freeze-dried and other processed foods. All canned and bottled goods should be stored in a *cool*, *dark* and *dry* environment and not stored directly on concrete – either on the floor or against a wall. The lime from the concrete can bleed over time and destroy the cans. Due to high acid content in fruits and some vegetables, shelf life is about five to ten years. Rotation can maintain quality control of the inventory.

To make horseradish remove the leaves from the root of an 8-10 inch long horseradish tuber and rinse the dirt off the root. Use a vegetable peeler and peel the surface skin off the tuber. Chop into pieces and place the pieces in a food processor. Add two tablespoons of water and process until well ground. If the mixture contains too much liquid, strain out some of the water. Immediately add one tablespoon of white vinegar and a pinch of salt to the mixture and pulse to combine. Using a rubber spatula, transfer the grated horseradish to a jar. It will keep for three to four weeks in the refrigerator. Work in a well ventilated room!

NUTS AND SEEDS

Nuts and seeds contain more protein than all vegetable foods with the exception of soybeans. Unfortunately, due to the high fat content, shelf life for nuts and seeds is not good for long-term storage. Recognizing the shorter shelf life and by properly caring for nuts and seeds, they can still complement and combine with the basic food staples. Nuts commercially sealed in No. 10 cans or in glass jars have the oxygen removed – the shelf life is approximately one year. Peanut butter (if hydrogenated) has a shelf life of about five years.

DRINKS

Another food storage item to be considered is various types of drink mixes. For example, for children (as well as adults) teams could consider hot chocolate and other flavored drink mixes such as Tang or Kool-Aid. Other possible choices include coffee and tea. Make sure these powdered drink mixes only require water to be added.

FISHING

Another method for obtaining food sources – and especially protein – is fishing. By *planning in advance*, team members should seek out and find water sources containing edible fish close to the primary residence or place of refuge. Once these sources are located, purchase fishing equipment and supplies and store in the emergency preparation inventory. Don't forget to consider ice fishing during the winter months – check with your local sporting goods store for information.

> **<u>Give</u> a man a fish and you feed him for a day. <u>Teach</u> a man to fish and you feed him for a lifetime. So true!**

HUNTING AND TRAPPING

During a long-term disaster, hunting and trapping will be a means for team members to obtain food. As part of *advanced planning*, one team member should be educated and experienced in basic hunting and/or trapping techniques and in <u>processing, preparing and storing the meat</u>. In the inventory, basic equipment and supplies should be available including guns and ammunition, bow and arrows, slingshots and traps.

In many remote areas, there is an abundance of wild game in the valleys, deserts and surrounding canyons including elk, deer, moose, rabbit, pheasant, dove, duck, sage hen, turkey and geese. As part of the local culture, there are many residents who are avid and active hunters. Make sure that one of them is included on your team or prior arrangements are made to combine skills between several teams.

INSECTS

During famine or other severe conditions, insects could make the difference between survival and death. Ants, termites, moths, grasshoppers, crickets, earthworms, cockroaches, butterflies, mosquitoes, locusts, beetle larvae, caterpillars and spiders have been on the survival menu throughout time. All wildlife (including insects) should be well cooked before eating and one of the easiest ways to prepare insects is to roast them over a fire and they also serve as "fair game" in soups and stews. Insects are higher in vitamins, minerals, protein and fat than most meat.

> Ask yourself this simple question: how hungry would I have to be before I would be willing to eat a worm, a cricket, an ant, a spider or a grasshopper?

LIVESTOCK

Many teams may include livestock as part of a potential food source during a disaster. Animals including cows, sheep, goats, pigs, chickens and turkeys are raised to provide not only meat but also milk and eggs. As *part of advanced planning*, make sure all livestock can be housed in adequate shelter to protect against heat, cold, wind, and predators (including human predators who would not hesitate to invade your livestock during famine situations). At least one team member should be knowledgeable and experienced in slaughtering techniques that provide humane treatment to the animals and sanitary methods for butchering and processing to avoid contamination and disease.

SPROUTING

Sprouting is the means of taking vegetable and grain seeds <u>specifically used for sprouting</u>, placing them in a container, adding water, and once the seed germinates and begins to grow a plant, the small plant (sprout) is harvested and eaten before the plant can grow to full "adulthood". A fresh crop of sprouts can be produced every few days with minimum effort and time. Sprouts <u>can</u> be economical providing they are purchased in bulk! <u>All you need is a container, sprouting seeds and water</u>. A harvest of sprouts can add a new aspect of how team members eat during difficult times. <u>Fresh</u> fruits and vegetables contain enzymes and aid the body in the digestion of food. When fresh fruits and vegetables are not readily available, sprouts are a great alternative and should always be eaten fresh – **NEVER COOKED** – as cooking the sprout kills the enzymes which are vital to our health.

The table below provides <u>general</u> information on growing time, yield and maturity of various sprout types and the approximate shelf life of seeds (providing seeds are stored properly):

SPROUT	GROWING TIME	YIELD	SHELF LIFE (Years)
Adzuki	2-4 days	½ cup = 1 cup	5
Alfalfa	7 days	*2 tablespoons = 4 cups*	4
Amaranth	2-4 days	2/3 cup = 1 cup	2
Arugula	5-6 days	1 cup = 1 cup	5
Barley	6-9 days	2/3 cup = 1 cup	2
Bean (Black)	3-5 days	½ cup = 1 cup	3
Broccoli	5-14 days	1 cup = 1 cup	5
Buckwheat	8-12 days	*½ cup = 2 ½ cups*	2
Cabbage	5-6 days	*3 tablespoons = 3 cups*	5
Clover	7 days	*2 tablespoons = 4 cups*	4
Cress	5-14 days	1 cup = 1 cup	5
Dill	14-16 days	¼ cup = ½ cup	3
Fenugreek	8-12 days	*3 tablespoons = 3 cups*	5
Flax	5-14 days	1 cup = 1 cup	3
Garbanzo	2-3 days	*½ cup = 2 cups*	5
Kale	5-14 days	1 cup = 1 cup	5
Kamut	2-3 days	2/3 cup = 1 cup	2
Lentil	2-4 days	*1 cup = 6 cups*	5
Millet	1-3 days	2/3 cup = 1 cup	3
Mizuna	5-14 days	1 cup = 1 cup	5
Mung Bean	1-5 days	*1/3 cup = 1 ½ cups*	5
Mustard	5-6 days	*3 tablespoons = 3 cups*	5
Oats	1-3 days	2/3 cup = 1 cup	2
Pea	5-6 days	*1 cup = 4 cups*	5
Peanut	2-4 days	½ cup = 1 cup	3
Pinto Bean	3-5 days	*½ cup = 1 ½ cups*	5

SPROUT	GROWING TIME	YIELD	SHELF LIFE (Years)
Pumpkin	1-2 days	*½ cup = 2 cups*	2
Quinoa	2-4 days	2/3 cup = 1 cup	2
Radish	5-6 days	*3 tablespoons = 3 cups*	5
Rice	2-4 days	2/3 cup = 1 cup	3
Sesame	1-3 days	2/3 = 1 cup	2
Soybean	3-4 days	*½ cup = 2 cups*	4
Spelt	2-3 days	2/3 cup = 1 cup	2
Sunflower	8-12 days	*½ cup = 4 cups*	2
Tatsoi	3-6 days	*3 tablespoons = 3 cups*	5
Triticale	2-3 days	2/3 cup = 1 cup	2
Wheat	2-3 days	*1 cup = 4 cups*	2

*Those marked in **bold** and *italic* are good choices to get a higher yield using a minimum amount of seeds.

GROWING INDOORS

Indoor farming allows the team to plant and harvest crops of vegetables sufficient to make a difference in the diet and health of team members. The team will need to consider the number of members in the team and the amount of space everyone would be willing to assign for indoor gardening. The key success factor for indoor farming is <u>knowing what vegetables can be grown indoors</u>. Any vegetable that does not need to be pollinated or is considered as a cool weather crop is a candidate for indoor farming. As part of *advanced planning*, include various pots and containers, shelving, seeds and even some commercially packaged soil in the emergency pantry to be used for indoor farming during a disaster when conditions do not allow for outdoor gardening.

Here is a list of some vegetables that could be successfully grown indoors:

- Arugula
- Broccoli
- Brussels Sprouts
- Carrots
- Chard
- Chives (Herb)
- Lettuce (Bibb, Loose Leaf and Romaine)
- Mint (Herb)
- Mustard Greens
- Onions
- Oregano (Herb)
- Parsley (Herb)
- Peppers
- Radishes
- Rosemary (Herb)
- Spinach
- Thyme (Herb)
- Tomatoes (patio/container growing only)

OUTDOOR GARDEN

One of the most important steps in emergency preparation is learning how to grow an outdoor garden. The ability to do so effectively can make the difference between life and death. However, one of the key factors in outdoor gardens is the availability of water. It should be noted that outdoor gardens are not an absolute certainty, especially if water sources are not available. It is also important to have the right tools to plant and cultivate a garden.

GARDEN SEEDS

<u>**Hybrid**</u> seeds are produced by companies through careful pollination of two specific varieties that bring together two traits in each of the chosen varieties so that the resulting seed has both traits. Plants grown from hybrid seeds typically <u>do **not** produce seeds that can grow the same type of plants again</u> and may even produce seeds that will not grow at all.

The advantages for hybrid seeds are better performance in the garden in terms of more fruits and vegetables produced and more plants surviving disease and pests. They tend to be more expensive and choices are limited.

Non hybrid seeds are referred to as open pollinated seeds or heirloom seeds and come from plants that are naturally pollinated. Non hybrid seeds *will* produce plants whose seeds will produce more plants again that look the same as the parent plant, so you can collect seeds from the plant and use them again next year to grow the same variety of plant. The non-hybrid seeds provide a multitude of vegetable and fruit varieties. Although the seeds are generally less expensive, they are not as well rounded, are much more susceptible to disease and pests and do not produce as many vegetables and fruits as the hybrid counterparts.

GREENHOUSE

A greenhouse is a great way to become self-sufficient because you get a longer growing season inside of a greenhouse. You can start plants growing early in the springtime and keep them growing long after the usual fall harvest. There are several seeds that can be started in a greenhouse including: broccoli, cabbage, cauliflower, celery, cucumbers, eggplant, melons, peppers, and tomatoes. A greenhouse can be large or small – economical or expensive. A good way to find something you might want to purchase is to search on the Internet or contact your local Extension Service. There are many outlets available that can deliver ready-to-assemble greenhouses or provide plans for building your own at a very reasonable price.

ORCHARD

Team members could consider planting an orchard to produce fresh fruit. To plant a successful orchard, you need a basic understanding of soil, pests, diseases and general care. Consider the climate because the type of orchard to be planted is determined by climate influences, including wind patterns, frost, average temperatures, amount of daylight and rainfall. For example, trying to grow an orchard of lemon and grapefruit trees in northern Utah would be "fruitless"!

In addition, evaluate the soil for adequate nutrients and drainage. The site may need to be amended before planting because of inadequate or excessive nutrients and will then need to be monitored and tested on a regular basis. Protect the orchard from wildlife such as rabbits, deer and rodents attracted to fruit-bearing trees by investing in mesh-wire fencing that extends at least six feet high to deter the animals. If you have outdoor cats, the trunks of these fruit trees will be used as a scratching post (trust me - I know). Protect the trunks by investing in trunk wrapping material. Clear the site of any towering trees that may reduce sunlight on the orchard. A minimum of eight hours of light is needed each day for fruit-bearing trees to be productive. Plant trees according to common characteristics such as resistance to diseases and pests, size or expected bloom dates. And finally, if the fruit tree is bare root – soak in water for 12-24 hours and trim damaged roots before planting.

PH LEVELS

All plants must have the proper pH level in the soil to grow. The pH level is the measure of acidity or alkalinity on a scale between 0 and 14. The soil is considered as *acidic* when the pH level is between 0 and 7. The soil is considered *neutral* when the pH level is at 7 and if the pH level is above 7, it is considered as *alkaline*. When soil is partnered with a plant suited to its pH level, the plant can accept nutrients in the soil allowing it to grow and be healthy.

Highly acidic or alkaline soil will cause problems for fruit trees. Most fruit trees prefer neutral to slightly acidic soil with an ideal range between 6.0 and 6.5. Citrus trees can tolerate more alkaline soils, growing well in soil with a pH between 6.0 and 8.0. Blueberries are a notable exception preferring acidic soil with a pH level of around 5.0. To reduce the pH level by one full point, add two pounds of sulphur per 100 square feet (reduce this amount by one half if you have extremely sandy soil). Three times a year, water plants with a leaf mould tea that lowers the pH but adds potassium that promotes strong root growth. A common sign that plants are in too alkaline soil is when leaves or needles take on a yellow-green hue referred to as *chlorotic*.

Plants cannot access nutrients (usually iron or manganese) if the soil has a high (alkaline) pH level. To correct the problem, lower the pH level and fertilize. Acid-loving trees and shrubs often have shallow root systems. When planting, remember to dig a wide and deep hole and thoroughly amend heavy clay soils. It is also important not to over-fertilize because roots will easily burn. To encourage long root systems, water infrequently but deeply. Plants preferring a lower pH will require similar care when feeding, mulching and pest control. When designing the garden, keep the acid-lovers together in the garden bed, which will make their special care more manageable.

pH	Zone	
14.0		
13.5		**LOWER PH**
13.0		• **Sulfur**
12.5		• **Pine Needles**
12.0		• **Peat Moss**
11.5		• **Bark Mulch**
11.0		• **Leaf Mould**
10.5	**ALKALINE**	• **Coffee Grounds**
10.0		• **Tea Bags**
9.5		• **Pickle Juice**
9.0		
8.5		
8.0		
7.5		
7.0		
6.5	**NEUTRAL ZONE**	
6.0		
5.5		**RAISE PH**
5.0		• **Limestone**
4.5		• **Oyster Shells**
4.0		• **Egg Shells**
3.5		• **Wood Ash**
3.0	**ACID**	• **Nitrogen Fertilizer**
2.5		• **Elemental Sulphur**
2.0		
1.5		
1.0		
.50		
0.0		

If you have highly acidic soil and need a more alkaline soil, the pH level can be <u>raised</u> by adding:

- Crushed Limestone
- Egg Shells
- Elemental Sulphur
- Ground Oyster Shells
- Nitrogen Fertilizer
- Wood Ash

If you have highly alkaline soil and need a more acidic soil, the pH level can be <u>lowered</u> by adding:

- Bark Mulch
- Coffee Grounds
- Leaf Mould
- Peat Moss
- Pickle Juice (vinegar)
- Pine Needles
- Sulphur
- Tea Bags

The following table displays <u>approximate</u> pH level requirements for various fruits, vegetables and herbs. Make sure the soil is within these boundaries for each specific plant.

PLANT	ACID										ALKALINE							
	2.5	3.0	3.5	4.0	4.5	5.0	5.5	6.0	6.5	7.0	7.5	8.0	8.5	9.0	9.5	10.0	10.5	11.0
Apple								▓	▓	▓								
Apricots								▓	▓	▓								
Artichoke									▓	▓	▓							
Arugula								▓	▓	▓								
Asparagus								▓	▓	▓	▓	▓						
Avocado						▓	▓	▓	▓	▓								
Banana							▓	▓	▓									
Basil							▓	▓	▓	▓								
Bean								▓	▓	▓	▓							
Beet								▓	▓	▓								
Blueberries					▓	▓												
Broccoli								▓	▓	▓	▓							
Brussels Sprouts								▓	▓	▓	▓							
Cabbage								▓	▓	▓	▓							
Cantaloupe								▓	▓	▓								
Carrot							▓	▓	▓	▓								
Cauliflower							▓	▓	▓	▓	▓							
Celery							▓	▓	▓	▓								

PLANT	ACID										ALKALINE							
	2.5	3.0	3.5	4.0	4.5	5.0	5.5	6.0	6.5	7.0	7.5	8.0	8.5	9.0	9.5	10.0	10.5	11.0
Cherry								■	■	■								
Chervil								■	■									
Chives								■	■	■								
Cilantro								■	■									
Collard									■	■	■							
Corn							■	■	■	■	■							
Cucumber							■	■	■	■								
Dill							■	■	■									
Eggplant							■	■	■	■								
Endive							■	■	■	■								
Fennel							■	■	■									
Garlic							■	■	■	■	■							
Grapefruit								■	■	■	■	■						
Grapes								■	■	■	■	■						
Horseradish								■	■	■								
Kale								■	■	■	■							
Kohlrabi								■	■	■								
Lavender								■	■									
Leek								■	■	■	■							
Lettuce								■	■	■	■							
Marjoram								■	■	■	■							
Melon							■	■	■									
Mustard								■	■	■	■							
Okra								■	■	■	■							
Onion								■	■	■								
Orange							■	■	■									
Oregano								■	■	■								
Parsley						■	■	■										
Parsnip								■	■	■	■	■						
Pea								■	■	■	■	■						
Peach									■	■								
Peanut						■	■	■	■									
Pear									■	■								
Pepper								■	■	■								
Plums							■	■	■									
Potato						■	■	■										
Radish								■	■	■								
Rhubarb							■	■	■	■								
Rosemary								■	■	■								
Sage								■	■	■								
Spinach							■	■	■	■	■							
Squash-Summer								■	■	■	■							
Squash-Winter							■	■	■	■								
Strawberries							■	■	■									
Sunflower								■	■	■	■							
Tarragon								■	■	■	■							
Tomatillo								■	■	■	■							
Tomato							■	■	■	■	■							
Turnip							■	■	■	■								
Watermelon							■	■	■	■								

EDIBLE PLANTS

There are many edible <u>plants</u> in the yard, garden or in the surrounding area. To *prepare in advance*, purchase a nature guide of flowers, roots and seeds available in your area that can be eaten by team members in the event of an emergency situation. A problem that can easily occur is when teams <u>begin to scavenge the area for plants</u>. It is very important to know which plants in your area can be safely consumed.

Children and teenagers should be carefully supervised to guarantee they do not eat poisonous plants. It is also important to recognize that although some parts of a plant may be safe to eat - other parts of the same plant could be poisonous. For example, it is perfectly alright to eat a tomato off the vine, but the actual vine itself and the leaves are poisonous. Likewise, it is alright to eat a potato that grows under the ground, but the stems and leaves that are very poisonous are members of the nightshade family.

EDIBLE FLOWERS

There are many edible <u>flowers</u> that may be in the yard or garden.

• *Dandelion*	• *Rose*	• *Violet*
• *Dune Evening Primrose*	• *Sego Lily*	• *Wild Mustard Flowers*
• *Indian Paintbrush*	• *Snapdragon*	• *Yellow Sweet Clover*
• *Oxeye Daisy*	• *Tulip*	• *Yucca*
• *Pansy*		

EDIBLE ROOTS

There are many wild edible <u>roots</u> available in the wilderness. Again, make sure you obtain a nature guide of edible roots in your area and make sure all team members recognize the roots that can be eaten. It does no good to know the names of the edible roots but you can not identify them. Some possible choices include:

• *Sego Lily*	• *Wild Carrot*
• *Sweetroot*	• *Salsify*
• *Chicory*	• *Burdock*

EDIBLE SEEDS

Edible <u>seeds</u> are very abundant in nature. Knowing about wild edible seeds can increase your ability to survive in nature. Edible seeds include beans, grains and nuts.

• *Curly Dock*	• *Pine Nuts (Pinion)*
• *Yellow Dock*	• *Foxtail Grass*
• *Clasping Pepperweed*	• *Wild Mustards*

WILD FRUIT

Most of the cultivated fruit we enjoy today began in a wild environment and many of the fruits are berries. Depending on where you live, the wild fruits vary by region. Some of the wild fruits available in the western deserts and mountains include:

• *Black Cherry*	• *Elderberry*	• *Pawpaw*
• *Blackberries*	• *Gooseberry*	• *Persimmon*
• *Blackcap*	• *Huckleberry*	• *Plum*
• *Blueberry*	• *Juneberry*	• *Prickly Pear*
• *Chokecherry*	• *Juniper Berries*	• *Raspberry*
• *Coralberry*	• *Lingonberry*	• *Salmonberry*
• *Crabapple*	• *Mayhaw*	• *Serviceberry*

• *Current Berries*	• *Mulberry*	• *Staghorn Sumac*
• *Deerberry*	• *Oregon Grape*	• *Thimbleberry*
• *Dune Primrose*	• *Passionflower*	• *Wild Strawberry*

POISONOUS PLANTS

During peaceful times, we are unlikely to seek out wild plants for consumption. However, during serious and long-term disasters, including famine, it's a good bet team members will begin to forage for any plant that can be harvested. Hunger is an amazing equalizer of human beings. **WHEN WE BECOME REALLY HUNGRY – WE CAN ALSO BECOME REALLY STUPID.** It is especially important to educate children and teenagers about poisonous plants. During a famine when people are hungry – children and especially teenagers are more susceptible to erratic behavior and are more likely to forage irresponsibly – and perhaps to their death.

It is important to *plan in advance* and become informed about the <u>poisonous</u> plants growing in your area. **KNOW WHAT THEY LOOK LIKE AND MAKE SURE THAT ALL TEAM MEMBERS CAN IDENTIFY THEM BY SIGHT!**

> As part of the emergency preparation library, get a reference book on edible and poisonous plants <u>growing in your area</u>. Make sure all adult team members can identify each plant. Counsel children and teenagers on the importance of "careful selection" when foraging for plants.

FOOD STORAGE GUIDELINES

The basic food staples and other complements gathered to fill emergency food pantries are expensive – there is no other way to say it. <u>Over the next several years, the price of food will continue to rise and at some point in time it may not even be commercially available – even if you have the money to buy it</u>. It is critical to use the correct methods to store food supplies. When the time arrives to eat the food stored in <u>all</u> emergency pantries - it must be edible and the equipment used to process and prepare the food must be working when you need to use it.

There are some foods that need to be constantly used, replaced, rotated and cared for in a logical manner. Even with the excellent methods used today to treat food and extend shelf life – many food types do not last forever and proper care and rotation is essential. For these foods, the rotation guidelines are simple: **FIRST IN – FIRST OUT** – also referred to as **FIFO** in the inventory control world. For example, when you stock your shelves with a case (48 cans) of tomato sauce, bring the current cans to the <u>front</u> of the shelf and place the new cans <u>behind</u> them. When using tomato sauce, always use the cans at the *front* of the shelf. Another method to know which food supplies are the oldest versus the newest is to use a marker to write down the date the food items were purchased. You can quickly see which food items need to be used first – namely, the ones with the oldest date.

<u>**THE ULTIMATE FACTOR IN MAINTAINING AND EXTENDING THE SHELF LIFE OF FOOD ITEMS IS THE ENVIRONMENT**</u>. <u>Keeping food in a *cool, dry* and *dark* environment is the key to proper food storage</u>. The less light, heat and moisture exposure - the longer the shelf life – period. These three enemies of food encourage bacteria and mold to grow and cause spoilage and deterioration.

The ideal storage temperatures for retention of vitamins and the least probability of spoilage range from thirty-five degrees to seventy degrees. Light can actually destroy the nutritive value of food. Moisture invites insect infestation in dry goods and encourages rust in canned goods. The optimal humidity level for storing food is between fifty and seventy percent.

ROOT CELLAR

A root cellar basically consists of a "hole in the ground" where you can store various types of fruits, vegetables and meats including potatoes, onions, carrots, turnips, parsnips and apples. If storage space in limited, canned and bottled food can also be stored in a root cellar. A well-built root cellar would be a good investment in emergency preparation. If you construct the cellar yourself, the cost of materials is less than you would spend in one winter buying food at supermarket prices.

A good root cellar should provide cool, above-freezing temperatures and good circulation of moderately humid air. The <u>dirt floor</u> takes advantage of the naturally cool and even temperature of the earth. It also provides needed humidity. The ideal location for a root cellar is on a hillside or slope facing away from prevailing winds. Make sure that you select the highest ground possible to avoid flooding.

There are many methods for building a root cellar. The cellar can be constructed with concrete walls and a dirt floor or the walls could be constructed using railroad ties. The cellar must have a heavy-duty and durable roof and also requires an air vent for circulation. A variety of instructional books and magazines are available for details on constructing a root cellar in your area.

STORAGE CONTAINERS

When filling the food pantry with bulk purchases of sugar, oats, flour, wheat, vegetables, fruits and other foods, the contents must be transferred into <u>sturdy</u>, <u>food-grade</u> and <u>airtight</u> containers to keep out insects, rodents and moisture. There are various sizes and shapes of containers that provide the criteria needed for storing food which is:

<u>NOT</u> up for negotiation!

DO IT OR LOOSE IT!

**CLEAN
<u>FOOD GRADE</u>
AIRTIGHT
MOISTURE PROOF
PUNCTURE PROOF
INSECT PROOF
RESEALABLE**

The proper containers can be purchased at most supermarkets. These containers are generally five-gallon buckets with a strong lid. Once the food has been emptied into the bucket, the lid requires the use of a hammer or mallet to seal it on the bucket. By contacting local restaurants, fast food outlets, bakeries and doughnut shops, you may be able to buy used or get free buckets for little or no cost.

Make sure <u>all</u> buckets are cleaned thoroughly. Avoid used buckets that previously contained strong-smelling contents such as pickles or vinegar. Canning facilities and outlets offer No. 10 cans that could be filled with food items and then commercially sealed as well. <u>Do not store food in any container that is not specifically meant to store food items</u>.

The use of plastic or metal 55-gallon trash cans is NOT a good option for storing dry goods – simply because the container cannot be made airtight. Rodents and insects can invade the contents with little or no effort. Likewise, a plastic bag is not airtight and will not deter rodents and insects. Another poor choice for storing dry goods is a Mylar bag. These bags look similar to metal cloth. They are airtight and stack well – but a cute little mouse or hungry little beetle can chew through a Mylar bag in less than an hour.

Food items packaged in cardboard, foil, plastic or paper bags must be stored in the proper container. These items include gravy or flavoring mixes, pouch cookie mixes, corn bread mixes, beans, cake mixes, muffin mixes, chocolate chips, drink mixes, flavored rice or pasta pouches. By following this procedure, these food items will avoid being eaten by rodents and insects.

<u>Large Food Containers</u>

It is expensive to store large amounts of food. A five gallon plastic bucket stores five gallons of food – the end. When a team is attempting to store enough food for a one year supply –that is A LOT of buckets! It is <u>very difficult</u> to find a *large* storage container to safely store food for human consumption – especially one that will hold one or even two tons of food.

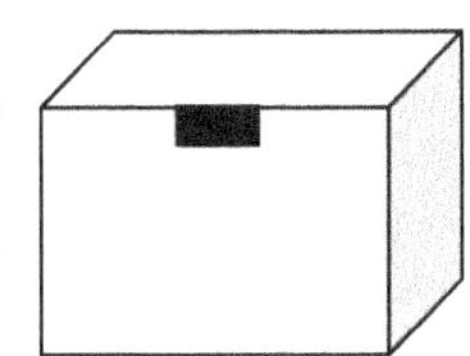

My brother, Stan, suggested I use a large capacity <u>chest freezer</u> in his garage that had stopped working. The freezer was like new – <u>including the seal</u>. I had previously purchased over 1,500 pounds of rice (in 25 pound bags) at a case lot sale and was in a dilemma on how to store this much rice. My prayers were answered – I gleefully watched as Stan and Cody, my nephew, put all the bags of rice in the freezer and shut the lid. The freezer (and the rice) is located in an enclosed garage which keeps out rain, sun, wind and other weather elements and also provides safety and security from those who may be inclined to help themselves to the contents - including rodents, insects and yes - humans.

In many cases, the motor of a large chest freezer gives out before the freezer and seal. It generally costs more to fix the motor than to buy a new freezer. There are many makes and models of chest freezers and range in capacity from smaller six to eight cubic foot models to large capacity twenty to twenty-five cubic foot models. Check with the appliance and repair stores in your area or put an ad in the local newspaper to see if anyone has non-working chest freezers that would suit the storage needs for your team. Remember – you don't care if the motor works but the seal must be in good condition!

When storing food supplies, the freezer MUST be located in an enclosed area such as a basement (preferred), garage or even a shed to avoid water damage from rain and other elements. There should be no cracks or holes in the structure and more importantly, the seal must be intact and able to seal tightly when closed. Before placing food supplies in the freezer, make sure the inside of the freezer and the seal are completely cleaned and sanitized.

EQUIPMENT

All food preparation equipment should be kept *dry*, *clean* and *well maintained* at all times. It should be covered when not in use. If and when electrical power and/or natural gas or propane are not available (especially during a medium to long-term disaster environment), there are many *layers* or *alternatives* of equipment that can be considered for preparing, processing and cooking food, to include the following:

- **Barbeque Grill (Charcoal/Propane)**
- **Electric Hot Plate (used with <u>solar</u> generator power)**
- **Mini-Stove (with fuel tablets)**
- **Candles**
- **Wood-Burning <u>Heating</u> Stove (top)**
- **Wood-Burning <u>Cooking</u> Stove (with oven)**
- **Camping Stove (propane)**
- **PROPANE OVEN**
- **Fireplace**
- **Campfire**
- **Dutch Oven**
- **SOLAR OVEN**

As part of <u>*advanced planning*</u>, make sure *alternatives* and *layers* of equipment used to prepare and cook food are part of your supplies and you have a good supply of cooking utensils including several sizes of heavy-duty pots, frying pans, spatulas and pancake turners. If you include any of this equipment in your inventory to use in an emergency – know how to use it! PLAN IN ADVANCE!

For example:

- **Level 1** disasters (1 hour to 7 days) using the barbeque grill with charcoal briquettes and dutch oven cooking would be possible. Providing there is wood available, a campfire, fireplace, the top of a wood-burning heating stove or a wood-burning cooking stove could be used for meal preparation.

- **Level 2** disasters (7 days to 1 month) the team may run out of charcoal. At that point, depending on whether or not there is propane and wood available, various types of camping stoves, wood-burning heating and/or cooking stoves or campfires could be used. If there is no wood or propane, a solar oven could be used for meal preparation.

- **Level 3** disasters (up to a 1 year) most day-to-day fuel sources would be expended and no longer available. At this point, the use of a solar oven would more than likely be the only means for cooking meals.

ALUMINUM FOIL

A good supply of <u>heavy-duty aluminum foil</u> can protect food cooked directly on hot coals or flames in a fire pit, fireplace or campfire. It is also used to enhance the light of a candle flame when mirrors are absent to achieve brighter lighting. Several sheets of heavy-duty foil can be used to make an improvised outdoor fire pit for heating and cooking, line homemade solar ovens or used in layers as an insulating mat on an improvised lid used as a cooking pot. Aluminum foil can be formed into energy efficient skirts to put around burners and cook pots to maximize heat and conserve fuel and to wrap and protect food for later use.

MANUAL WHEAT GRINDER/OATS ROLLER/MEAT GRINDER

As part of the overall emergency preparation planning, if storing whole grains, include a good heavy-duty <u>manual</u> wheat grinder and oats roller. For grinding meal, invest in a manual meat grinder. An electric machine will serve no purpose during a serious and long-term disaster.

CANNING AND BOTTLING SUPPLIES

Include a large assortment of canning supplies such as a canner, pressure cooker with gauge, strainers, grinders, jar lifter, bottles, lids and rings. <u>Store a large quantity of rings and jars</u> - these items will also be used for bartering. A manual juicer is another piece of equipment that can be included in emergency pantries. Check out garage sales!

ELECTRIC HOT PLATE

Go ahead – ask me. Why would I suggest you get an ELECTRIC hot plate, when I have been telling you to purchase supplies and items that do <u>not</u> require electricity! Here's why. <u>IF you have a solar-powered generator</u> – the generator would provide enough power to operate a single burner hot plate used for cooking meals.

SOLAR OVEN

A solar oven is an <u>absolute</u> necessity for emergency planning because it can cook food without the use of any type of fuel (wood, gas, propane) or electrical power. The only requirement for cooking with a solar oven is sunlight.

> **During a long-term disaster – when all other cooking methods are exhausted due to lack of fuel – the solar oven may be your one and only source for cooking food.**

A solar oven <u>will not work on cloudy days</u> but it will cook food during cold weather providing the sun is shining. The temperature inside a solar oven will reach 200 to 400 degrees Fahrenheit, depending on the sun angle, food content and length of time exposed to the sun. Water pasteurization (when water borne bacteria are killed) and food begins cooking at around 180 degrees. The food is cooked slowly, will not burn and will be tender and flavorful. No water is added to fruits, vegetables or meats, and more vitamins and minerals are retained.

In a solar oven, food cooks faster when several small pots are used. In solar ovens, the food must be cooked in <u>dark colored pots</u> – black, green, brown or blue. Generally, 1 ½ quarts of rice will cook in 1 ½ to 2 hours and a chicken will usually bake in 2 to 2 ½ hours. There are many solar ovens on the market – access the Internet to find a variety of solar ovens to meet the needs and budget of the team.

WOOD BURNING COOKING STOVE

Consider a wood burning <u>cooking</u> stove that provides the means to prepare food on a stove using wood (or coal) and ranges in price from around $800.00 to $2,000.00.

PROPANE OVEN

I purchased a small propane oven at a local camping outlet for $130.00. The oven works very similar to a regular oven. It is large enough to bake a loaf of bread, or cook a casserole and even a roast. It is powered by propane. I also purchased a 300 gallon propane tank with a spigot on the top that allows me to siphon propane out of the large tank and into a smaller propane tank which can then be attached to the propane oven. This propane oven will allow me to cook bakery products as well as main dishes very easily.

DUTCH OVENS

A dutch oven collection is a very smart addition to emergency pantries. These dutch ovens can cook practically anything that is cooked on a hotplate or in the oven. Include a dutch oven cookbook with recipes that can be made during emergency situations. Dutch ovens use either charcoal briquettes or a campfire as the fuel source for heat. Another piece of equipment that could be considered is a device that holds the dutch oven over the campfire.

ROLLED OAT MUFFINS

1 ½ cups rolled oats
¼ cup condensed milk, sweetened
¾ cup hot water
2 tablespoons light corn syrup
2 eggs, separated
½ teaspoon salt
¾ cup white flour
4 teaspoons baking powder
2 tablespoons oil

Pour hot water and condensed milk over rolled oats and let stand ½ hour. Add corn syrup, oil and beaten egg *yolks*. Sift flour, baking powder and salt. Add to rolled oats mixture. Beat only until smooth. Fold in stiffly beaten egg *whites*. Fill well-greased muffin tins b full. Bake at 425 degrees for 20 minutes. Makes 10 muffins.

BRAN MUFFINS

¾ cup honey
½ cup butter
2 eggs
2 ½ cups whole wheat flour
½ teaspoon salt
2 ½ teaspoons baking soda
2 cups buttermilk
1 cup boiling water
2 cups bran

In small bowl, pour boiling water over 1 cup bran and set aside. Cream honey, butter and eggs together in medium bowl. In separate bowl, add whole wheat flour, salt and baking soda. Alternately add whole wheat flour mixture and buttermilk to the creamed mixture. Add bran and water mixture. Fold in remaining 1 cup of dry bran. Bake at 400 degrees for 15-20 minutes.

WHEAT MUFFINS

2 cups whole wheat flour
1 cup brown sugar
¼ teaspoon salt
1 teaspoon baking soda
1 cup milk
1 cube butter, melted
1 egg
1 teaspoon vanilla

Mix dry ingredients together in medium bowl. Using separate bowl, combine liquid ingredients. Pour over dry ingredients and stir until moistened. Spoon into greased muffin tins. Bake at 350 degrees for 15 minutes. Makes 12 muffins.

CHAPTER TEN

PRODUCTION

As an integral part of emergency planning, <u>it is important to understand the regions of the country and the world who specifically provide our food and recognize that disasters can compromise the elements bringing commodities to market.</u> For example, most citizens are aware of the impact oil plays on the global economy. If the countries providing oil to the United States experience a serious manmade or natural disaster, the supply of oil imported into our country could be reduced – which creates a domino effect by raising the price of gasoline at the pump, and in turn, raising the prices of any commodity made from oil and the price of most goods and services.

EXPORTS AND IMPORTS

As an integral part of emergency preparation, it is important to recognize the importance of exports and imports from countries around the world. An *export* is defined as natural or manmade resources and/or goods grown or manufactured in the *origin* country and then sold and distributed to a *destination* country. For example, the country of Afghanistan (origin country) has an <u>abundance</u> of fruit, nuts, carpets, wool, cotton, hides, pelts and gems. The <u>surplus</u> of these goods and resources in Afghanistan are sold and exported (distributed) to other destination countries. When the destination countries receive the goods and resources from Afghanistan, they are referred to as *imports* to the destination countries.

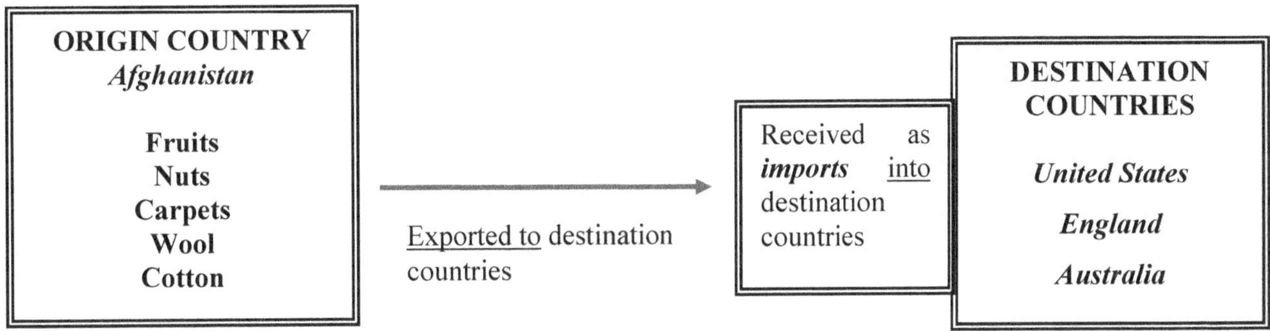

<u>**Imports into the United States**</u>

The exports <u>from other countries coming *into* the United States as *imports*</u> include a variety of natural resources, agriculture and manufactured goods. The top fifteen countries that <u>export goods *into* the United States</u> are as follows:

1	China	4	Japan	7	United Kingdom	10	Taiwan	13	India
2	Canada	5	Germany	8	Saudi Arabia	11	France	14	Russia
3	Mexico	6	South Korea	9	Venezuela	12	Ireland	15	Italy

Based on the above table, it becomes obvious that a serious disaster affecting **China**, **Canada**, **Mexico**, **Japan** and the other listed countries could have a *direct* impact on the amount and timeliness of products coming into the United States. Depending on the products, our country could experience a decrease in critical goods and products used in our own manufacturing processes (electronics), natural resources used for energy consumption (oil) or as an agricultural product consumed by the citizens (fruits and vegetables).

The United States produces a tremendous amount of fruits every year – especially with the help of California, Florida and Texas, and yet we <u>import</u> a substantial amount of fruits from other countries. A serious natural or manmade disaster in any of these countries could again have a direct impact on the supply of fruits coming into our country.

Countries importing fruit <u>into</u> the United States include the following:

1	Mexico	4	Thailand	7	New Zealand	10	Greece	13	Iran
2	Taiwan	5	China	8	Argentina	11	Canada	14	Pakistan
3	Israel	6	Chile	9	Turkey	12	Samoa	15	Hong Kong

A SERIOUS DISASTER IN ONE REGION OF THE WORLD CAN HAVE DIRECT AND INDIRECT CONSEQUENCES ON COUNTRIES IN OTHER PARTS OF THE WORLD DEPENDING ON THE EXPORT/IMPORT RELATIONSHIPS BETWEEN COUNTRIES IN THE GLOBAL ECONOMY.

Exports from the United States

The exports *from* the United States going *into* other countries as imports include a variety of natural resources, agriculture and manufactured goods. The top fifteen countries importing goods coming *from* the United States are as follows:

1	Canada	**4**	Japan	**7**	South Korea	**10**	Hong Kong	**13**	France
2	Mexico	**5**	United Kingdom	**8**	Brazil	**11**	Singapore	**14**	Australia
3	China	**6**	Germany	**9**	Netherlands	**12**	Belgium	**15**	Taiwan

Products exported from nations around the world to other countries provide crucial monies for the origin country used to support infrastructure, social programs, employment and other services needed by the citizens. During a serious disaster in the origin country, the goods exported to other countries could easily be destroyed or disrupted which would limit the monies coming into the country.

Conversely, the countries that would normally receive these goods would be impacted since the goods would cease to be distributed – at least in the short term. The destination countries that rely exclusively on crucial exports from other countries for their citizens i.e. automotive and computer parts, metals, fuel, food and clothing, could face serious consequences if other sources could not be located. An example was during the severe flooding in Thailand in 2011 when the United States was unable to receive shipments of one-source computer parts and several manufacturing plants in this country were forced to lay off workers and close production lines.

COUNTRIES RELYING ON EXPORTS TO "MAKE A LIVING" FOR THE CITIZENS OR COUNTRIES RELYING ON SPECIFIC IMPORTS WITH NO SECOND SOURCE OPTION ARE THE MOST LIKELY TO BE IMPACTED DURING A DISASTER OR CRISIS SITUATION.

STATE EXPORTS TO OTHER COUNTRIES

In the United States, each state produces various manmade goods such as aircraft, electronics, automobiles and automotive parts, equipment, tools, parts and supplies, plastics, paper, cosmetics and machinery. Most states also harvest and process various natural resources within their state boundaries such as oil, wood, precious gems, minerals and metals, agriculture products (wheat, corn and rice) and rubber.

In many cases, a large portion of both manmade and natural products are utilized within the respective state or distributed and sold to other states throughout the country. The budget of all state governments are dependent on monies received from selling their products to other states in the country and each state must also consider as part of their budget, the amount of funds expended to purchase products from other states.

In the event of a disaster affecting a specific industry here in the United States, the states exporting goods from that industry and the countries receiving the imported goods could be seriously affected from an economic and financial standpoint as well as distressing the standard of living of the states and the countries connected to the disaster. The disaster could easily have a direct and indirect affect on the population of many regions around the world. The following table shows the top exporting commodity for each state in the United States:

TOP EXPORTING COMMODITY										
STATE	Agriculture	Electronics	Automotive	Energy	Aircraft	Minerals Metals	Machinery	Medical	Equipment	Chemicals
Alabama			X							
Alaska						X				
Arizona		X								

STATE	Agriculture	Electronics	Automotive	Energy	Aircraft	Minerals Metals	Machinery	Medical	Equipment	Chemicals
Arkansas	X									
California		X								
Colorado		X								
Connecticut					X					
Delaware								X		
Florida						X				
Georgia					X					
Hawaii					X					
Idaho		X								
Illinois							X			
Indiana								X		
Iowa	X									
Kansas	X									
Kentucky					X					
Louisiana	X									
Maine		X								
Maryland			X							
Massachusetts								X		
Michigan			X							
Minnesota								X		
Mississippi				X						
Missouri			X							
Montana				X						
Nebraska	X									
Nevada						X				
New Hampshire		X								
New Jersey						X				
New Mexico				X						
New York						X				
North Carolina	X									
North Dakota	X									
Ohio			X							
Oklahoma									X	
Oregon		X								
Pennsylvania								X		
Rhode Island						X				
South Carolina			X							
South Dakota	X									
Tennessee								X		
Texas				X						
Utah						X				
Vermont		X								
Virginia		X								

<table>
<tr><td colspan="11" align="center">TOP EXPORTING COMMODITY</td></tr>
<tr><td>STATE</td><td>Agriculture</td><td>Electronics</td><td>Automotive</td><td>Energy</td><td>Aircraft</td><td>Minerals Metals</td><td>Machinery</td><td>Medical</td><td>Equipment</td><td>Chemicals</td></tr>
<tr><td>Washington</td><td></td><td></td><td></td><td></td><td>X</td><td></td><td></td><td></td><td></td><td></td></tr>
<tr><td>West Virginia</td><td></td><td></td><td></td><td>X</td><td></td><td></td><td></td><td></td><td></td><td></td></tr>
<tr><td>Wisconsin</td><td></td><td></td><td></td><td></td><td></td><td></td><td></td><td></td><td>X</td><td></td></tr>
<tr><td>Wyoming</td><td></td><td></td><td></td><td></td><td></td><td></td><td></td><td></td><td></td><td>X</td></tr>
<tr><td>TOTAL</td><td>8</td><td>9</td><td>6</td><td>5</td><td>5</td><td>7</td><td>1</td><td>6</td><td>2</td><td>1</td></tr>
</table>

OUR FOOD SUPPLY - WHERE IT COMES FROM

Let's take a look at where our <u>food</u> supply is produced here in the United States. Team members should study the various states producing specific food sources and pay special attention to natural and manmade disasters prevalent in the region that could destroy and severely damage the meat, dairy, fruit, vegetable and nut production.

MEAT PRODUCTS

<u>Beef and Dairy Cattle</u>

The United States has the largest <u>beef</u> cattle (fed) industry in the world and is the world's largest producer of grain-fed beef for domestic and export use. Because the cattle/beef industry is a major user of feed grains, beef production is vulnerable to both manmade and natural disasters that in turn affect grain supplies and prices. With its abundant grasslands and large grain supply, the United States has developed a beef industry that is largely separate from the dairy sector.

The industry is roughly divided into two production sectors: cow-calf operations and cattle feeding operations. According to the National Cattlemen's Beef Association, fifty percent of the total value of cattle sales came from five states: **Texas, Kansas, Nebraska, Iowa** and **Colorado**. Natural disasters in these states such as drought, wildfires, flooding or disease could have a serious impact on the cattle industry - and on the citizens at the supermarket.

According to the United States Department of Agriculture, in the United States, the top five <u>dairy</u> states by *total milk production* are **California, Wisconsin, Idaho, New York** and **Pennsylvania**. Dairy farming is also important in **Florida, Minnesota, Ohio** and **Vermont**. Pennsylvania has the heaviest dependence on dairy farming - its number one industry.

HOGS

China is the largest pork producer in the world. Although the European Union produces the second largest amount of hogs, the United States is the world's second-largest producer of pork. By the end of 2010, the USDA estimated 64.3 million hogs were in the United States of which 58.5 million were market hogs. In the United States, the top five hog producing states are **Iowa, North Carolina, Minnesota, Illinois** and **Indiana**. Other states with substantial hog production include **Nebraska, Missouri, Oklahoma, Kansas, Ohio, Texas, South Dakota, Pennsylvania, Colorado** and **Utah**.

POULTRY

Poultry refers to domesticated fowl raised for meat or eggs and includes chickens, turkeys, ducks, geese, emus, ostriches and game birds. According to the United States Department of Agriculture, the United States is the world's largest poultry producer and the second-largest egg producer and exporter of poultry meat. The top ten broiler-producing states are **Georgia** followed by **Alabama, Arkansas, Mississippi, North Carolina, Texas, Missouri, Virginia, Delaware** and **Kentucky**.

The top egg <u>producing</u> states **Iowa, Ohio, Pennsylvania, Indiana, California, Texas, Minnesota, Michigan, Nebraska** and **Florida**. The top ten egg <u>processing</u> companies are Cal Maine Foods (**Mississippi**), Rose Acre Farms (**Indiana**), DeCoster Egg Farms (**Iowa**), Moark LLC (**California**), Hillandale Farms (**Pennsylvania**) Michael Foods

(**Minnesota**), Rembrandt (**Iowa**), Sparboe Summit Farms (**Minnesota**), Daybreak Foods (**Wisconsin**) and Center Fresh Egg Group (**Iowa**).

TURKEYS

There are an estimated 244 million turkeys were raised in this country. The top turkey producing states are **Minnesota** as the top turkey producer, followed by **North Carolina, Arkansas, Missouri** and **Virginia**.

SHEEP

The top five sheep producing states in the United States are **Texas, California, Colorado, Wisconsin** and **Utah**. Other top states include **Arizona, Minnesota, Ohio, New Mexico, Pennsylvania, Virginia, Wisconsin, Missouri, North Dakota** and **Oklahoma**.

HORSES

The American Horse Council reports the horse industry has a direct impact of $39 billion on the economy in the United States and an overall impact of $102 billion in indirect and induced spending. The top horse producing states are **Texas, California, Florida, Oklahoma** and **Kentucky**.

AGRICULTURAL CROP PRODUCTS

The top agricultural products of the United States reported by the Food and Agriculture Organization of the United Nations (ranked in quantity by metric tons) are as follows:

1	*Corn*	4	Wheat	7	Potatoes	10	Cattle Meat	13	Sorghum	16	Hen Eggs
2	Soybeans	5	Sugar Beets	8	Chicken Meat	11	Rice	14	Oranges	17	Apples
3	Cows Milk	6	Sugar Cane	9	Tomatoes	12	Hog Meat	15	Grapes	18	Lettuce

Alfalfa and hay would be in the top ten if tracked by the Food and Agriculture Organization of the United Nations. The combination of disease and climate has a direct result on agriculture, and severe weather conditions are currently having an impact on countries producing agricultural crop products throughout the world. It is important for teams to know the regions of the country where these commodities are produced and recognize the impact severe disasters in these specific regions could have on the food supply for this country.

The table below shows the state ranking for specific agricultural (grain) commodities produced in the United States:

STATE	RANKING								
	Corn	Wheat	Sorghum	Oats	Barley	Soybeans	Hay	Rice	Alfalfa
Arizona					5				
Arkansas			4			10	9	1	
California					9			2	1
Colorado		7	7		4				9
Idaho		6			1				4
Illinois	2					2			
Indiana	5					5			
Iowa	1			5		1			10
Kansas	9	1	1				5		
Kentucky							3		
Louisiana			3					3	
Michigan				10					
Minnesota	4	8		2	10	3			5
Mississippi			10					4	
Missouri	10		9			7	1	6	
Montana		3			2				3
Nebraska	3		6			4	7		7

STATE	RANKING								
	Corn	Wheat	Sorghum	Oats	Barley	Soybeans	Hay	Rice	Alfalfa
New York				9					
North Dakota	6	2		4	3	9			6
Ohio	8			7		6			
Oklahoma		9	8				8		
Oregon		10							
Pennsylvania				6					
South Dakota		5	5	3		8	10		2
Tennessee							4		
Texas			2	8			2	5	
Virginia					8		6		
Washington		4			6				
Wisconsin	7			1					8
Wyoming					7				

SOURCE: United States Department of Agriculture

The map below shows the states that are ranked in the <u>Number One</u> position for various agricultural grains in the United States. However, as you can see from the above table, the state of Kansas leads the nation in the production of wheat and sorghum but is also rated fifth in the production of hay and ninth in the production of corn. The state of Minnesota, although not ranked in any top two positions, still commands six positions in the top ten for corn, wheat, oats, barley, soybeans and alfalfa. Likewise, the states of North and South Dakota also claim six positions as the top ten grain production leaders. A major disaster – whether natural or manmade – affecting any of these states would take a heavy toll on grain production in this country.

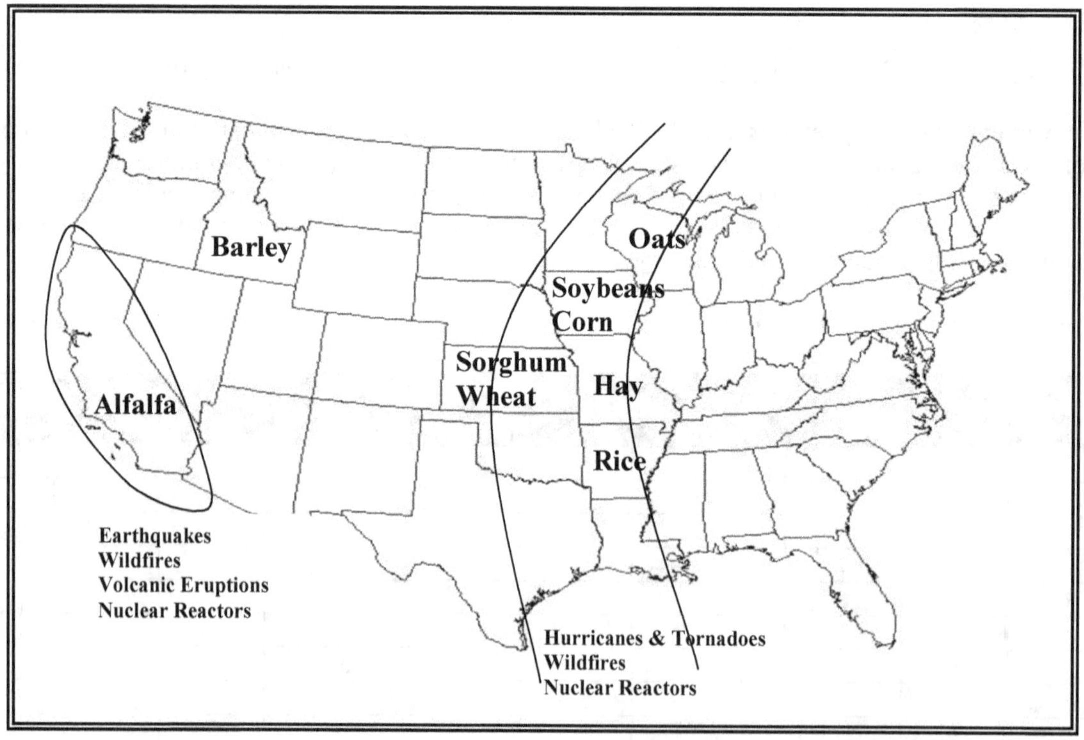

For example, the state of California that leads the nation in alfalfa production is susceptible to earthquakes, tsunamis and volcanic eruptions. The states of Kansas, Iowa, Minnesota, Nebraska, Arkansas, Missouri, North and South Dakota, Oklahoma, Texas and Wisconsin - states that are ranked Number One in specific grains and/or produce an abundance of grains for the country, are considered states located in Tornado Alley, Dixie Alley or Hoosier Alley – all areas prone to tornadoes. A severe and long-term drought in these same areas would seriously impact grain production. Many of these states in this "grain belt" are susceptible to wildfires. There is even the possibility of nuclear meltdowns in many of these states that have nuclear reactors, including California, Texas, Kansas, Arkansas, Nebraska, Iowa, Illinois, Louisiana, Minnesota, Illinois and Wisconsin.

In the event of a nuclear war – many of the states who are leaders in grain production would also be considered as primary targets due to military installations, nuclear weapons and equipment located within their borders. The enemy would basically get two for the price of one – target the military arsenal to avoid retribution AND as an added bonus – impact or cripple our ability to produce food (grains) for our nation.

SUGAR

Did you know the average person in the United States consumes about 25 ounces of sugar per day – or about 270 calories? The top producing states in the United States for sugar <u>beet</u> production are **Minnesota, Idaho, North Dakota** and **Michigan** and the top producing states for sugar <u>cane</u> production are **Florida, Louisiana, Texas** and **Hawaii.**

ALFALFA

Alfalfa is widely grown throughout the world as forage for cattle, is most often harvested as hay, but can also be made into silage. Disasters that affect alfalfa production will also have a direct affect on the cattle and dairy industry and on beef and dairy prices at the market. The United States is the largest alfalfa producer in the world with **California** as the leading producer, followed by **South Dakota, Montana, Idaho** and **Minnesota.** Other states that have substantial alfalfa crops are **Utah, Arizona, Washington, Oregon, Wyoming, Pennsylvania, Nebraska, Ohio** and **Nevada.**

HAY

The top ten states in the United States for hay (all other hay except alfalfa) production are Missouri, Texas, Kentucky, Tennessee and Kansas. Other states that have substantial hay crops are **California, North Dakota, Mississippi, New York, Alabama, North Carolina, Oregon,** and **Washington.**

LEGUMES

A good supply of legumes in the emergency pantries is important. In the absence of meat protein, a combination of legumes and grains provide the protein we need for our bodies. The top states in the United States for dried edible bean (kidney, pinto, navy and black bean) production are **North Dakota, Michigan, Nebraska, Minnesota, Idaho, Washington, California** and **Wyoming.**

FRUITS

According to the United States Department of Agriculture, in the United States:

- The state of **CALIFORNIA** accounts for over one-half (53%) of bearing fruit acreage, followed by **FLORIDA** with one-fourth (26%) and **WASHINGTON** with one-tenth (10%) of bearing fruit acreage. The states of *Michigan, New York, Oregon, Pennsylvania* and *Texas* are also important fruit-producing states and together account for over one-tenth of the fruit acreage in the nation.

- **CALIFORNIA** is the largest producer of grapes, strawberries, peaches, nectarines, kiwifruit, prunes and plums and is a major producer of other non-citrus fruit including apples, pears and sweet cherries. California ranks second in citrus production behind Florida. Florida's primary fruit crop is citrus.

- **WASHINGTON** is the largest producer of pears and sweet cherries and a big producer of apples and grapes.

- Most fruits are grown for both fresh and processing markets. In the United States, the fresh-market sector accounts for more than half the value of fruit production with over three-quarters of that amount generated by non-citrus fruits. The fresh market is the destination for over half the volume of all produced avocados, bananas, nectarines, kiwifruit, strawberries, tangerines, sweet cherries, apples, pears and lemons.

- Processed fruit products include canned, frozen, juice, and dried fruit and wine. Fruits processed include oranges, grapefruit, grapes, apricots, figs, prunes, peaches, tart cherries and most berries, including blueberries and cranberries. Juice is the primary form in which fruit is consumed in the United States. On a fresh-weight basis, fruit juice accounts for nearly half of the total per capita fruit consumed annually with fresh use accounting for over one-third, and canned, dried, and frozen fruit each represent less than one-tenth.

- The top five fruits consumed in the United States are *oranges*, *grapes*, *apples*, *bananas* and *grapefruit*.

VEGETABLES

As we continue our review of food production here in the United States, we now turn to vegetable production. As you review the table below, the state of **CALIFORNIA** leads the nation in vegetable production with close to fifty percent of vegetables produced in the golden state. There really is a legitimate reason why the State of California receives such a high percentage of the water from the Colorado River. Other top ranked vegetable producing states include **Florida, Arizona, Oregon, Georgia, Washington, New York** and **Texas.**

The states of **California, Oregon** and **Washington** are all susceptible to earthquakes, tsunamis and volcanic eruptions. The state of Texas is located in Tornado Alley and is also vulnerable to drought and the states of **Florida** and **Georgia** are located in Dixie Alley – areas prone to tornadoes.

The states of **Texas, Florida** and **Georgia** are also vulnerable to severe hurricanes. The states of **California, Arizona, Texas** and **Florida** are vulnerable to wildfires. Nuclear reactors are located in all top ranked vegetable producing states (except Oregon) in the country. Likewise, a long-term drought, heat wave, pests and disease, freezing temperatures or severe flooding in any of these vegetable producing states would seriously impact vegetable production and the availability and prices of fresh vegetables at the markets across the country.

In the event of a nuclear attack on the nation, strategic military installations in the United States are located in **California, Georgia, New York, Texas** and **Washington.** As with the comparisons involving grain and fruit production, when comparing major vegetable-producing states and the probability of these states becoming strategic nuclear targets – it could easily destroy a large portion of the vegetable production.

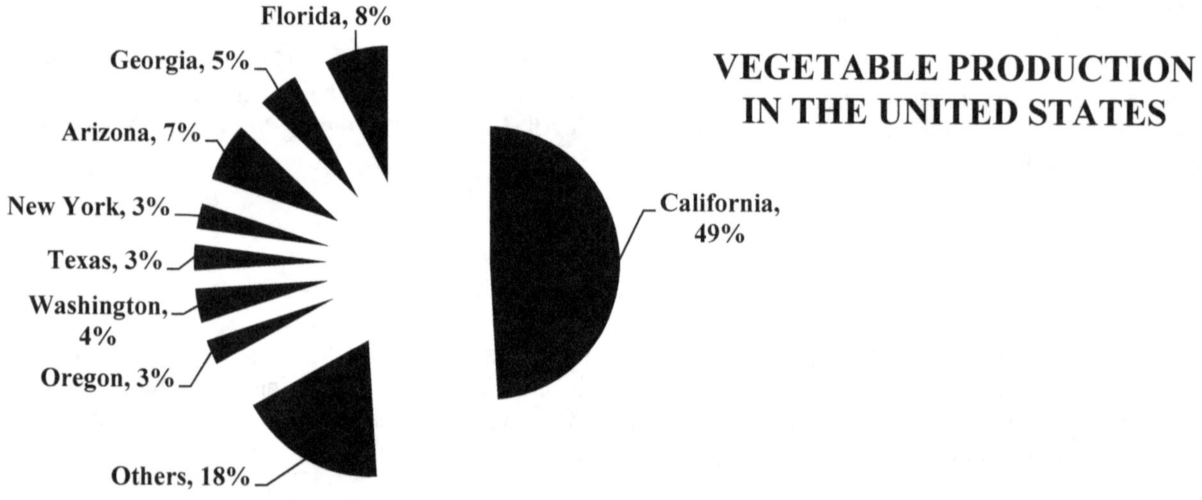

Take a minute to evaluate how serious it would be if California – the leading producer of both fruits and vegetables in this country and other top ranked states were to experience a serious disaster. That's why it is so important to *prepare in advance* and make sure the food pantries are filled with plenty of fruits and vegetables – dehydrated, freeze-dried, canned or bottled – all good choices.

POLLINATORS

A study of the Royal Society/Biological Sciences and the University of California at Berkeley concluded that animal pollinators such as bees, birds and bats affect thirty-five percent of the world's crop production. A total of 115 crops were studied and eighty-seven depend to some degree upon animal pollination, accounting for one-third of global crop production. Of those crops, thirteen are entirely reliant upon animal pollinators, thirty are greatly dependent and twenty-seven are moderately dependent. Crops that did not rely upon animal pollination were mainly staple crops such as wheat, corn and rice.

Honey bees are the most economically valuable pollinators of agricultural crops in the world. Scientists frequently emphasize that bee pollination is involved in about one-third of the diet in the United States and contributes to the production of a wide range of fruits, vegetables, tree nuts, forage and field crops and other specialty crops. The monetary value of honey bees as commercial pollinators in the United States is estimated at about $15-$20 billion annually.

Beginning in 2006, the commercial migratory beekeepers along the East Coast of the United States began reporting sharp declines in honey bee colonies called Colony Collapse Disorder (CCD). Beekeepers in most states were affected and the number of managed honey bee colonies dropped 32% during the winter of 2006/2007, 36% in 2007/2008, 28% in 2008/2009, 34% in 2009/2010 and 30% during the 2010-2011 winter season. The losses in honey bee colonies are not uncommon, but the current losses are occurring mostly because bees are failing to return to the hive which is uncharacteristic of bee behavior.

> **You can thank a pollinator for one out of every three bites of food you eat!**

Researchers are focusing on three major possibilities including pesticides and chemicals that are having negative affects on honey bees, parasites or pathogens that may be attacking honey bees and global climate and temperature changes. There is a combination of stresses that may compromise the immune system of bees and disrupt their social system. These include high levels of mite infestation, poor nutrition due to overcrowding, pollination of crops with low nutritional value, pollen or nectar scarcity, exposure to limited or contaminated water supplies and migratory stress. There are many beekeepers that claim over a seventy percent loss every year in their bee population.

According to the United States Department of Agriculture, it is estimated that one-third of the estimated value of commercial honey bee pollination is in alfalfa production, with another 10% of the value for apples, followed by 6%-7% of the value each for almonds, citrus, cotton and soybeans. Overall, pollinator-dependent crops are reported to make up an estimated 23% of total agricultural production in the United States.

A number of agricultural crops are almost totally dependent on honey bee pollination including almonds, apples, avocados, blueberries, cranberries, cherries, kiwi fruit, macadamia nuts, asparagus, broccoli, carrots, cauliflower, celery, cucumbers, onions, legume seeds, pumpkins, squash, and sunflowers. To a lesser degree, other specialty crops rely on honey bee pollination including apricots, oranges, lemons, limes, grapefruit, tangerines, peaches, pears, nectarines, plums, grapes, strawberries, olives, cantaloupe, watermelon, honeydew, peanuts, cotton, soybeans, and sugar beets.

CROP	DEPENDENCE ON INSECT POLLINATION	HONEY BEES PROPORTION	VALUE OF HONEY BEES (Millions)	MAJOR PRODUCING STATES
Alfalfa, Hay & Seed	100%	60%	4,654.2	CA, SD, ID, WI
Apples	100%	90%	1,352.3	WA, NY, MI, PA
Almonds	100%	100%	959.2	CA
Citrus	20-80%	10-90%	834.1	CA, FL, AZ, TX
Cotton	20%	80%	857.7	TX, AR, GA, MS
Soybeans	10%	50%	824.5	IA, IL, MN, IN
Onions	100%	90%	661.7	TX, GA, CA, AZ
Broccoli	100%	90%	435.4	CA
Carrots	100%	90%	420.7	CA, TX
Sunflower	100%	90%	409.9	ND, SD
Cantaloupe	80%	90%	350.9	CA, WI, MN, WA
Other Fruits & Nuts	10-90%	10-90%	1,633.4	
Other Vegetables/Melons	70-100%	10-90%	1,099.2	
Other Field Crops	10-100%	20-90%	70.4	
TOTAL			14,564	

Compiled by CRS using values reported in R.A. Morse and N.W. Calderone *"The Value of Honey Bees as Pollinators of US Crops"*

In the United States, most pollination operations are provided by commercial migratory beekeepers that travel from state to state and provide pollination services to crop producers. According to the Agricultural Statistics Board, in 2010, there were about 28,000 operations with 2.68 million bee colonies in the United States. The states of **North Dakota** and **South Dakota** account for twenty-seven percent of all bee colonies with **California** claiming fourteen percent and **Florida** accounting for seven percent of all bee colonies.

The states of **Montana**, **Minnesota**, **Idaho**, and **Texas** account for about five percent each of all colonies nationwide. Other states with a large number of bee colonies include **Michigan**, **Oregon**, **Georgia**, **Nebraska**, **New York**, **Washington**, **Wisconsin**, and **Wyoming**, with about two percent each. Although these operations also produce honey for commercial sale, it is their value as crop pollinators that provide the greatest economic impact in the production of food and feed crops in the country.

Honey Producing States

RANK	STATE	HONEY PRODUCING COLONIES (Thousands)	PRODUCTION (1,000 Pounds)	VALUE OF PRODUCTION (1,000 Dollars)
1	**North Dakota**	**510**	**46,410**	**70,079**
2	California	410	27,470	42,853
3	South Dakota	265	15,635	24,078
4	Florida	200	13,800	21,666
5	Montana	157	11,618	18,008
6	Minnesota	126	8316	12,807
7	Texas	100	7,200	11,016
8	Idaho	98	2,646	3,969

SOURCE: Agricultural Statistics Board, NASS, USDA

As the bee population continues to become more susceptible to natural and manmade elements, the ability of these pollinators to "bee" able to pollinate the crops we need to sustain our citizens could "bee" in serious jeopardy. It would appear that if we lose our bee population - we would also loose many of the fruits, vegetables and some grains as well. So - we should now have an understanding of how food production and natural or manmade disasters are related to our ability to produce and obtain vital food sources in the country.

BASIC BREAD

5 ½ cups all-purpose white flour
2 tablespoons granulated white sugar
1 tablespoon salt
2 packages Fleischmann's Rapid Rise Yeast
2 ¼ cups water
1 ¼ cups butter *or* margarine

Combine 2 cups flour, sugar, salt and yeast in large bowl. Heat water and butter until very warm (120-130 F). Add to dry ingredients, stirring well. Gradually stir in enough remaining flour to make soft dough. Knead until smooth and elastic, about 8-10 minutes. Cover dough and let rest for 10 minutes on a lightly floured surface. Divide dough in half. Roll each half into a 12x8 inch rectangle. Beginning at short ends, roll up tightly like a jelly roll. Pinch seams and ends to seal. Place loaves, seams down, in greased 9x5 inch loaf pans. Cover and let rise in a warm, draft-free place until doubled in size, about one hour. Bake at 375 degrees for 30-35 minutes or until done. Remove from pans and cool on wire rack. Makes 2 loaves.

CHAPTER ELEVEN

COMMUNICATION

Although our country has an adequate communication system, unusual conditions can create a strain on communication resources so it is crucial to recognize the part communication will play in the survival of the team. It will be necessary to receive accurate and consistent status on world, national, state and local issues as well as the status of individual team members.

Depending on the communication source, information could be sensationalism, partial truths or outright lies perpetrated by networks to gain higher ratings or by reporters desperate for the first story on the disaster. Another problem is how to "consider the source" of family members, friends, neighbors or other citizens who provide information. For example, during peaceful times, think of individuals you know to be unreliable in providing accurate, realistic or truthful information. It could be they quite simply do not know how to tell the truth or are so out of touch with reality, they don't know the truth. Others may simply exaggerate the real facts in an attempt to appear important or knowledgeable.

Some persons may be able to provide accurate information when calm, but during hectic or stressful times, they become confused, disoriented or bewildered in their facts. We must be able to determine whether any information people provide during an emergency can be trusted and followed so we can make critical decisions based on their information.

EMERGENCY PREPARATION PRINCIPLES

There are <u>five</u> principles that can be incorporated into your overall emergency plan to prepare for and in some cases eliminate communication issues that could become prevalent during an emergency situation. For example:

- **<u>During many serious disasters, and if you are one who is located in the area of the disaster, the rest of the world will likely know the details of the disaster before you do – those unfortunate enough to be in the cross-fire generally loose communication sources</u>**.

- Be wary about anyone providing information - take ALL people's information, instructions and advice with "a grain of salt" – use your instincts and common-sense to determine the accuracy or truthfulness of statements.

- Whenever possible, use communication equipment that does **<u>not</u>** require electricity or batteries.

- When creating your communications emergency plan, use preparation methods that include **alternatives** or **layers** of sources and items so that if one fails or is not available or realistic to use, another item or source may be used instead.

- Do not count on the Internet or cell phones for medium to long-term disasters.

NEIGHBORHOOD

It becomes obvious to individuals serious about *preparing in advance* for an emergency that two heads are better than one – thus, the importance of a team. As your team becomes more disciplined and prepared for a disaster, the team is able to accomplish much more than a single person. In addition to the team, the group can be expanded to include the neighborhood. Any neighborhood that can be cultivated to prepare together for emergencies will be a well-developed and muscular force during a disaster - especially when combining forces to protect persons living in the neighborhood, the homes and emergency supplies. It could likely be the neighborhood force that would do what governmental agencies and private companies would be unable to do.

It is important for all persons living in a neighborhood to become acquainted with their neighbors and to know and understand their basic patterns and habits of movement. Everyone should pay attention to unusual situations or circumstances occurring around the homes. It is just as important to pay attention and investigate individuals living in your neighborhood who could pose problems during a disaster. It was smart for all neighbors to keep their doors locked at all times. <u>If a solid foundation among neighbors has not been reached *prior* to a disaster, and once the situation</u>

becomes unmanageable, it will be difficult to restore any useful communication or cooperation with others. In essence, human nature under pressure is perhaps the biggest ambiguity in a crisis.

A good first step in getting to know your neighbors is to begin a Neighborhood Watch Program. It will give everyone the opportunity to meet all of the neighbors (including the kids). Once a good foundation has been established, an overall emergency plan could be created among neighbors to identify common and general guidelines to follow during a disaster. When discussing information with neighbors, let caution, common sense and intuition be your guarding light as you interact with your neighbors. Although it is important to communicate basic information, in this current day and age, loose lips can sink ships. Travel these waters very carefully.

FAMILY

The knowledge of knowing where your team members are located *before*, *during* and *after* a disaster will become so paramount that it may even impede more important considerations such as shelter, heat, light, water and food. Our human nature will demand information to guarantee all team members and other family members and friends are safe and secure. We will be driven to get this information – sometimes at all cost. If we have the information, it will be easier for us to deal with circumstances of disaster and we would likely be able to focus on the tasks at hand. There are several methods that can be considered to assist in locating and communicating with team members, neighbors, friends, relatives and other family members.

W^5 PLAN

Although we cannot possibly know the whereabouts of our family members and other loved ones all the time, we can initiate an effortless plan to at least provide a starting point in locating and hopefully communicating with the team members and other loved ones after a disaster. The W^5 Plan is simple – you provide the following information to another team member when leaving the area for at least one day:

- **Where** you will be going
- **When** you will return
- **What** transportation mode you will be using
- **Who** is in your party
- **Why** you are taking the trip

BLOCK CAPTAIN

Every neighborhood should appoint a block captain who agrees to serve as an "overseer" in the event an emergency occurs in the neighborhood. A neighborhood could be considered as a residential block or even an apartment complex. Regardless of how the area is divided, all neighbors, including the block captain should know the area under the "emergency control" of the block captain. This person should hopefully be someone who is home (or close by) during both day and night hours, someone who is responsible and mature enough to carry out the assigned duties and someone who is able to quickly canvas the entire neighborhood area by walking or driving from house to house. In the event of an emergency in the neighborhood, the block captain would be responsible for checking each house to make sure everyone is safe and if necessary, aid those individuals needing assistance.

HOME SIGNAL

During a crisis situation, one of the easiest and most effective methods to alert first responders and neighbors about the status of team members is to use a pre-determined signal device in the home. Using a signal as a means to communicate is a common-sense system that can save precious time and resources. For example, every neighborhood could devise a plan where a large (so it can be clearly seen from the street) white "flag" (or large white poster board) is hung from the front window or door of the home with a large black shape signifying a condition inside of the residence. For example, purchase white poster boards and cut in half. On one side, glue a large black circle that signifies **SAFE** and on the other side, glue a large black rectangle that signifies **HELP**. Make sure the words "**SAFE**" and "**HELP**" are also on the poster board so residents know which shape is correct for the situation. Then, laminate the entire poster board. Pass out a completed poster board flag to each neighbor in the area and explain the procedure to be used in the neighborhood to display the flags. As emergency response personnel, block captains or neighbors scan through the neighborhood, the situation of each home and team becomes immediately evident.

- White rectangle with large black circle - team is **SAFE**
- White rectangle with large black rectangle – team needs **HELP**

NO COLORED FLAGS! Some responders or team members may be colorblind and will not differentiate between the colors – or their meaning. Using a <u>shape</u> in the flag eliminates this problem.

Whether it is your state, county, city, church, charitable organization or neighborhood who is overseeing the emergency preparation plan in your area, and as part of *planning in advance*, the people in each vicinity should devise a neighborhood signaling system, selected a block captain, make sure each team has been trained and has the specific flags or signaling device ready to use during an emergency.

EMERGENCY ALERT SYSTEM

During a serious disaster (and sometimes even during a Level 1 emergency), instructions from various governmental agencies will be provided to citizens through the Emergency Alert System (EAS). Almost all radio and television broadcast stations, including cable companies, are required to carry EAS messages. These stations and especially those with emergency power generators and equipment, provide extensive information about local disaster conditions, warnings, instructions and guidelines on how to locate missing family members. Providing the Emergency Alert System is working and whether power is available at their end and at your end, it is designed so local city or county dispatchers can contact the stations with specific crisis-related information which is then broadcast to the general population in the area, i.e. open and closed transportation routes, location of public shelters, power outages and weather conditions. These broadcasts are where you would receive the most reliable information and instructions. During a disaster, tune to the local television/radio stations for information. **In our area, radio station KVNU (610) is the channel for emergency information.**

COMMUNITY WARNING SYSTEMS

Depending on the circumstances, there may be other community warning systems available in your area. For example, the use of bullhorns and sirens may be utilized by police or fire departments to notify citizens of impending danger. Another method of communication used by government agencies is door-to-door notification by fire, police, National Guard or trained CERT volunteers. If you are warned by local authorities to take certain actions, you should explicitly and immediately follow their instructions.

UNITED STATES POSTAL SERVICE

The United States Postal Service has one enormous advantage over the other carriers. During a widespread disaster in the country, the federal government grants right-of-way to the post office at the expense of all other carriers. The theory is simple. The United States Postal Service could be instrumental in delivering hard-copy correspondence and packages during a crisis. The old saying "the mail always gets through" may become true during a widespread disaster.

ESTABLISHING A PRIORITY LIST

Take time *before* an emergency to write an <u>emergency priority list</u>, including important items to be hand-carried by you, items to be moved by car or truck if one is available, and things to do if time permits, such as locking doors and windows, turning off utilities, etc.

Place the list in a secure location. Include on your list the following information:

- Important telephone numbers (police, fire, paramedics, and medical centers)
- Telephone numbers of electric, gas/propane, sewer and water companies
- Name and telephone numbers of neighbors
- Name and telephone number of landlord or property manager
- Radio and television broadcast stations to access for emergency broadcast information

OUT OF STATE CONTACT

One of the most important keys to receiving and sending information to family members who may be in different places when a disaster occurs is through an out-of-state contact. This person is a trusted friend or relative designated to handle messages should you not be able to call or locate local family members. While most local private phone lines may be out of order for hours after a disaster, <u>pay phones are usually working much sooner</u>. The out-of-state contact receives and relays messages from family members.

<u>Tips for Communication</u>

- Establish *in advance* who will be your out-of-state contact and make sure everyone knows who it is – including the out-of-state contact!

- Everyone should carry with them a <u>laminated</u> card with the out-of-state contact's name, address, and day and evening phone numbers. Include the following information: (1) emergency meeting place with the address (outside the home); and (2) alternate meeting place and address (outside the neighborhood).

- Let teachers know who the out-of-state contact is for your team. That way, if children are at school and you cannot pick them up, school representatives will know who to contact concerning your children.

- Each family member should know where the public phone booths are located in the area, and carry a phone card or enough change for several phone calls.

HAM RADIO OPERATORS

It will be helpful to find out *in advance* if you have a ham radio operator in your area. They are very helpful and can deliver messages from both private and community sources *before*, *during* and *after* a disaster. If a pay telephone isn't readily available, and your out-of-state contact is several states away, you can communicate via this type of relay system.

Your local ham operator can contact another ham operator that will contact another ham operator, and so on, until they find one within your out-of-state contact's area. The ham operator closest to your contact could then hopefully phone the contact and deliver any messages. Consider becoming a ham operator.

FAMILY STATUS REPORT LETTER

A family status report is a worthwhile consideration for each team. The concept is simple – <u>each teenager and/or adult team member</u> carries a one-page status report form that can quickly be filled out and mailed to the out of state contact or other contacts located outside the vicinity of the primary residence.

The information on the form can advise family members about the status of team members. The form should be very quick and easy to fill out and yet still provide the recipient with critical information about the status of the team members.

FAMILY STATUS REPORT FORM

There has been a disaster in our area as follows:

As the designated out of state contact for our team, this letter will serve to advise you that our condition is as follows:

WHO	STATUS	INJURIES	LOCATION

We have not been able to locate the following team members:

ADDITIONAL COMMENTS:

Please advise other team members who contact you of the status of other team members as this information becomes known to you and provide additional instructions as necessary.

_______________   _______________
SIGNATURE   DATE

Ensure team members have continual and immediate access to a blank copy of the form in the (1) primary residence (2) place of refuge (3) auto (4) work and (5) evacuation kits. If possible, female team members should carry a form in their purse and those individuals who use wallets or briefcases should also consider carrying a blank form.

Place the form in an envelope and address the envelope to your intended recipient(s). Make sure your return address is included on the envelope. Place a "forever" stamp on the envelope. Try to have a sharpened pencil or pen available as well. After the disaster, fill out the form with pertinent information on team members, attempt to find a United States

Postal Service **blue mailbox** and drop the letter in the slot. If there is any chance at all for your letter to be delivered –the United States Post Office would be a good bet.

HIDDEN MESSAGE BOX

Another excellent method to communicate with team members is to create a hidden message box. The message box will serve as a depository for team members to leave and receive messages from one another.

There are several "do" and "do not" guidelines when preparing the box:

DO -

- Container **MUST BE** water proof, dirt proof, insect proof and rust proof
- Container that is six inches long, six inches wide and six inches deep would be a perfect size
- Container should be made out of heavy duty plastic, galvanized metal or material that keep contents dry
- Container should have air-tight lid but should be easy for team members to open and close – **NO LOCKS**
- Container should contain several small notebooks and at least 5-10 <u>sharpened</u> pencils – **NO PENS**
- Container should be <u>hidden</u> and **BURIED** in the ground somewhere on or near the primary residence
- A heavy duty baggie or trash bag could also be wrapped around it for added protection from the elements
- Located where it will <u>not</u> be disturbed, discovered or moved by anyone

DO NOT -

- Put container in a shed, barn or other structure – these buildings could collapse or be swept away
- Put container near standing water and/or water drainage areas
- Put container <u>directly</u> next to primary residence, power lines, sewer lines, gas lines or propane tanks
- Bury it under a tree –tree could be easily uprooted and the box could be difficult if not impossible to locate
- Bury it so deep in the ground it is hard for team members to reach it

Special attention and thought should be taken in picking the location for the hidden message box. Some recommended locations could be adjacent to a fence, across the street in a field, next to a large boulder or rock, or even out in the middle of the backyard lawn. The location must be easy to remember and easy to access.

In general, the location of this message box should be known only to **TEAM MEMBERS**. Bringing outsiders into the secret, regardless of good intentions, tends to confuse and complicate the flow of communication. Also, only share the secret with team members who are mature enough to maintain the secret of the location, understand its significance and purpose and be able to utilize the box if needed during and after a disaster. If a disaster occurs and some of the team members at the primary residence are forced to flee to an alternate site or refuge, any remaining team members who later arrive at the primary residence can check the message box for any messages.

Likewise, any member can check and/or leave messages so other team members will be informed of their status, location and other important information. All team members using the box should be instructed and trained to tightly close and rebury the box to avoid contamination after accessing the message box and either receiving or leaving messages. Team members should be watchful when accessing the box to make certain outsiders are not observing their action.

ELECTRO MAGNETIC PULSE

Planning in advance must also take into account the possibility of a worst-case-scenario when considering communication efforts during a disaster. Over the past century, our world has experienced a phenomenon called an Electro-Magnetic Pulse (EMP). An Electro-Magnetic Pulse (EMP) is a high-intensity burst of electromagnetic energy caused by the rapid acceleration of charged particles. Nuclear weapons, non-nuclear weapons (radio-frequency weapons), or geomagnetic storms (often called solar storms) can power an EMP, and the resultant changing magnetic field in the atmosphere can disrupt electrical systems. An EMP has three main components:

1. An electromagnetic shock disrupts electronics, such as **communication** systems

2. An effect similar to lightning rapidly follows and compounds the first component

3. The pulse flows through electrical transmission lines, overloading and damaging transmission distribution centers, fuses, and power lines

While the ability of an electromagnetic pulse (EMP) to inflict catastrophic damage on the infrastructure in the United States has been a known fact for decades, insufficient efforts have been taken to mitigate the threat. A survey of congressional, federal, state, local, and international measures to deal with the threat reveals more complacency than action. With regards to the *nature and magnitude* of an EMP attack, one commission concluded that an EMP attack on the United States would be devastating:

> *Should significant parts of the electrical power infrastructure be lost for any substantial period of time, the Commission believes that the consequences are likely to be catastrophic, and many people will ultimately die for lack of the basic elements necessary to sustain life in <u>dense urban and suburban communities</u>. In fact, the Commission is deeply concerned that such impacts are likely in the event of an EMP attack unless practical steps are taken to provide protection for critical elements of the electric system and for rapid restoration of electric power, particularly to essential services.*

Solar Flares

The first method an Electro-Magnetic Pulse (EMP) can be generated is through a <u>natural</u> occurrence called a *solar flare* where the sun emits radiation that travels to the earth and disrupts vulnerable electrical and electronic devices and equipment.

Scientists and astronomers have long been studying the effects of the radiation produced by solar flares. On August 28 through September 2 in 1859, the Carrington Event was the largest geomagnetic storm ever recorded and disabled telegraph systems all across Europe and North America.

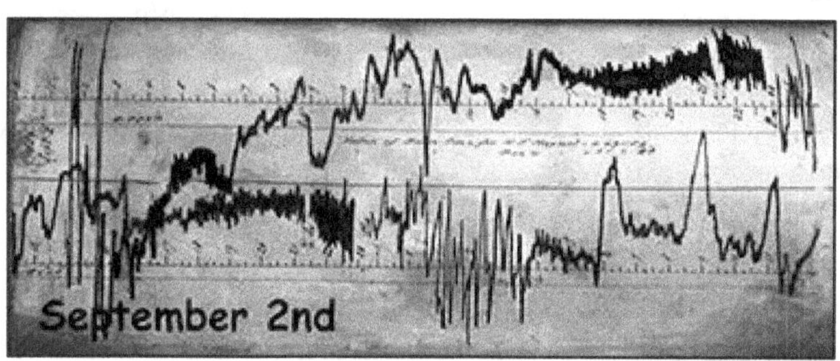

A study conducted by Lloyd's of London and the United States Atmospheric and Environmental Research (AER) estimated the results of such a storm would have a $2.6 trillion dollar effect on the world economy. More recently, a series of solar storms in the 1970's was substantial enough to bring widespread disruption in the use of CB radios, in addition to disrupting commercial radio and television transmissions.

Act of War - Terrorist Attack

The second method an EMP can be generated is through a <u>manmade</u> *act of war or terrorist attack* using a nuclear missile that explodes above the earth's atmosphere and releases the electro-magnetic pulses. Public knowledge about an EMP (sometimes known as NEMP - Nuclear Electro-Magnetic Pulse), initially surfaced when the United States began carrying out nuclear tests, as phones and other electronic equipment began to malfunction miles from ground zero. An EMP occurs with all nuclear explosions; however, the effect can be potentiated if the nuclear explosive is detonated just outside the Earth's atmosphere.

It is possible for the magnetic field of the earth to spread the EMP to cover the whole continental United States with the electromagnetic pulse. An EMP of this magnitude could be capable to seriously disrupting the electric grid and a significant amount of both public and private electrical and electronic devices.

<u>**Electrical Power Versus Electrical/Electronic Devices and Equipment**</u>

One must differentiate between loosing electrical **POWER** and losing electrical and/or electronic **EQUIPMENT AND DEVICES**.

Electrical **POWER** can be disrupted as a consequence of many types of *natural* disasters, including earthquakes, winter storms, solar flares, wind and other natural occurrences. Electrical power could also be disrupted by *manmade* disasters including terrorist attacks on the electrical grid, vehicle accidents that disable power lines, worn out electrical equipment and a nuclear attack emitting strong **E**lectro-**M**agnetic **P**ulse waves. For example, an enemy could detonate nuclear devices high in space where gamma radiation released by the blast would strip electrons from the upper levels of the atmosphere and create electromagnetic radiation levels that could fully or partially destabilize the entire electrical grid in the country resulting in loss of electrical power.

Electrical/Electronic **EQUIPMENT AND DEVICES** can be destroyed and/or disrupted when an electrical power surge streams through the electrical wiring and hits the electrical or electronic device with such force and strength, the electrical and electronic components are fried or severely damaged and will no longer operate.

<u>**EMP Protection**</u>

Basically, anything operating on a charge or on batteries <u>when not plugged into an AC outlet</u> is likely to be spared from an EMP attack. If the device is kept away from other large metal objects and large swaths of wiring, it should remain relatively unharmed and continue to operate as long as its charge or batteries last. Some electronics are inherently EMP-proof, including large electric motors, vacuum tube equipment, electrical generators, transformers and relays, and other large systems often housed in surge-resistant housing.

Harden your equipment (another way of saying, protect it from EMP using tree formation circuits (not standard loop formations), induction shielding around components, self-contained battery packs, loop antennas, and Zener diodes. In addition, grounding wires for each separate instrument into a system could help as well. A new device called the Ovonic Threshold Device (Energy Conversion Devices of Troy, MI) is a solid state switch that opens a path to ground when a massive surge of EMP is encountered by a circuit.

One big myth is that an EMP will wipe out the electronic components of most vehicles. On the contrary, the metal construction of most cars and trucks act as virtual Faraday Cages for the electronic components contained within the vehicle. Thus, if you were to insulate your vital medical electronics in tin foil, put them in a makeshift Faraday Cage, and store it inside a vehicle, it should be protected from *most* moderate EMP strikes. Ultimately, it's all about how you insulate and shield your devices. For example, a washer or dryer could be used to store some larger or obscurely shaped devices if needed, so long as all sides are made of metal and have a tightly fitting lid.

For *most* home and commercial electronic devices, surge protectors and lighting arrestors serve to protect the systems from failure in the event of a power outage and fortunately most will also protect them against the effects of an EMP. While a powerful surge could wipe out the grid and shut off electrical services, the devices themselves would not be harmed *if plugged into a high-end surge protector*. However, the device would need to be operated using an alternative electrical power source such as a solar powered generator.

<u>**Faraday Cage**</u>

Since we have yet to experience an EMP strike, its unknown as to how effective surge protectors and resistors will be in a real-world event. In the end, the best way to protect vital electronics is to keep them disconnected from external power sources, away from antennas, and shielded in a well-sealed and insulated Faraday cage.

The Faraday Cage, named for Michael Faraday, the 19th-century inventor, is any conductive structure that protects its contents from electrical pulses. Whatever is stored in the Faraday Cage must be insulated from the inside metal surface of the box, but should otherwise remain protected. Accordingly, the box should be constructed so that no large gaps or holes are present. The simplest option is an old microwave oven, a tightly sealed metal garbage can, an ammo can, metal filing cabinets, truck bed cabinets, or a metal safe. As a general rule, the thickness of the box does not make much difference in determining its effectiveness against EMP waves, although thicker metal is likely to work better as an overall deterrent against destructive waves.

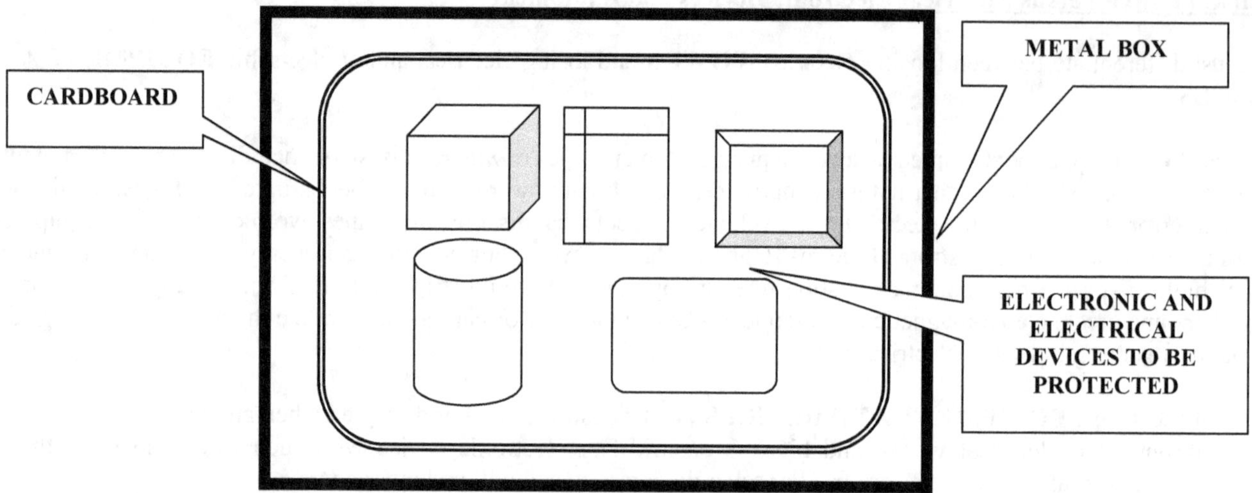

A Faraday Cage is easy to build. Follow these steps:

1. Determine what size box you're going to need. Gather all items to be shielded and determine how much space is required. Important items include shortwave radios, walkie-talkies, crucial medical equipment (i.e. a glucose meter), and spare electronic parts for your generator and car. Note that batteries are *not* affected by an Electro-Magnetic Pulse.

2. Obtain a *metal* box or container that closes as securely as possible. Any gaps will render the grounding ineffective.

3. Tape every seam down firmly using regular tape, although aluminum or copper tape will provide better security.

4. Line the inside of the box with cardboard to ensure that electronics do not make contact with any metal surface including the foil or metal tape.

5. Place electrical and electronic items inside the cardboard area and using aluminum or copper tape, seal the outside lid of the metal   container.

> **NOTE:**   Another method to construct a Faraday Cage is to take a plastic, wooden or cardboard box or container that closes as securely as possible and wrap the entire container (inside and outside) with *heavy duty* aluminum foil. Place a cardboard box inside of the newly constructed metal (aluminum foil) container. Place items inside the cardboard box.

COMMUNICATION EQUIPMENT

Many types of communication equipment require a power source. During any level of disaster, it is likely power will be out. For obvious reasons, when planning for communication devices and equipment, attempt to purchase solar powered, rechargeable battery-operated (including solar powered battery charger) or alternative power forms that are not subject to an electrical power grid. Again, always remember to plan for *alternatives* or *layers*.

AM/FM Radio

As part of emergency planning for communications, every team MUST have a basic AM/FM radio that does not require conventional electricity. One choice is a battery-operated radio, but another excellent alternative is a solar-powered radio or hand crank to generate power. Remember that AM broadcasts will override FM broadcasts for disaster news and many can be picked up from a very long distance. **If a widespread emergency occurs, civil defense-affiliated stations are generally set up to broadcast survival information on the AM broadcast band.** These radios should be specified for *emergency use only* and off-limits for all other use. I cannot emphasize enough the importance of making sure you have several *alternatives* or *layers* of radios available for emergency situations. These radios would very likely be your **ONLY MEANS** of receiving emergency news and other important information concerning the outside world.

Phones

The cell towers that operate our cell phones rely on regular AC power for operation. During times of serious disasters, the towers and/or backup power systems could be damaged or destroyed. The cell phone itself involves complexities with moving parts. The batteries are short-lived and sensitive to fluctuations in temperature and geographic location.

The land line phones also create a problem during a disaster. Telephone poles and wires go down, switch stations can be destroyed, transmitting and receiving cells can be damaged – and in an instant – landline telephone communication can be shut off. Remember that when the power is out, a cordless land line phone will not operate, but a corded phone could still work (depending on the circumstances) without power to support it. **Only an ill-advised person would rely on any phone to support communication during any level of disaster**.

Internet

The Internet relies on the electrical grid – either directly or indirectly to operate the system. The battery that operates your computer would at some time have to be recharged – using electrical power. The Internet parallels the cell phone dilemma in that towers, cables and lines supporting Internet relies on regular AC power for operation, and just like a cell phone, these towers and lines could easily be damaged or destroyed. Even Internet powered by satellite can be affected by weather conditions or other logistical complications. Again, do **NOT** count on the Internet for communication – even during a Level One disaster.

CB Radio

The range for a CB radio is generally about ten to twenty-five miles, depending on the geography in the area. One of the problems with a CB radio is during an emergency; interference from other users can be common since users share only a few channels. And again, another setback is their reliance on a direct or indirect electrical power source. One of the good points about a CB radio is that they are useful as a neighborhood communication system or in the car when on the road to get real-time information from other drivers about roads and highways or other hazards. On a CB radio, Channel 9 is the official nationwide channel for emergency use and traveler's information. The Radio Emergency Associated Communications Team (REACT) is a volunteer group who monitors Channel 9 continuously all across the country.

Walkie Talkie

A walkie talkie is a good communication device when communicating with a minimum amount of interference and the person is a short distance away. A walkie talkie comes in a wide variety of styles, channels, power outputs and prices. Again, one of the major setbacks with a walkie talkie is their reliance on a direct or indirect electrical power source.

Shortwave (Ham) Radio

A shortwave radio system allows you to be in touch with the unfiltered world of international radio whether you live in a small town or large city. Depending on the equipment, a shortwave radio system can also be used for two-way communications instead of just listening to conversations. Users of shortwave radios are also called "ham operators". During any emergency situation, the ham operators are vital to receiving and dispersing valuable information to citizens.

Ham operators use many frequency bands across the radio spectrum - these frequencies are allocated by the FCC for amateur use. Non-hams can **"listen in"** via their own receivers or radio scanners. Hams operate from just above the AM broadcast band to the microwave region in the gigahertz range. Many ham bands are found in the frequency range above the AM radio band (1.6 MHz) to just above the citizens band (27 MHz). During daytime hours, 15 to 27 MHz is a good band for long-distance communications. At night, the band from 1.6 to 15 MHz is good for long-distance communications. These bands are often referred to historically as **short-wave** bands (as in "short-wave radio").

Scanners

A scanner allows you to receive broadcasted information from police, sheriff, ambulance, fire, Border Patrol agents, United States Customs, the Federal Emergency Management Administration (FEMA), the National Oceanic and Atmospheric Administration (NOAA) and ham radio operators. During an emergency, and depending on the severity of the crisis, these governmental agencies will generally have important information on the disaster and would broadcast much of this information on scanners.

<u>**Paper and Pencils**</u>

During a disaster, we as a society will be humbled into accepting an age-old method of communication – a simple piece of paper and a pencil. Have an abundant supply of paper, pens and pencils. These items should be included in emergency pantries including: (1) primary residence, (2) place of refuge, (3) auto and (4) evacuation kit. It is assumed that these office supplies would already be available at your worksite.

<u>**Typewriter**</u>

It is very difficult to find a manual typewriter in any office supply outlet but they can be found on-line and can be purchased using a ribbon or a ball for about $120.00. Ribbons cost about $10.00 each. This typewriter will serve as a means to communicate using a simple piece of paper during a serious disaster, when electric typewriters, word processors and computers will be standing silently by watching the real typing master at work!

<u>**Bull Horn**</u>

Somewhat of a crazy idea – I'll admit – but the individual holding a bull horn can be heard over the crowd and throughout the neighborhood! Team members who are assigned to serve as team leaders or block captains during a disaster in the neighborhood, at the church or in the community should consider the purchase of a bull horn. Someone speaking with a bull horn is much more likely to be heard, recognized and accepted than someone screaming and shouting in the wind.

<u>**Whistle**</u>

All team members should have a good whistle in their evacuation pack. This whistle could serve as a means of communication in the event some member becomes lost or disoriented during the chaos that may be prevalent during the evacuation. As part of *planning in advance*, teams could devise various "codes" that could be used to identify specific issues, i.e. one whistle means safe, two whistles mean hurt and needs assistance, etc.

CORN BREAD

1 b cups white flour
b cup granulated white sugar
5 teaspoons baking powder
1 teaspoon salt
1 b cups yellow cornmeal
2 eggs, beaten
1 b cups milk
a cup margarine *or* butter, melted

Mix flour, granulated white sugar, baking powder and salt in large bowl. Stir in cornmeal until well blended. Add beaten eggs and milk and stir to form a smooth batter. Stir in melted butter or margarine just until blended. Do not over mix. Pour into a well-buttered 9x5x3 inch loaf pan. Bake at 425 degrees for 40 to 50 minutes or until toothpick inserted in center comes out clean. Cool in pan 10 minutes, then loosen around edges and turn out to cool. Makes 1 loaf.

PINTO BEAN FUDGE

1 cup pinto beans (cooked, drained and mashed)
¼ cup milk
1 tablespoon vanilla
2 pounds powdered sugar
1 (6-ounce) chocolate bar, unsweetened
6 tablespoons butter *or* margarine
1 cup nuts, chopped (optional)

In large bowl, stir beans and milk together, adding enough milk to resemble mashed potatoes in consistency. Stir in vanilla. Melt chocolate and butter and stir into bean mixture. Add nuts. Gradually stir in powdered sugar until well blended. Spread onto lightly butter 9-inch baking dish or form into two 1 ½ inch rolls. Chill 1 or 2 hours. Cut into pieces. Refrigerate.

CHAPTER TWELVE

DOCUMENTATION

All members of the team have important documentation that must be preserved during an emergency. These documents include legal, financial, religious, medical and insurance documents. Unfortunately, most of us have these important documents stored in various locations throughout the house. It is vital to *prepare in advance* to manage important documents during an emergency situation, whether the team remains at the primary residence or is forced to evacuate the primary residence and transport to an alternate location or place of refuge. During an emergency is **NOT** the time to be gathering up all of this critical documentation.

EMERGENCY PREPARATION PRINCIPLES

There are <u>eight</u> guidelines that can be incorporated into an overall emergency plan to prepare for and in some cases eliminate documentation issues that would become prevalent during an emergency situation:

- Purchase a good safe that is fire and water resistant - place important documentation in the safe.

- Make and continually update an inventory of all possessions including jewelry, guns and clothing.

- Consider storing documents that cannot be replaced in a location away from the primary residence such as a safe deposit box at a nearby bank.

- Consider personal property insurance.

- Update scrapbook and photo albums. Consider leaving sentimental photos and negatives or duplicate photos in storage or with a relative. Put photos on CDs!

- Make duplicates of all documentation including personal address lists.

- Consolidate all documentation into one location, including personal records, financial documents, school records, etc.

- Plan for pets. Keep pets' records updated and with you during an evacuation that includes you and your pets.

There are several methods that can be utilized to safeguard important documents and paperwork during an emergency. By *planning in advance*, the team members would have a good prospect for maintaining and accessing important documentation during a crisis situation.

1.   Gather all important documents and make *three* GOOD copies of each. If necessary, have each document notarized. Place all <u>original</u> documentation in a safe deposit box at a bank near the primary residence.

Distribute the three copies as follows:

- If your alternate place of refuge is a long distance away from the primary residence, put a copy of all documentation in a safe deposit box at a bank near the alternate site.

- Maintain a copy of the complete set of documentation at the primary residence in a fire-proof, water-proof, and dinosaur-proof container or safe – with a combination lock.

- Mail a copy (using certified mail) of the complete set of documentation in a clearly marked and sealed envelope to a trusted friend or relative who lives outside the area of your primary residence (perhaps the out-of-state contact) – preferably in another state across the country.

2.   Make a list on <u>one</u> sheet of paper of all policy numbers, contract numbers, account numbers and identification numbers on all the documents. Include names, addresses and phones numbers of the institutions where the accounts are located. Make two copies of the list. Mail one copy to a friend or relative who lives outside the area of your primary residence (out-of-state contact) – preferably in another state across the country. Laminate the second copy and tape it to the *inside* of your evacuation kit.

3.   Make a list on <u>one</u> sheet of paper of all policy numbers, contract numbers, account numbers and identification numbers on all the documents. Include names, addresses and phones numbers of the institutions where the accounts are located. On this list however, write all numbers <u>backwards</u>; in other words, if the correct policy number is 12345, write it down as 54321. Make three copies of the list.

Laminate the lists and place one under the driver's seat of the car(s), tape one list on the bottom of a drawer in your desk at work and put another one in your wallet or purse. If using the car for evacuation or if you are stuck at work or are stranded at the store during an emergency, you would have the list. If the car, wallet or purse is stolen at any time, or if a co-worker finds the list in your desk - no problem – the numbers would not be valid – only you will know how to decipher the accounts.

4.   Assemble <u>copies</u> of all documentation into one heavy-duty and waterproof container (locking file box with handle). Consider this container as an additional evacuation unit that must be transported with the rest of your evacuation supplies. If the place of refuge is a public shelter, team members must be vigilant to guard the safety and security of its contents.

5.   Scan copies of all important documentation. Make sure that each page of the documents and photographs can easily be viewed and read. Copy the scanned documents and photographs onto four CD's. Store the first one in the safe deposit box at your local bank, the second one at the safe deposit box at a bank near the alternate site, the third one with a trusted friend or relative who lives outside the area of your primary residence (out-of-state contact) – preferably in another state across the country, and the fourth one in your evacuation kit.

6.   After scanning all the documents and photographs, email them to your private email address. Create a folder called **"EMERGENCY DOCS"** and move them to this location. Make sure they will not be automatically deleted – as some email systems are programmed to do after a specific length of time. Now – leave them alone. Depending on the crisis, it may be possible to access a computer, printer and the Internet near your location of refuge. You can simply bring up your email, access the folder and print out the files containing your important documentation.

NOTE: When emailing documentation to your private email address, attach the documents assigned to the same category in one email, i.e., send all medical documents under one email. Depending on your Internet provider, you may be limited on the amount of data that can be transmitted.

When all emails arrive at your private account, set up sub-folders for each category under the **EMERGENCY DOCS** folder.

WHAT TO CONSIDER FOR THE DOCUMENTATION ELEMENT

Legal		Monthly Expenses
- *Marriage Certificate* - *Vehicle Plate Number*		- *Budget*
- *Birth Certificate* - *House Title / Deeds*		- *Bills*
- *Divorce Papers* - *Lease*		- *Outstanding Debts*
- *Naturalization Papers* - *Mortgages*		
- *Vehicle Title* - *Drivers License*		
- *Car Registration* - *Social Security Card*		
- *Vehicle ID Number* - *Passport*		

Will	**Bank/Credit Union Deposits**
- *Will* - *Living Will* - *Power of Attorney* - *Guardianship*	- *Safe Deposit Box Information* - *Checking – bank, phone, account number* - *Savings – bank, phone, account number* - *IRA – bank, phone number, account number* - *CD - bank, phone number, account number*
Financial	**Utilities**
- *Income for both spouses* - *Assets/ Debts* - *Stocks and Bonds* - *Income Tax Returns* - *Property Tax Statements*	- *Electric - name, phone, account number* - *Water - name, phone, account number* - *Gas - name, phone, account number* - *Propane – name, phone, account number* - *Sewer - name, phone, account number* - *Phone – name, phone, account number*
Insurance	**Religious**
- *Life – agent, phone and policy number* - *Auto – agent, phone and policy number* - *Other – agent, phone and policy number* - *Home – agent, phone and policy number* - *Medical – agent, phone and policy number*	- *Religious Books and Scriptures* - *Patriarchal Blessing* - *Genealogy Records* - *Membership Identification Number* - *Temple Recommend*
Medical	**Important Miscellaneous**
- *Past Histories – diseases, surgeries, dates* - *Current Histories – current treatments, etc.* - *Medication – dosage, schedule, reason* - *Immunizations – type, date, purpose* - *Hospital – name, address, phone* - *Physician – name, address, phone, specialty* - *Dentist – name, address, phone, specialty* - *Other - name, address, phone, specialty*	- *Recent photos* - *Fingerprints of children* - *Local Phone Book (if applicable)* - *Neighbors/Friends/Relatives* - *Police – address and phone number* - *Fire – address and phone number* - *Personal property – description, value, photo*
Records	**Pets**

- *Employment – name, address, phone number*
- *Military – dates, title, military number*
- *School – name, address, phone, student*
	- *Medical Records*
	  * *Surgeries*
	  * *Immunizations*
	  * *Spay/Neuter*
	  * *Birthdate (if possible)*
	
	- *Photograph*

Always store original documents in a fireproof location, i.e., safe, safe deposit box, etc. Documentation to be placed in your emergency pantries and kits should be copies only. Consider any and all security issues before placing documents in your pantries and kits.

CHICKEN RICE CASSEROLE

1 cup rice, uncooked
1 (10-ounce) can cream of celery soup
1 ½ cups water
1 package dry onion soup mix
1 (10-ounce) can cream of mushroom soup
1 raw chicken, cut in cubes

Mix rice, cream soups and water together and place mixture in large baking pan. Place chicken on top of rice mixture and sprinkle with dry onion soup mix. Cover with aluminum foil. Poke holes in foil with fork. Bake at 350 degrees one hour.

CHOCOLATE OATMEAL CAKE

1 ¾ cups boiling water
1 cup dry oatmeal
½ cup butter *or* margarine
2 large eggs
1 ¾ cups flour
1 cup brown sugar, firmly packed
¾ teaspoon salt
1 teaspoon baking soda
4 tablespoons dry cocoa
1 cup granulated white sugar
1 tablespoon vanilla
1 cup chocolate chips (optional)
¾ cup nuts (optional)

Pour boiling water over dry oatmeal. Let stand. Cream butter, sugars and eggs. Set aside. Sift together flour, salt, baking soda and cocoa. Add to creamed mixture. Add vanilla. Fold in oatmeal, chocolate chips and nuts. Pour into greased and floured 9x13 inch pan. Bake at 350 degrees for 40 minutes or until toothpick inserted in center comes out clean.

NAVY BEAN BUNDT CAKE

1 b cups navy beans, cooked
1 cup granulated white sugar
1 teaspoon vanilla
2 cups flour
1 teaspoon baking soda
2 teaspoons cinnamon
a cup water
1 ½ teaspoons baking powder
½ cup pecans *or* walnuts, chopped
1 a cups flaked coconut
1 cup butter (softened)
b cup brown sugar, firmly packed
2 eggs
a cup evaporated milk
1 ½ teaspoons nutmeg

Puree beans in blender or mash with fork. Set aside. In large bowl, combine butter, sugars and vanilla. Beat until creamy. Add eggs and mix at high speed until well blended. Add milk and water and mix thoroughly. Stir in beans. Set aside. In medium bowl, combine flour, baking powder, baking soda, nutmeg and cinnamon. Stir half of dry ingredients into bean mixture until well blended. Add nuts and coconut and blend. Blend in remaining dry ingredients. Pour into greased Bundt pan. Bake at 350 degrees for 50-55 minutes.

CHAPTER THIRTEEN

SANITATION

The lack of sanitation is directly or indirectly responsible for deaths of thousands of people worldwide every year. Although sanitation supplies may arguably only be *want* or luxury items, the lack of these basic sanitation supplies even during a short-term but definitely during medium and long-term disasters can have a devastating impact on the physical body and the morale, spirit and confidence of team members to continue to work towards ultimate survival.

EMERGENCY PREPARATION PRINCIPLES

There are <u>six</u> principles that should be incorporated into an overall emergency plan to prepare for and in some cases eliminate sanitation issues that would become prevalent during an emergency situation:

- A **<u>disaster</u>** environment is **NOT** a **<u>normal</u>** environment. When preparing for disaster - always think about what would be *realistic*, *logical* and *practical* in a **<u>disaster</u>** environment, i.e. no electricity, water, etc. Think outside the box!

- Maintain consistent order and cleanliness by keeping the primary residence, surrounding buildings and the yard clean and free of debris and trash at all times.

- Maintain equipment (toilets, garbage cans, etc.) and keep supplies in good working condition that would be used to manage sanitation issues.

- Continue regular and consistent trash disposal by placing trashcan out on the street for pickup on your assigned day each week.

- On a regular basis, and if using a septic tank, use a septic tank product to control waste buildup in the tank and eliminate roots from breaching or clogging the lines.

- When practical, buy products that serve <u>multiple</u> uses i.e. instead of buying a disinfectant and a cleaner, buy a product that serves both purposes or instead of buying shampoo and soap, buy bath gel that serves both purposes. Less money - less storage space.

POWER AND WATER

During any level of disaster, many times both **water** and **electricity** are compromised and as a result, many of our daily hygiene practices are affected as well. The sanitation practices in the United States support a high standard of living – but in a matter of days, sanitation problems could dramatically increase to dangerous levels. Since sanitation is one of the elements that would be vulnerable to loss of water and electricity, the general population becomes susceptible to diseases that under normal conditions would not be common in our society. Remember!

When: **Electricity** goes down
             Water goes down

             And as a result -

             Sanitation problems go up
             Medication (disease and illness) goes up
             Emotion (stress, anxiety, fear, frustration) goes up

During any serious or long-term disaster, unless team members *plan in advance* and stock basic sanitation supplies, team members may find the following situations:

- No drinking **water** or **water** to be used for other purposes
- No **water** or **electricity** to support a workable toilet or sewage facilities
- No **water** or **electricity** to wash or dry clothes – forced to wear dirty clothes longer between washings
- No toilet paper, no facial tissue, no paper towels
- No **water** to bathe or take a shower
- No **water** to wash or dye the hair
- No **water** to brush the teeth or clean dentures
- No trash pickup with increase of garbage and trash in neighborhoods and streets
- No means to vacuum or sweep floors, clean counters and cabinets, etc.
- No **water** to wash the dishes
- No means to reduce or eliminate insect and rodent populations
- No means to bury dead bodies
- Bad smells - coming from you and your rancid body odor

Depending on the disaster type, length of time and consequences to the elements, *all* water sources could be seriously jeopardized and citizens would be forced to manage and allocate sparse but critical water resources. Illness and disease would increase and the emotional and psychological health of survivors would decrease causing stress, nervous tensions, irritability and short tempers.

There are some additional strategies that can be used by team members for *advanced planning* of possible disaster scenarios to cope with scarce water resources and sanitation tasks:

1.   There is an adage that says:

> *"Boys are made out of snakes and snails and puppy dog tails.*
> *Girls are made out of sugar and spice and everything nice."*

      Women and girls like to be physically clean, have a sanitary environment and we like to look nice. Men and boys don't mind a little dirt and in many cases, boys hate to take baths because it wipes off all that hard earned dirt. As a result, women generally have the hardest time adjusting to lack of sanitation facilities and scarce water resources. Women tend to be responsible for keeping the children, laundry, dishes and general surroundings clean. As part of *planning in advance*, women and girls should <u>especially</u> prepare themselves to expect less - less - less.

2.   Men and women with medium to long length <u>hair</u> - *plan to cut it short* to eliminate the need for spending excessive time on grooming and will limit the amount of water needed for washing and cleaning hair.

3.   Men and women with long <u>nails</u> - *plan to cut them short* to eliminate the need for spending excessive time on manicuring and will allow everyone to perform critical tasks without having to worry about "breaking a nail". They will grow back.

4.   Women should avoid using <u>makeup</u> during the length of the disaster. This will eliminate the need for spending excessive time on grooming and will limit the amount of water needed for removing makeup.

5.   Men and women should remove any permanent <u>jewelry</u> items and refrain from wearing jewelry for the entire length of the disaster. This will eliminate the possibility of illness (from infection), injury (from cuts or tears when performing tasks associated with disaster environments) and theft (there will always be some idiot out there wanting to steal jewelry and hoping to collect barter items)

6.   It is more than likely that everyone is going to start <u>smelling bad</u> due to lack of personal hygiene and   increased need to perform hard manual labor - causing the sweat glands to work overtime. Stock deodorant.

7.   Discuss with <u>teenagers</u> *in advance* the realities that may be present during disaster situations including the limitations that will be placed on them in conducting excessive personal hygiene regiments, i.e., no daily showers or baths, no daily hair wash, no makeup, no hair dye, no shaving legs or face, being required to cut medium and long length hair, not being able to wash or wear clean clothing, no daily teeth brushing, etc.

8.   Parents will need to re-evaluate the number of times <u>diapers</u> will be changed on babies and toddlers   where scarce water would be needed to maintain cleanliness.

9.   At part of *planning in advance*, plan to use <u>alternative methods</u> that will eliminate, replace or reduce the need for excessive or additional water resources including:

- Use <u>paper plates</u> and <u>plastic cups and utensils</u> that can be thrown away or used as fire starter instead of using dishes that require dishwashing.

- Stock a *large* amount of bottled hand <u>sanitizer</u>, <u>sanitizer wipes</u> and <u>moisture wipes</u> that can be used to "wash" the body instead of using water.

- When stocking extra <u>tooth brushes</u> for household team members, invest in good brushes and not those found in the dollar stores. The cheap toothbrushes tend to bend and can easily break - don't risk it.

- Perspiration from stress smells even worse than "regular" sweat - seems there are different chemicals. Either way - stock up on <u>deodorant</u> to eliminate offensive odors.

- Use <u>laundry detergent</u> that does not require hot water and in fact - very little water to get clothes clean.

- Stock a *large* amount of *all-purpose* <u>cleaners</u> and <u>disinfectants</u> that can be sprayed directly on floors, counters and appliances to clean instead of using water. To save money and space, purchase products containing *both* a cleaner <u>and</u> disinfectant instead of buying separate products.

> There is a "hand" cleaner product available in most department, grocery and auto supplies stores called **ORANGE** (in an orange bottle no less) used for very dirty hands and arms with dirt, grease, oil, tar and other hard to remove dragons.

- Stock up on *baby* <u>moisture wipes</u> that can replace the use of water in cleaning up after a diaper change.

- If makeup is indeed a top priority ☹ during a serious and long-term disaster - stock up on <u>makeup remover pads</u> so precious water resources can be saved for more important things.

- Stock up on large quantities of <u>paper towels</u> that can be used for most general cleaning purposes instead of using a rag that will need to be washed out using water.

- Stock up on <u>bath gel</u> that can replace both soap and shampoo - less to buy and store and generally requires less water.

- Plan to use either *paper towels* or *air dry* when taking a <u>shower or bath</u> - large bath towels and even hand towels and wash cloths will take excessive water to launder.

TOILET

When it comes to "toilet duty" - there are many things that can go wrong during a disaster because there are many "working systems" that are part of that bathroom experience we all take for granted on a daily basis.

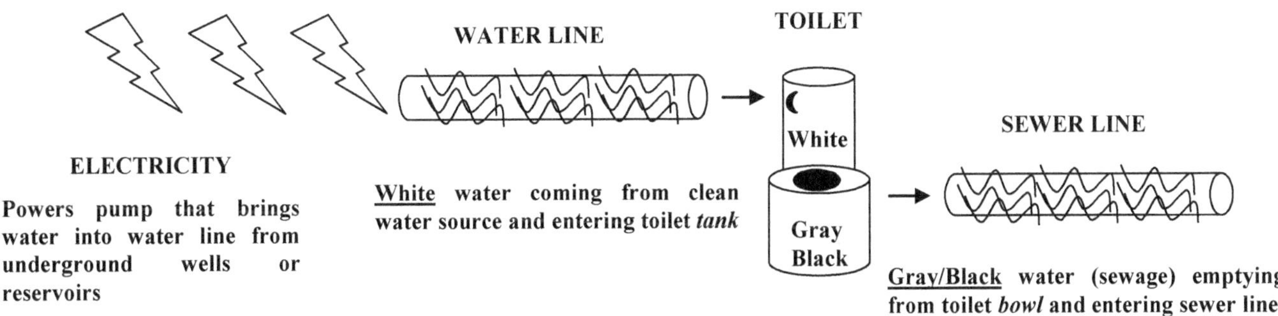

As you can see from the above diagram - if any or all of these "systems" break down during a disaster - it is going to severally impact the "bathroom experience". For example, if electrical power is down, there will be no water being pumped into the water line and into the toilet bowl. If the water line breaks, there will be no water coming into the toilet bowl regardless of whether or not there is electricity. If the toilet is cracked or broken, there will be no need for electricity, water line or the sewer line. If the sewer line breaks, there will no easy means to empty a toilet bowl containing feces and urine. And there you have it.

It is important for team members to *plan in advance* to prepare for any contingency that may occur during an emergency and have *alternatives* or *layers* available to support toilet functions - especially if you have small children, elderly or disabled or handicapped members.

Let's look at some possible contingencies on what could happen if one or several of the systems supporting the toilet were to be damaged or destroyed and how we can *plan in advance* and have available alternatives to serve our toilet sanitation needs during any length of disaster:

TOILET IS WORKING ☺

Using Gray Water To Flush

If the toilet and sewer or septic tank system is alright but the *water line is damaged*, turn the water off behind the toilet. One solution is to use gray water to create a "flush" for the toilet. Remember! Gray water is water that is *not* used for drinking or food preparation. Gray water can be water that has been used for other purposes such as bathing or washing dishes and clothes, water coming from rivers, dams, lakes or streams, water collected as rainwater or melted snow. This "gray" water can then be reserved to flush the toilet. As part of an overall emergency sanitation plan, a 50-gallon drum could be used to store gray water.

An entire gallon of water poured directly and quickly into toilet bowl will generally get the toilet to flush. To conserve water, use the "selective flushing method" - don't flush the toilet every time you use it. Flush only once or twice a day (depending on family size) to conserve gray water. **USE GRAY WATER WISELY**.

EXPERIMENT

Use the toilet for one entire week, **BUT DO NOT FLUSH THE TOILET** – period. Not only will the sight of the contents create a gag reflex – but the stench will become overwhelming. It matters not how many people are in the family – when the sewer stops working, the result is the same – bad smell – very bad smell.

Practice *in advance* to see how much water is required to flush the toilet. Turn the water off behind the toilet and flush to get rid of water in the tank. Plunge out remaining water in bowl. Toss a square of toilet paper in bowl. Dump a gallon of water <u>all at once</u> into bowl. Experiment to see the minimum amount of water the toilet needs to flush.

Using Bags, Buckets and Disinfectant

If the toilet is alright but the *sewer or septic tank system and/or water lines are damaged*, one solution is to use <u>heavy-duty</u> plastic garbage bags, disinfectant, a <u>heavy-duty</u> bucket and a large trash can.

- Place tape over handle of toilet (to avoid the habit of flushing)
- Wear latex or rubber gloves
- Turn the water faucet <u>off</u> behind the toilet
- Flush or scoop out any water in the <u>tank</u>
- Place a tennis ball in the outlet at the bottom of the toilet <u>bowl</u>
- Line the bowl with a <u>heavy-duty</u> plastic garbage bag (13+ gallon)
- Secure the bag in place with Acco clips or duct tape
- After each use, add a <u>small</u> amount of disinfectant
- Place used toilet paper in a separate plastic grocery bag and burn contents at regular intervals
- When the heavy duty garbage bag is ½ full, securely tie the bag with a twist-tie
- Transfer the garbage bag into a heavy-duty empty bucket with a handle
- Carry the bucket outside the house
- Deposit bag contents into a large trash can* lined with a <u>heavy-duty</u> trash bag and a tight fitting lid
- As a further means to contain any odor, pull another thirty-gallon plastic trash bag over the entire toilet

* trash can should be used exclusively for the purpose of storing human waste.

TOILET IS <u>NOT</u> WORKING ☹

If the toilet is damaged or destroyed, the first task is to construct a temporary toilet provision for team members and especially the children. Almost any covered metal or plastic container will do - a covered pail, a five-gallon bucket, or a small kitchen garbage container with a foot-operated cover.

As an emergency toilet, anything having a cover and will hold the waste contents until you can properly dispose of it will <u>temporarily</u> serve the purpose. If using the bucket method, line it with a <u>heavy-duty</u> garbage bag and fill it with one gallon of water (do <u>not</u> use drinking water – only gray water or water from other natural sources) and one cup of <u>liquid</u> chlorine bleach to break down the odor and waste. Use Acco clips or duct tape to keep the plastic bags in place.

> Use thirteen-gallon kitchen size <u>heavy duty</u> trash bags. The "Mil" on the label means millimeter and refers to the thickness of the plastic - the larger the number the stronger the bag. **BUY HIGH MIL AND HEAVY DUTY!!! SPEND THE MONEY!!!**

When bucket is half full (no more) seal off bag and properly dispose of it in a large trash can (specifically assigned to hold human waste) or other waterproof container with a tight fitting cover. If you have babies or adults in diapers, store used diapers in separate plastic grocery bag (along with used toilet paper) and dispose of it accordingly.

COMMODE

Although using a bucket may be acceptable for some team members during <u>short-term</u> disasters, as the length of the disaster increases and the toilet is still broken and/or electricity, water lines and/or sewer lines are still down - the use of a bucket as a temporary toilet solution becomes challenging at the very least. And again, when small children, the elderly or disabled and handicapped persons are part of the team - it becomes even more important to *plan in advance* for a more practical and respectful alternative.

A commode can be purchased at medical supply outlets and even in large department stores and range in price from $75 to $200. Another place where they frequently turn up is charitable organizations or garage sales. It is perfect for handicapped and disabled people - in fact, it was made for them. It also supports the weight of heavier team members. Another important feature is that it can be set up right in the house - perhaps in the bathroom next to that broken toilet. It has a removable waste tray underneath the seat. Simply place a small amount of water (white or gray) into the tray and add a <u>small</u> drop of bleach or other disinfectant. Once the tray is full of human waste, simply pull out the removable waste drawer and empty the waste in a hole dug specifically for this purpose, or use the contents to water and/or fertilize the garden or other trees, shrubs and vines.

A commode solves all the toilet issues:

- If the toilet is broken - use the commode
- If the electricity is out - use the commode
- If the water line is broken - use the commode
- If the sewer line is broken - use the commode

Other good choices are commodes that can be used *inside* or *outside* of the primary residence. The collapsible toilet structure could also be used in the auto kit and instead of a bucket or trash can - a hole could be dug in the ground to collect the waste and then covered up when the toilet was no longer needed.

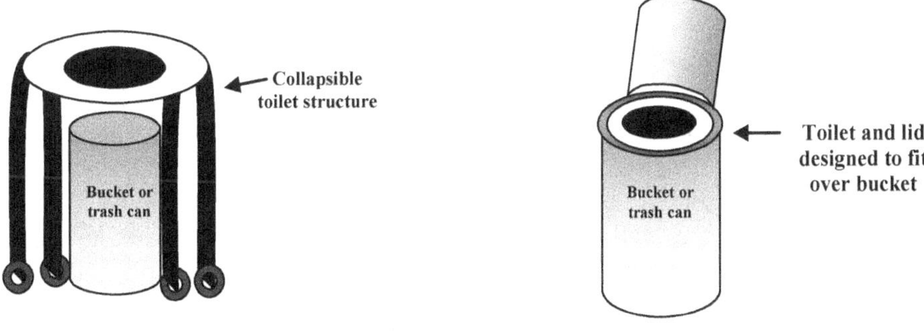

OUTHOUSE

Another good alternative to replace a broken toilet or accommodate the reality of power outages or broken water or sewer lines is an outhouse. Although there are several drawbacks to using an outhouse, it does solve all the toilet issues. If using this alternative, the team should construct the outhouse *in advance* and store it in a safe location. One of the biggest problems with using an outhouse as an alternative toilet - it does need to be set up outside and during inclement weather and cold temperatures - that can be uncomfortable. An outhouse can also create logistical problems for small children, the elderly and disabled or handicapped members.

SEWAGE DISPOSAL

Depending on the severity of the emergency and the condition of waste disposal systems, <u>every team should know and be prepared to use alternative methods of waste disposal</u> for both short-term and long-term emergencies. Failure to properly dispose of human waste can lead to serious diseases and epidemics of typhoid, hepatitis, dysentery and diarrhea. Human waste must be disposed of in ways that will prevent contamination to water supplies used for drinking, cooking, bathing, laundering and other domestic purposes.

Although human waste can be stored in a large outside trash can with a tight lid for a short period of time, at some point in time, the waste will need to be transferred into the ground. There are several factors that must be considered when disposing of human waste. When selecting the location of the waste site, caution should be used in areas with a high ground water table. Investigate the natural drainage of above ground water and avoid low drainage areas.

Consider the location of underground wells, springs used as primary water sources, creeks, rivers, dams, streams and other natural sources of water - keep the sewage away from these areas. Pathogens in feces can travel three hundred feet through the earth contaminating above and below ground water sources. The National Forest Service recommends <u>a minimum of two hundred feet between the sewage site and any open water source</u>. Depending on how long the sewage site would be used and how many team members would be "contributing" to the site; the depth of the hole must be deep enough to accommodate the decomposition process.

When preparing an outside sewage site, dig the hole at least four to six feet deep with a diameter of twelve to fourteen inches. If using a commode inside the primary residence and then transporting the waste directly to the outside sewage site, continue to dump the waste into the hole and place a sturdy board over the hole. If using an outhouse, a sturdy portable toilet with a seat could be placed securely over the hole.

The outhouse should be located at a site that avoids water contamination but still is adjacent to the primary residence and close enough so all team members can reach it easily and quickly to avoid the stress that comes with darkness and weather conditions in making the trip. Stock chlorinated lime or bleach to chemically and safely break down the waste matter. Lime that is powdered and <u>chlorinated</u> (not quick) is available at building supply stores and it can be used dry.

TOILET PAPER

As part of the emergency preparation pantry, I would suggest a **LARGE** supply of toilet paper is stored just for emergencies and nothing else. In other words – do not recycle this item. If you need more toilet paper for everyday use – buy it but do not use the toilet paper stored in the emergency pantries.

One method to establish how much <u>toilet paper</u> will be needed for emergency pantries is to start at the first of the month, and after a roll has been used, stack the empty rolls on the counter. Before beginning this exercise, ask all team members to use the toilet paper for its <u>intended purpose only</u> and not for removing makeup or blowing your nose. Instruct all members to be conservative in its use – <u>take what you need but need what you take</u>.

At the end of the month, count up how many empty rolls have been accumulated on the counter. Add an additional 20% to the total to account for the stress factor that can cause increased diarrhea during a disaster environment and using other toilet paper at school or work. This should provide a good estimate of how much toilet paper the team uses in a month. Now, simply do the math and figure out how much toilet paper needs to be stored for 3 months - 6 months - 9 months - **one year**. As part of the overall emergency preparation plan, try to work towards a one year supply! Remember - this toilet paper is for emergencies only! For everyday use, purchase separate toilet paper.

The table below provides the arithmetic for how many rolls of toilet paper will be needed <u>based on the number of empty toilet paper rolls on the counter at the end of the month</u>. These numbers **do not** reflect that additional 20% to account for stress and use outside of the home.

When purchasing toilet paper to fill emergency pantries, make sure you buy the same toilet paper size i.e. same type, single or double and/or number of squares, as used in the experiment so you really have the needed number of rolls based on this table.

ROLLS	3 Months	6 Months	9 Months	1 Year
1	3	6	9	12
2	6	12	18	24
3	9	18	27	36
4	12	24	36	48
5	15	30	45	60
6	18	36	54	72
7	21	42	63	84
8	24	48	72	96
9	27	54	81	108
10	30	60	90	120

PERSONAL HYGIENE

During a disaster, try to continue regular hygiene habits. This may help prevent the spread of disease and irritation as well as help relieve stress. Stock up on the following items:

- Acne Products
- Adult Diapers
- After Shave Lotion
- Alcohol Wipes
- Combs and Brushes
- Denture Supplies
- Feminine Wash
- Fingernail Clippers
- Fingernail Files
- Razors (disposable)
- Shaving Cream
- Tweezers

A small amount of hair is lost every day when we wash or comb our hair. However, during a disaster, when <u>stress</u> levels are high, even more hair will be lost. This type of hair loss is not permanent and will grow back - but plan on bigger hair piles in your comb and the shower drain.

BATH AND SHOWER

There are several alternatives that can be considered if shower and bathtub facilities are not available, water lines are damaged or destroyed, and/or water is scarce. **Unless drinking water is in ample supply, do not use drinking water for baths or showers! Instead, use water from natural sources, swimming pool, hot tub or radiators.** Depending on where you live, cold winter temperatures may not allow water to be heated by the sun.

Although a hard bar of soap is certainly acceptable to use when bathing or showering, during a disaster, it may be more prudent to use liquid soap or bath gel instead. Bath gel can be used to not only clean the body but can also serve as a shampoo to wash the hair. For a team on a budget, there would be only one product to buy instead of soap *and* shampoo. Costs less money and takes up less space - win/win.

Remember during a disaster environment, team members will get a lot dirtier than in a normal environment - simply from doing more "dirty" tasks required in a disaster situation. Even worse, showers or baths will more than likely be less often and less effective and doing laundry will also be challenging. When drying, use <u>paper towels</u>. Paper towels can be used again to perform cleaning chores or used as fire starter when building a fire. And don't forget to think outside the box for the best choice - you can always just stand still and let the air dry you off. . . . .who knew!!!

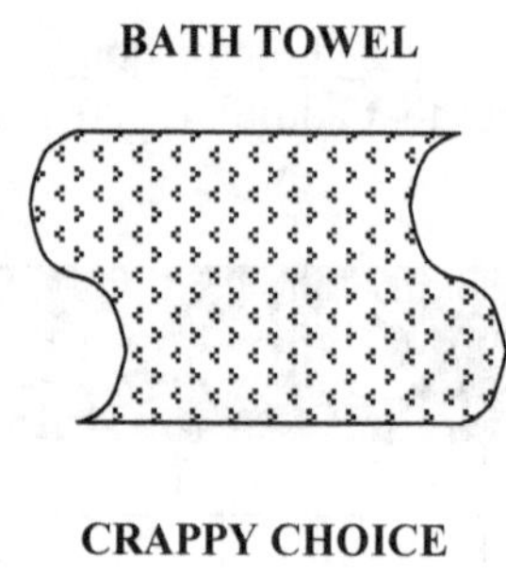		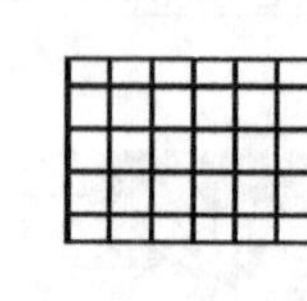	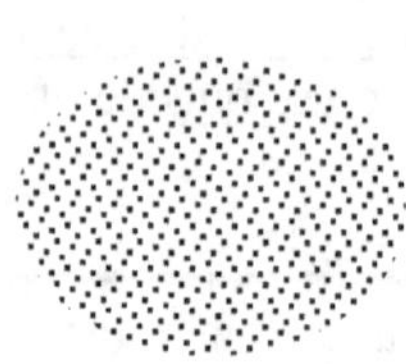
BATH TOWEL	**HAND TOWEL WASH CLOTH**	**PAPER TOWEL**	**AIR**
CRAPPY CHOICE	**BAD CHOICE**	**GOOD CHOICE**	**BEST CHOICE**
Large bath towel will get really filthy and will be very difficult to launder.	Hand towel and wash cloth will get extremely filthy and will be somewhat difficult to launder.	Paper towel can be used for other tasks and does not require laundering.	Air is free, needs no storage space and is always available. And even better - no laundering.

Here are suggestions for keeping clean. Review the choices and select the ones that are right for your team!

Disinfectant Washing

There is a method for cleaning external areas of the body that tend to take on offensive odors including the crotch, armpits and feet. Use a variety of alcohol-based products and a paper towel or rag, and while not actually getting clean from dirt, the alcohol kills odor-causing germs that cause skin diseases. Team members who are obese may have the same bacterial buildup between the folds and rolls of fat. Keep as clean as possible through regular methods of wiping with rubbing alcohol, lotions containing alcohol, shaving lotions, face creams or waterless hand sanitizer.

Moisture Wipes

If water is scarce or overly contaminated so as not to be able to use it for washing, bathing or showering - the best alternative is to store a large amount of moist towelettes or wipes. This alternative will eliminate the need for water and will still allow team members to stay clean and refreshed. There are countless types on the market - select one that provides cleaning for babies <u>and</u> adults and is safe for *face*, *hands* <u>and</u> *body*. When purchasing, buy the kind in plastic containers and covered in plastic wrap. The refills generally come with a heavy-duty plastic covering. When storing, place the container containing the wipes and any refills in a heavy-duty zip-lock baggie and then place the baggie in a heavy-duty (2 mil) garbage bag. Tightly seal the garbage bag. Place the wipes in a *cool*, *dark* and *dry* environment. *Prepare in advance* by stocking up on this product.

Spray Bottle Shower

A spray bottle can be used as a shower using a very small amount of water. Purchase or recycle a heavy-duty spray bottle with an adjustable spout that allows for a fine mist or a squirt-gun stream. Fill the spray bottle with water (<u>not</u> drinking water) and place in the sun (during warm days - temperatures above freezing). Once the water is heated, use a combination of spraying and wiping with a rag or small paper towel.

Large Spray Container Shower

A multi-gallon manually pressurized spray container with an attached handheld wand that is normally used for spraying weed killer or fertilizers can also be used as a shower. Obviously, if using this method for personal hygiene, <u>purchase a new container</u>. Simply fill the container with water (<u>not</u> drinking water) and place in the sun (during warm days - temperatures above freezing). Once the water is heated, pressurize the holding tank and enjoy a nice hot shower!

Solar Camping Shower

In the camping section at the local department or sporting goods store, you will find a fairly inexpensive portable shower consisting of a heavy-duty plastic bag and spray attachment. Fill the bag with water (<u>not</u> drinking water) and place in the sun (during warm days - temperatures above freezing). There is a hook on the bag for hanging on a tree branch or other structure. Using the wand attachment, release water over the body for a hands-free shower.

TEETH CLEANING

A good supply of <u>toothbrushes</u>, <u>toothpaste</u>, <u>dental floss</u>, <u>mouthwash</u>, and if applicable, <u>denture adhesive and cleaner</u> should be included in all pantries. Only safe drinking water should be used when brushing teeth or cleaning dentures - gray water can cause illness. **BE PREPARED!** It is surprising how much water is needed to brush teeth. Use an 8-ounce cup of water and brush your teeth. When finished, look and see how much water was used. As part of *planning in advance*, do the arithmetic and determine how many 8-ounce cups of water would be needed every day to <u>realistically</u> serve the needs of all team members for simply brushing teeth or cleaning dentures for one week, two weeks, one month, three months, six months and one year. The results will surprise you! That is why it is so important to store plenty of clean water.

When purchasing toothbrushes - buy the good ones. There are several companies that manufacture good toothbrushes including Colgate and Oral B. The cheaper toothbrushes tend to bend and break and will not hold up well. When doing the arithmetic for the number of toothbrushes needed at the primary residence and/or place of refuge to support a short, medium or long term disaster, a good rule of thumb is to plan on replacing a toothbrush every four months - thus, each team member would need three toothbrushes to support a disaster lasting one year. Make sure you also include toothbrushes and/or denture adhesive and cleaner in the evacuation, auto and work kits.

There are other options for keeping teeth clean including rags, washcloths or a willow or cottonwood tree containing salicin. Cut a fresh twig about the size of a pencil and chew the end until fuzzy - then use as a toothbrush. There will be a slightly bitter taste but it definitely works to clean the teeth. A substitute for toothpaste is baking soda or salt. There is no good alternative for dental floss - so - purchase and store dental floss. As a general rule, depending on how well toothpaste is conserved when used and how often teeth will be brushed, each team member should have one or two large tubes of toothpaste available at the primary residence and place of refuge to support a disaster lasting one year with smaller tubes in the evacuation, auto and work kits.

Another excellent piece of "dental equipment" to include in the emergency pantries is a "tongue scrapper" - located adjacent to the toothbrushes at the store. It is a plastic device that "scrapes the tongue" after brushing. You will NOT believe the "stuff" that will be on the scrapper after using it. And you actually thought your mouth was clean after just brushing!

LAUNDRY

Although laundry may not be a priority during a disaster, having clean (or at least cleaner) clothes must be addressed at some point in time. Clean clothing is especially important in a survival situation if there are cold temperatures. Depending on the circumstances and the availability of water sources, the team may just have to get used to wearing dirty clothes until power and water can be re-established! As part of *planning in advance*, it is a good idea for all team members to have several complete outfits of clothing available to wear in an emergency situation.

A primary objective would be to have water available for <u>drinking</u> purposes for the team, pets and livestock and then additional water could be gathered for other needs, including laundry. This water can be from natural sources including rivers, creeks, streams, springs or dams in the area or from swimming pools, hot tubs, radiators, hot water boilers, water beds or water collected from a rain barrel. Any gray water that has been used for dishwashing could be used again to wash out underwear and socks.

Here is a list of supplies for doing laundry by hand:

- Laundry detergent designed to be used in *cold* water
- Ivory or Zote hand soap
- Scrub Brush (for scrubbing stains)
- Tubs (3) – one (washing) two (rinsing)–consider kitchen sink
- Washboard
- Latex gloves (to prevent chapped and sore hands)
- Clothes Wringer
- Clothesline (outdoor drying)
- Clothes rack (indoor drying)
- Clothespins

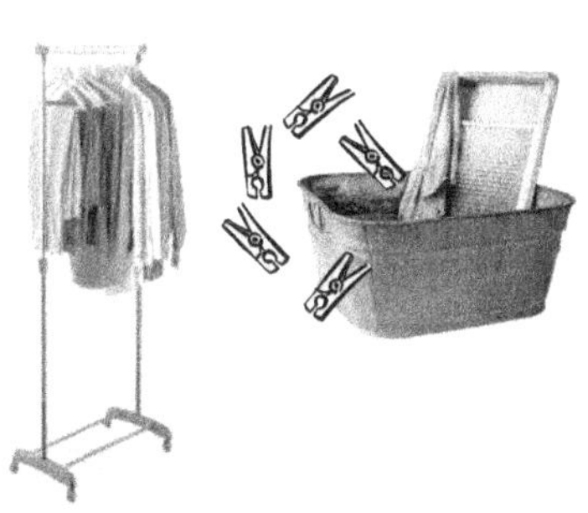

The kitchen sink or bathtub is probably the best place to wash clothes by hand providing there is a tight-fitting drain plug and the sewer lines are intact to dispose of the dirty water. Most kitchens have double sinks – one side would be for washing clothes and the other side would be for rinsing clothes. As a precaution, purchase several heavy-duty plastic tubs from the local department store. A washboard can also be purchased on the Internet from several companies. Remember, used laundry water can be used again for other purposes.

HOMEMADE LAUNDRY DETERGENT

Making your own laundry detergent for the emergency pantry can save a substantial amount of money by using specific products purchased at the local grocery store. There are countless recipes available on the Internet. I have used one particular recipe that has worked extremely well in getting my clothes fresh and clean. As I have continued to research laundry detergent, I discovered that it is not how <u>much</u> laundry detergent is used in a load of wash – what gets the clothes clean is the <u>ingredients</u> that are in the detergent.

I must warn you that when purchasing the ingredients, they are rather expensive, but when comparing the homemade product with a commercial brand, the <u>unit</u> cost per load is significantly less when using the homemade detergent. The secret? Use only 1/8 cup of the detergent for a full load! **With commercial detergent, you wash <u>ONE</u> load using one cup of detergent. With homemade detergent, you wash <u>EIGHT</u> loads using one cup of detergent.** I made several batches and stored it in plastic buckets with sealable lids. After placing the detergent in the buckets, I wrote down the actual recipe and put in the bucket as well. I then labeled the front of the buckets as "homemade laundry detergent".

The recipe is as follows:

- 12 cups Borax
- 8 cups Baking Soda
- 8 cups Washing Soda
- 2 ½ cups Fels Naptha® bar soap (grated)
- 2 ½ cups Zote bar soap (grated)
- 3 cups Ivory® bar soap (grated)

Mix all ingredients well and store in a sealed heavy-duty plastic bucket. **<u>Use 1/8 cup of powder per full load</u>**.

For bar soaps required in the recipe, do <u>not</u> use heavily perfumed soaps. Use a cheese grater to grate the soap <u>or</u> cut the soap into <u>small</u> chunks and use a high-end food processor to process soap down to a fine powder.

CLOTHES WRINGER

I made an investment in a <u>heavy-duty</u> and <u>commercial grade</u> clothes wringer and stand. That's right – the kind grandma used to wring out the water in clothes after they had been washed. There are several companies on the Internet that sell these clothes wringers. For me personally, I feel it is one of the most valuable items included in my overall emergency pantry. I have small hands and wringing water from clothes would be extremely difficult for me. A person with arthritis or rheumatism will also experience a similar problem. By using a clothes wringer, the clothes will dry faster because of less water; a fact that becomes important during cold or rainy weather or overcast days. A good heavy-duty wringer and stand will cost around $220.00. <u>However, an alternative clothes wringer would be cleaning buckets with an attached wringer used to wring out the mop - excellent choice for a beginner or teams on a budget!</u>

SOLAR CLEANING

During extended emergencies, we may have to wear a shirt for two or three days. Take it off occasionally and shake vigorously in a beam of sunlight. Sunlight contains ultraviolet radiation that kills waterborne germs and these same disinfecting benefits of ultraviolet radiation can work on the fabric of clothing. The more potent the sunlight, the better and faster the clothes are "washed". Simply collect dirty articles of clothing, turn them inside out, take them outdoors and vigorously shake each item. Spread clothing out in the full sun and off the ground – on a bush, fence or porch.

The more the entire surface area of the fabric is exposed to direct sunlight – the better. Flip the article of clothing in the middle of the day or after an entire day if you have the time. A hot summer day will "clean" a shirt in a few hours. A sun-washed garment will smell and feel cleaner as the ultraviolet radiation has baked to death those dinosaurs living in your sweat and dead skin cells.

CLEANERS AND DISINFECTANTS

During disaster conditions, it becomes important to keep surfaces free of spills and dirt - if nothing else - the surface looks better. For general cleaning, keep extra spray bottles of Pine-Sol, Formula 409, Windex or other cleaners in the cupboard. This type of cleaning method does not require any additional water but will clean up most messes.

Another alternative is to fill a spray bottle with water (white or gray) and add a small amount of either bleach or vinegar. Baking soda can also be used directly on a surface by adding a small amount of water and scrubbing the area. Of course, it is also important to store a good supply of hand sanitizer for ourselves and use it often during an emergency situation.

Don't forget to include a good floor broom, whisk broom, dust pan, mops and scrubbers in your cleaning arsenal. Another good addition - a **manual vacuum cleaner** used in restaurants!

It is also important to kill disease-causing germs while cleaning the primary residence. In this case, a disinfectant is needed such as Lysol which "kills germs on contact"! Household chlorine bleach is one of the best and most readily available choices as a disinfectant to control germs during emergency situations. Use a solution of one part liquid chlorine bleach to ten parts water (approximately one cup bleach to one-half gallon of water). Bleach should contain at least 5 ¼ % sodium hypochlorite. You can also use "ultra" bleaches which are 6% sodium hypochlorite. Do <u>not</u> use dry or powdered bleach – it is caustic.

Over the years, manufacturers have combined ingredients to create powerful cleaners that also serve as disinfectants. Depending on the product, it can be used on all surfaces or is limited to just specific surfaces.

ALWAYS READ THE LABEL ON CLEANERS AND DISINFECTANTS - THERE IS A DIFFERENCE BETWEEN CLEANING AND SANITIZING. Make sure you are getting the right cleaner and/or disinfectant product for the right job and when practical, purchase all-purpose products that clean <u>and</u> disinfect.

FEMININE HYGIENE

When preparing for emergency situations, feminine hygiene products are many times not included in emergency pantries. Most women try to store at least a one month supply so when the time arrives each month, they are not forced to run to the store to pick up pads or tampons. When *planning in advance*, each girl or woman who needs to worry about this monthly event should determine how many individual pads or tampons are used each month and then multiply that number by twelve months.

PAPER AND PLASTIC PRODUCTS

Paper and plastic products are critical for sanitation during a normal environment and will become even more important during a disaster. There are many different paper and plastic products used for different tasks - including personal hygiene, cooking cleaning and general use and include such items as toilet paper, paper towels, napkins, adult diapers, baggies and garbage bags.

As a beginning student to emergency preparation, it is sometimes difficult to determine how much or how many items will be needed to support the team for one month, three months, six months or one year. It is also tricky to decide how much product will be needed for each of the pantries - the primary residence, place of refuge (if applicable), evacuation (sometimes referred to as the 72-hour kit), auto kit and the work kit.

Similar to the toilet paper project, and for other paper and plastic products, conduct an experiment or make an analysis to determine how many rolls, boxes or packages are used on a monthly basis by all team members. Start at the beginning of the month and keep track of the empty rolls, packages or boxes. At the end of the month - use the formula in the table below to estimate how much product will be needed to support a one month, three month, six month or one year disaster. Purchase additional quantities to support the place of refuge, evacuation, auto and work kits.

PRODUCT	COMMENTS	FORMULA FOR PRIMARY RESIDENCE
Facial Tissues	During any disaster, the need for facial tissues could escalate due to stress and other factors. Stressful events can also trigger allergies, sinus infections and colds calling for additional tissues to wipe the eyes and nose. For this experiment, place <u>one</u> tissue box in the residence to be used by all team members for the entire month. Remove all other tissue boxes in the residence during the experiment. When the tissue box is empty, replace it with another full box. Use these tissues for the intended purpose, i.e., wiping the nose, eyes etc.	At the end of the month, count up the number of empty tissue boxes. Add **six** additional boxes (<u>the stress factor</u>) to the total. Multiply by one, three, six or twelve months to determine the number of boxes required to meet a one month, three month, six month or one year supply <u>for the primary residence</u>.
Paper Towels	During any disaster, the need for paper towels will increase due to possible fluctuations with the water supply and increased urgency to keep a sanitary environment. For this experiment, place <u>one</u> paper towel in the residence to be used by all team members for the entire month. Remove all other paper towels in the residence during the experiment. When the paper towel roll is empty, replace it with another full roll. Use these paper towels for the intended purpose, i.e., cleaning the counters, walls, windows, appliances and wiping up spills etc.	At the end of the month, count up the number of empty paper towel rolls and add **three** additional rolls (<u>stress factor</u>) to the total. Multiply by one, three, six or twelve months to determine the number of rolls required to meet a one month, three month, six month or one year supply <u>for the primary residence</u>.
Plastic Grocery Bags	These plastic grocery bags serve many general light-duty uses. After emptying groceries or other supplies from the plastic grocery bag, place used grocery bags in a tote or container. If double bagged, these grocery bags can be placed in the toilet bowl or waste container of a commode for easy disposal. They could also store used adult and baby diapers and used toilet paper. Consider each team member will require <u>one</u> grocery bag per day.	Number of team members to obtain daily total needed. Multiply total by 30, 90, 180 or 365 days to determine the number of grocery bags required to meet a one month, three month, six month or one year supply <u>for the primary residence</u>.
Paper Napkins	Assumption is made that meals will be served four times per day (breakfast, lunch, snack and dinner), and for each meal, each team member will require one napkin.	Multiply <u>four</u> napkins by the total number of team members to determine number of napkins needed <u>per day</u>. Multiply total by 30, 90, 180 or 365 days to determine the number of napkins required to meet a one month, three month, six month or one year supply <u>for the primary residence</u>.
Diapers Adult	Adult team members required to use diapers should stock a sufficient amount to be used during a disaster. The consequences of not doing so become obvious when it comes time to do the laundry.	Number of team members using adult diapers multiplied by total number of diapers used per day. Multiply total by 30, 90, 180 or 365 days to determine the number of diapers required to meet a one month, three month, six month or one year supply <u>for the primary residence</u>.
Plastic Trash Bags 13 gallon **1 mil**	These <u>heavy-duty</u> trash bags are used for *kitchen* trash cans and/or for placing in a *toilet* or *commode* to collect human waste when water and/or sewer lines prevent the regular use of the toilet. Two (one for kitchen trash and one for toilet/commode to collect human waste) trash bags <u>per day</u> for every <u>three</u> team members.	Number of members times two. Divide total by three (not less than 1; round up). Multiply total by 30, 90, 180 or 365 days to determine number of 13 gallon trash bags required to meet a one month, three month, six month or one year supply <u>for the primary residence</u>.

PRODUCT	COMMENTS	FORMULA FOR PRIMARY RESIDENCE
Plastic Trash Bags 33 gallon **1.05 mil**	These <u>heavy-duty</u> trash bags are generally used for medium-size trash cans collecting *regular trash, human waste, dirty diapers*, etc. Since these bags could be storing human waste and wet materials, a minimum of 1.05 mil will be required. One trash bag <u>per day</u> for every <u>three</u> team members.	Number of team members and divide total by three (not less than 1; round up). Multiply total by 30, 90, 180 or 365 days to determine the number of 33 gallon trash bags required to meet a one month, three month, six month or one year supply <u>for the primary residence</u>.
Plastic Trash Bags 55 gallon **2 mil**	These <u>heavy-duty</u> trash bags are generally used for large and extra large trash cans supporting *yard debris, regular trash* etc. One trash bag <u>per week</u> for every three team members.	Number of team members and divide total by three (not less than 1; round up) to determine weekly amount. Multiply weekly total by 4, 12, 26 or 52 weeks to determine the number of 33 gallon trash bags required to meet a one month, three month, six month or one year supply <u>for the primary residence</u>.
Plastic Baggies	Store heavy-duty zip-lock plastic baggies in all the various types and sizes available, i.e., gallon, quart and sandwich sizes. Baggies will serve as excellent storage containers for not only food but other items as well.	4-5 large boxes of each size

The team has now determined how many paper and plastic products to purchase for emergency preparation - it is time to spread the products across the various emergency pantries. A top priority for all teams is to have a good supply of paper and plastic products for *all* emergency pantries. Shown below is a table listing <u>general</u> guidelines for recommended supplies to be stored at the primary residence, place of refuge (if applicable), evacuation kits, auto kits and work kits:

Primary Residence	Place of Refuge	Evacuation	Auto	Work
Toilet Paper (1 year supply)	**Toilet Paper** (6 month supply)	**Toilet Paper** 1 roll for each kit (person) to support a minimum of 7-14 days	**Toilet Paper** (1 large roll)	**Toilet Paper** (1 large roll)
Paper Towels (1 year supply)	**Paper Towels** (6 month supply)	**Paper Towels** 1 roll per three persons to support a minimum of 7-14 days	**Paper Towels** (1 large roll)	**Paper Towels** (1 large roll)
Facial Tissues (1 year supply)	**Facial Tissues** (6 month supply)	**Facial Tissues** 1 small box for each kit (person) to support a minimum of 7-14 days	**Facial Tissues** (1 large box)	**Facial Tissues** (1 large box)
Paper Napkins (1 year supply)	**Paper Napkins** (6 month supply)	**Paper Napkins** 30-50 napkins for each kit (person) to support a minimum of 7-14 days	**Paper Napkins** (10-50) depending on how many members regularly ride in car	**Paper Napkins** (10)
Plastic Grocery Bags (1 year supply)	**Plastic Grocery Bags** (6 month supply)	**Plastic Grocery Bags** 3 bags for each kit (person) to support a minimum of 7-14 days	**Plastic Grocery Bags** (3-5) depending on how many members regularly ride in car	**Plastic Grocery Bags** (2)

Primary Residence	Place of Refuge	Evacuation	Auto	Work
Diapers (Adult) (1 year supply)	**Diapers (Adult)** (6 month supply)	**Diapers (Adult)** (1 or 2 per day to support 7-14 days)	**Diapers (Adult)** (1 or 2 per day to support at least 3-5 days)	**Diapers (Adult)** (1 or 2 per day to support at least 3-5 days)
Plastic Trash Bags 13 gallon kitchen + toilet 1 mil - heavy duty (1 year supply)	**Plastic Trash Bags** 13 gallon kitchen + toilet 1 mil - heavy duty (6 month supply)	**Plastic Trash Bags** 13 gallon-toilet 1 mil - heavy duty 2-3 for each kit (person) to support 7-14 days	**Plastic Trash Bags** 13 gallon-general 1 mil - heavy duty (1)	**Plastic Trash Bags** 13 gallon-general 1 mil - heavy duty (1)
Plastic Trash Bags 33 gallon general + waste 1.05 mil - heavy duty (1 year supply)	**Plastic Trash Bags** 33 gallon general + waste 1.05 mil - heavy duty (6 month supply)	**Plastic Trash Bags** 33 gallon-general 1.05 mil - heavy duty 1 for each kit (person) to support 7-14 days	**Plastic Trash Bags** 33 gallon-general 1.05 mil-heavy duty (1)	**Plastic Trash Bags** 33 gallon-general 1.05 mil-heavy duty (1)
Plastic Trash Bags 55 gallon yard + general 2 mil minimum (1 year supply)	**Plastic Trash Bags** 55 gallon yard + general 2 mil minimum (6 month supply)	**Plastic Trash Bags** 55 gallon-general 2 mil minimum 1 for each kit (person) to support 7-14 days Used as ground tarp	**Plastic Trash Bags** 55 gallon-general 2 mil minimum (1)	**Plastic Trash Bags** 55 gallon-general 2 mil minimum (1) *Used as floor tarp in public shelter*
Plastic Baggies Zip-Lock All types and Sizes (1 year supply)	**Plastic Baggies** Zip-Lock All Types and Sizes (6 month supply)	**Plastic Baggies** Zip-Lock All Types and Sizes (1-2 for each kit (person) to support 7-14 days)	**Plastic Baggies** Zip-Lock All Types and Sizes (1-2)	**Plastic Baggies** Zip Lock All Types and Sizes (1-2)

The place of refuge is either an (1) alternate to the primary residence if the primary residence is no longer habitable, i.e., cabin, motor home, trailer, camper, etc., **or** (2) considered as the primary residence and members will automatically travel to this location at the onset of the disaster. Not everyone will have a "private" place of refuge available and if the primary residence becomes uninhabitable, these team members would be forced to locate to a public shelter or other site such as a field, mountains or empty building. In these cases, emergency supplies could not be stocked in advance and members would have to rely on the evacuation kit for supplies or supplies provided by others. With regards to the place of refuge and stocking supplies, consider these guidelines:

IF	THEN
Team has a private place of refuge such as a cabin, motor home, trailer or camper that will be used in the event the primary residence is inhabitable.	In addition to stocking the primary residence as outlined in the above table, try to also stock <u>at least</u> a six month supply of provisions at the place of refuge.
Team has a cabin, motor home, trailer or camper that will serve as the primary residence at the onset of the disaster (will not use team member's places of residence as a primary residence).	Consider this location as the primary residence and follow the guidelines for stocking a one year supply. Ignore the guidelines for place of refuge in above table.
Team does not have a place of refuge and will be forced to locate to a public shelter or other undetermined site.	Stock the primary residence as outlined in the above table, ignore guidelines for place of refuge and include additional provisions in the evacuation and auto kits if possible to be used at a public shelter or other undetermined site.

TRASH DISPOSAL

Remember to always dispose of trash on garbage pickup day – even if you have a small amount. At the onset of an emergency – you want an empty trashcan. In addition to a human waste problem during an emergency, consider the most sanitized method of disposing of <u>regular</u> garbage.

For short-term emergencies, communicate with government officials to find out when regular garbage pickup will begin again and make sure the trashcan full of regular garbage is out on the curb on time. If garbage pickup will not be in service for an extended period of time, drain the garbage of all liquid - it can then be stored for a longer period of time. The ability to burn garbage is the ideal solution. <u>As a last resort</u>, both garbage and human waste should be buried no less than twelve inches deep in the ground - preferably eighteen to twenty-four inches.

PESTS

An overall lack of administration, facilities, materials and supplies increases the likelihood of disease and vermin. There will be an increase in rats, mice, flies, wasps, mosquitoes, cockroaches and ants. The presence of wildlife will also be prevalent as raccoons, skunks, squirrels and other animals begin to encroach on urban and rural areas in search of food. As part of *planning in advance*, store adequate rat and mouse traps, fly swatters, as well as fly, wasp, mosquito and ant traps or killer.

DEATH

One of the most difficult circumstances team members may be forced to deal with is the death of a loved one or another person. Major disasters would stretch emergency response personnel to the limit and firemen, police, sheriff, hospital, coroner, mortician and medical personnel who would normally save us from having to witness death in its raw state may be unavailable as a first responder in a disaster situation.

The process that goes into human remains after a disaster is difficult and complicated. During *short-term* disasters, <u>attempt to contact and wait for the authorities before disposing of a body</u>. Depending on the circumstances, and the time of season (hot versus cold temperatures) – many local churches may be able to store dead bodies at their respective locations as a <u>short-term solution</u> until arrangements are made to transport the body to another location (refrigerated storage, hospital, mortuary or cemetery). It is wise to contact church leaders and local government authorities *in advance* to find out what arrangements have been made for a <u>temporary</u> morgue to store dead bodies during a disaster. You may be surprised to learn that government officials do not have <u>any</u> plan in place to manage death during a crisis.

Depending on the level of the disaster, individual citizens may be required to process dead bodies in their area because the burial of the body in the cemetery may not be an option. During a Level 1, Level 2 or even at the beginning of a Level 3 disaster, if you do anything with a dead body, you would be scrutinized by government officials after the dust settles. <u>*Document everything in writing*</u> including the following information:

- Name of Deceased Person(s)
- Sex
- Age
- Cause of death
- Time of death
- Circumstances surrounding the death

> ***You only live twice. Once when you are born and once when you look death in the face.***
>
> **- Ian Fleming**

If you have access to a camera, take photographs of everything you do. Recognize that there is a series of regulations for removing a body, including inspection of the site, examination of the body, collecting evidence, photographing the scene and questioning witnesses. Document the circumstances surrounding the situation. During severe and long-term disasters, government may not exist or at least not to the point where any oversight for death and burial issues would be an issue.

During a disaster, and if a team member, relative, friend, co-worker or neighbor is lost, the stress and feeling of loss can be overwhelming but we will have no choice but to move forward and sometimes very quickly in order to survive another day. Frankly, you may be put in the position where you have to manage the death of this person.

DEAD BODIES

Immediately following a disaster, the priorities of the team will be to care for other survivors by modifying shelters, disinfecting drinking water, finding heat and light, providing effective emergency sanitation and getting food. Only after the immediate needs for the <u>living</u> are addressed should the team begin to deal with the death issue.

If storage at the local mortuary, church or refrigerated storage facility is not an option, temporary burials may be necessary until conditions allow transfer of the body to its final resting place or depending on the <u>level</u> of the disaster – it may be necessary to permanently bury the body.

PRIORITIZE WHAT NEEDS TO HAPPEN TO PROTECT THE *LIVING* FROM FURTHER DANGER, DEAL DECISIVELY WITH THE DEAD BODY, AND THEN ALLOW YOURSELF AND YOUR TEAM MEMBERS TO CONSCIOUSLY MOVE THROUGH A HEALING PROCESS.

Recognize that a death caused by suffocation, stabbing, blunt-force trauma, shooting, drowning or burning will <u>not</u> result in bodies spreading disease and during most disasters, these are the major causes of death.

The World Health Organization (WHO) has stated:

"Dead or decayed human bodies do not generally create a serious health hazard unless they are polluting sources of drinking water with fecal matter or are infected with plague or typhus in which case they may be infested with the fleas or lice that spread these diseases".

Most medical opinions confirm that dead bodies are <u>not</u> dangerous in spreading disease because body temperature drops rapidly after death killing most resistant viruses and bacteria. The disease-causing microorganisms living in bodies of both humans and animals that create health risks need a specific environment to cause disease and these little guys need to continue to live in that right environment after the host dies. In most cases, the temperature drop kills the microorganisms.

Only in rare cases will the microorganisms continue to live; for example, if the environment supports the spread of the disease such as severed sanitation systems, overcrowded shelters or when the bodies are host to a disease common for the area. Granted - there are documented exceptions such as outbreaks of cholera, hepatitis, typhus and bubonic plague due to bodies being accessed and diseases transmitted by flies, mice and rats. The HIV virus has also been found active within a dead body sixteen days after death. Tuberculosis is contagious and dead bodies suspected of having the disease should have a cloth placed over the mouth and handled in open areas.

The process of *putrefaction* is caused by different microorganisms than those causing a disease. In putrefaction, dead bodies left exposed to the elements will quickly decompose – especially in hot weather. The rate of decomposition of a body depends on the amount of bacteria already present within the intestines at the time of death. The process of decomposition will manifest within a few days depending on the environmental conditions and the stench and visible sight of the dead would cause pain and suffering in the general population. The body will need to be buried.

BURIAL

When burying a body, and if practical under the circumstances, attempt to practice accepted precautions against blood and body fluids at all times when burying a body by following these guidelines:

- Wear gowns, aprons, coveralls or a large heavy-duty garbage bag when doing anything that would likely splash blood or other bodily fluids.

- Wear masks, protective eyewear, face shields, dust masks or goggles when coming in contact with a corpse

- Wear disposable latex or vinyl gloves when handling the body or anything associated with the body.

- Thoroughly wash hands and other parts of your body by dipping hands in a chlorine bleach solution upon removing gloves and dispose of them properly.

- Do not smoke, eat or drink when disposing of a dead body, and avoid touching your own mouth, eyes or nose.

- Cover all cuts and abrasions with waterproof bandages or dressings

- Disinfect all equipment, vehicles and contaminated surfaces after disposal of the body with freshly prepared 0.1 percent chlorine bleach solution.

- Put the body in body bags, fifty-five gallon garbage bags or plastic sheeting and secure tightly with duct tape.

- Dig the grave at least one hundred feet away from all surface water sources and the bottom of any grave should be at least five feet above the water table with a two-foot unsaturated zone. Attempt to have the body under at least three feet of earth. Mound up the earth several inches on top of the hole.

- Mark the grave in a way that identifies who is buried there and initiate a funeral service or rite-of-passage ritual to begin closure and healing for family members.

Remember that good sanitation practices will be critical for all team members during any level of disaster. Keep in mind that a *decrease* in sanitation conditions will easily result in an *increase* of diseases that usually would not be prevalent in a normal environment. Also, consequences in the SANITATION Element produce an unusually high peak in irritability among the general population – and especially in women and girls.

CRACKED WHEAT CASSEROLE

1 pound ground beef
½ teaspoon salt
¼ teaspoon oregano
¼ teaspoon black pepper
¼ cup Parmesan cheese
2 tablespoons parsley, chopped
1 teaspoon beef bouillon
½ cup onion, chopped
1 small garlic clove, minced
1 ½ cups water
½ cup cracked wheat, uncooked
1 cup tomatoes, chopped

Brown ground beef with onion and garlic until pink color has gone from meat. Drain. Combine with remaining ingredients except cheese and tomato. Bake in tightly covered 1 ½ quart casserole dish for 45 minutes or until cracked wheat is tender and water has been absorbed. Stir in cheese and tomato and let stand for one minute before serving.

PINTO BEAN CASSEROLE

1 (15-ounce) can pinto beans with juice
1 pound ground beef
1 package corn tortillas
1 cup cheese, grated
1 (15-ounce) can Italian-style Marinara Sauce
½ cup sour cream (optional)

Butter tortillas and layer bottom of a 13x9x2 inch cake pan. Brown ground beef and drain. Place beans over tortillas, then sauce and ground beef and grated cheese. Bake at 350 degrees for 30 minutes. Top each serving with sour cream, if desired.

RICE A RONI

½ cup rice
1 teaspoon chicken soup base
½ teaspoon dried onion
c teaspoon ginger
½ teaspoon salt
¼ cup chicken
¼ cup dry spaghetti
1 tablespoon shortening
½ teaspoon parsley
c teaspoon garlic
c teaspoon pepper
1 cup water

Break spaghetti into 1-inch pieces. Fry rice and spaghetti in melted shortening, stirring frequently until brown. Add onion, garlic and ginger. Add soup base to water to make broth and add to rice and spaghetti mixture. Add chicken and parsley. Cover with tight-fitting lid. Cook at very **LOW** heat for 25 minutes until rice is tender.

BASIC MAYONNAISE

1 egg
1 teaspoon dry mustard, ground
Dash cayenne pepper
¼ teaspoon salt
1 teaspoon granulated white sugar
1 ¼ cups salad oil
3 teaspoons lemon juice

Put egg, mustard, salt, cayenne, sugar and ¼ cup salad oil in blender and blend until thoroughly combined. With blender still running, take off cover and slowly add ½ cup salad oil and then lemon juice until thoroughly blended. It may be necessary to stop and start blender to stir down mayonnaise. *Note: Mayonnaise will not bind on high humidity days. If recipe fails, pour mixture into another container, put another egg into blender, beating thoroughly. Pour back original mixture very slowly. Spoon back into clean jar, cover and refrigerate.*

WHEAT SPROUT PATTIES

2 cups wheat sprouts
2 tablespoons onion, minced
2 tablespoons mushroom, chopped
1 egg, slightly beaten
2 tablespoons green pepper, minced
Dash of garlic powder
Dash of pepper
Dash of celery salt
Butter *or* oil

Grind sprouts. Add egg and vegetables. Mix well. In skillet, heat butter, garlic powder and pepper. Using large spoon, drop sprout mixture into skillet and press with back of fork to form patties, no more than ½ inch thick. Cook for 2 minutes on each side over medium heat until lightly brown. Sprinkle with celery salt to taste.

CHAPTER FOURTEEN

FUEL CONSUMPTION

Fuel – a "driving" force in this country – and around the world. Without fuel sources, the entire world would come to a screeching halt. There would be no truck drivers transporting food, clothing, toilet paper or medicines to markets around the country. There would be no citizens driving cars to work or to a favorite destination. There would be no furnace, water heater or cooking range in operation. We could say farewell to lipstick, makeup, nail polish and hair dye products.

The grass around our yards would continue to grow from lack of lawn care. We would no longer be able to purchase detergents to wash clothes and dishes. There would be no cab drivers, no trains, no subways, no boats and no airplanes. The equipment relying on oil for lubrication would be silent. The fireplaces would be dark and empty. There would no longer be any war machine – helicopters, planes and tanks could no longer support aggression or killing sprees. Not only would there be no need for roads because vehicles lack fuel – but there would be no new roads or any repaired roads using asphalt and other oil based products. The shingles on a roof would no longer be replaced – again, many roofing products are made from oil.

There would also be no electricity. In order to generate electricity, fuel is needed to operate the equipment that generates electrical power. Coal is the major fuel source used to generate electrical power around the world. Natural gas is also a fuel source for generating electricity through the use of gas and steam turbines. Most grid peaking power plants and some off-grid engine generators use natural gas.

During good times and bad times, fuel is a valuable commodity – but during a disaster, a continuous fuel source becomes a major priority and a challenge to acquire for team members. There are many types of fuel available through commercial markets and natural resources. Each type of fuel serves a specific need and in some cases, one type of fuel can support various elements.

For example, gasoline is used as the fuel to operate a home generator. Gasoline and diesel are also major fuel sources for vehicles on the road. Propane is used as the fuel source to heat homes but it is also used as a fuel source on barbeque grills used to cook our food. Oil is used to lubricate vehicles, generators, and equipment and is as a major component in cosmetics, medicines and plastics.

The **FUEL CONSUMPTION** Element is vulnerable to not only specific natural and manmade disasters such as earthquakes (natural) and war (manmade), fuel sources can also be affected by environmental and political situations. For example, political confrontations between our government and the governments in the Middle East, South America and other countries exporting oil to the United States could influence the availability of oil and the price to purchase fuel sources. There could also be environmental impacts affecting our ability to obtain fuel including oil spills, solar flares and depletion of forests.

For emergency planning, team members should recognize that during a Level One and Level Two disaster, there would most likely be fuel sources available – either at the primary residence or available through commercial outlets. However, as we enter a Level Three (1 month to 1 year) disaster and edge towards the one year period of time, most commercial fuel sources, i.e., gasoline, propane, natural gas, oil and wood would be depleted.

Most fuels and especially oil, gasoline and diesel have a limited shelf life and it becomes impractical to store large quantities for emergency preparation purposes. Natural gas and propane have a long shelf-life, but these fuels must be distributed and transported using pipelines and trucks. Propane, however, once received at the primary residence and stored in propane tanks could provide a valuable fuel source during a short-term, medium-term or long-term disaster.

There is another fuel source used for lighting that can be stored for long periods of time. Lamp oil can be purchased in most department, hardware and grocery stores and generally comes in one quart to one gallon size plastic bottles. In the past, lamp oil was very inexpensive, but over the years, it has become more expensive and today, it can cost as much as twenty dollars for a medium size bottle. For many years, I have purchased lamp oil and transferred it into five-gallon plastic gas containers.

EMERGENCY PREPARATION PRINCIPLES

There are <u>six</u> principles that can be incorporated into the overall emergency plan to prepare for and in some cases eliminate fuel issues that would become prevalent during an emergency situation. For example:

- **Purchases for the FUEL Element are a high priority** – we are dealing with ultimate survival – the fuel sources for generating electrical power, providing light and heat, supporting our massive transportation needs and providing the means to prepare food.

- **Know your fuel inventory and where it is stored**. Know how much you have of all resources. Make sure they are readily available and logistically located for easy access and transport.

- **Practice absolute safety procedures and guidelines** when using and storing all fuel sources. Keep all fuel out of the reach of children and away from pets.

- **Rotate fuel supplies** that have a short shelf life.

- Use only **approved storage containers** to store liquid fuel sources (gasoline) and heavy-duty tarps to store solid fuel sources (wood).

- Practice <u>enhanced</u> **security procedures** when storing all fuel sources. Remember, during an emergency, others may feel the urge to help themselves to your fuel supplies.

FUEL TYPES

There are many fuel types available through government agencies, public utilities, commercial enterprises, privately-owned companies and private land-owners. There are various *alternatives* or *layers* of fuel that can be used for many uses during an emergency. As part of *planning in advance*, team members should arrange to have an adequate supply of fuel for at least short-term disasters.

<u>Propane</u>

As part of *planning in advance*, I installed <u>three</u> propane tanks comprising 2,500 gallons that under normal circumstances, would serve to heat my home for two years. When the tanks were installed, the supplier installed a valve on top of one tank allowing me to siphon propane out of the large tank into a smaller five-gallon tank.

I also purchased a 300 gallon propane tank with a valve on top to be used exclusively for my barbeque grill. A five-gallon propane tank can last about 120 hours and is refillable. Depending on the situation, smaller cylinders of propane can be purchased at commercial outlets and will last two to five hours on a two-burner stove. These cylinders are non-refillable and automatically reseal themselves when removed from the equipment.

<u>Wood</u>

In the United States, there is a tremendous amount of wood throughout the country. Unfortunately, this wood is not available "for the taking" by citizens. The wood sources are owned by government (federal, state, county or city), corporations or individual citizens. To harvest your own wood on public lands, a permit is required. Other wood sources are owned by public and private companies including utilities, ranches, farms and lumber companies. Commercial stores and outlets own the trees growing on their properties. And last – but certainly not least – the property owners (citizens) own the trees growing on privately-owned land.

If purchasing wood from a public or private retail source, it can be expensive; generally costing around $150-$200 a cord (a cord is 128 cubic feet when neatly stacked in a line or row. A standard cord would be eight feet long, four feet wide and four feet high - loosely defined as a pickup truck load). How long the wood burns will depend on the efficiency of the fireplace or stove, type of wood, dryness of wood, log size, and humidity of surrounding area. Hardwood will generally burn longer than softwood. Wood should be kept dry by covering it with a tarp or heavy plastic. Always wear gloves when picking up wood – spiders make their home in woodpiles.

Although wood is a common fuel source, it can only be common as long as there is an ample supply available to citizens for heating, cooking and recreation.

During a crisis environment, and once the population figures out regular channels for getting fuel is no longer available, most citizens will begin a frantic and frenzied search for anything that can be used to make a fire. Prepare to witness any and all wood products (trees, shrubs, telephone poles, fence posts, abandoned buildings and sheds, furniture and road signs) being confiscated and plan to see a landscape once flourishing with trees and shrubs being wiped clean by individuals looking for fuel to heat their homes and cook their food.

Oil

Purchase and store necessary gasoline and oil products needed to support generators, and other mechanical equipment. Due to short shelf life with some products, use a rotation system to maintain a free supply.

> Make a self contained wick that will burn a long time and can be placed in kindling to start the fire. Supplies include an airtight and waterproof container, cotton balls or Styrofoam balls and petroleum jelly. Have the container opened and ready to place fire starters in as you make them. Take petroleum jelly and cover the outside of the cotton ball. When the ball is totally covered, place in the container. The ball will serve as a wick and the petroleum jelly will be the fuel. Place a ball under the starter kindling and light it. Because you are using petroleum jelly it is resistant to dampness.

Pressed-Wood Logs

These logs are expensive ($1.50-$6.00) and burn for two or five hours but do not emit a large amount of heat. It is cheaper to buy these logs by the case at discount department stores and watch for sales.

Newspaper Logs

A newspaper log is an economical method to recycle newspapers while at the same time having an available heat (and light) source during emergency situations. They can be stacked and stored the same way you stack wood logs. When making newspaper logs, you can build your "log pile" all year long. To make newspaper logs, you will need newspaper, thin or fine wire or strong cord, a five gallon tub or bucket, laundry detergent and water. The newspapers should be the width of a standard sheet of newspaper (not a double sheet). GOOD IDEA!

The instructions for making newspaper logs are as follows:

- Open several sections of the paper (14 inches wide, 26 inches long) and make a stack 3 to 4 inches thick.

- Cut the wire or cord into sixteen-inch pieces.

- Stack several sections of newspaper on top of each other about two inches deep. These sections should be folded in the middle, like they are laid on your porch or at a newspaper stand (fourteen by thirteen inches).

- Grasp the papers on the fold and begin rolling the whole stack <u>tightly</u> into a tube about four inches wide. *The more compactly paper is rolled, the heavier the finished log and the longer it will burn.*

- Holding the tube of newspapers tightly, lay it on the edge of a 14 x 20 inch newspaper section, roll it up in the new section until about eight inches of paper remains.

- Slip another section of newspaper into the space between the unrolled paper and the rolled log.

- Continue rolling and roll until about eight inches of paper from the newest section remain and then slip another section in and keep rolling. Continue the process until you have a log about six inches in diameter.

- Holding the log firmly so that it will not unroll (kneeling on it works), slip a piece of wire or cord under the newspaper log, wrap it around, and twist or tie it tightly. The ends of cut wire are sharp – be careful.

- Tie another piece of wire or cord on the other end of the log.

- Thoroughly soak the log in a detergent solution and let it dry (fill a plastic tub or bin with enough water to cover the logs. Add a tablespoon of regular laundry detergent to the water and swish it through the water so it mixes well. Make sure any lumps are thoroughly dissolved).

- Set the log on its end on a level platform to drain and dry. It may take several days for the logs to thoroughly dry. Stack the newspaper logs as you would regular wood.

Coal

Coal is another alternative as a heat source. Since coal burns hotter than wood, coal is an option only if you have a firebrick-lined fireplace or a stove specifically designed for coal. Coal fires are not easy to start and you must follow a specific and regular procedure of loading, shaking, raking and adjusting coal. If you don't follow the correct procedure - the fire will go out.

If coal is your only heat source, you would probably burn about one ton per month in a coal-burning stove or in the fireplace depending on the weather and the type of coal. Hard coal burns longer and better than soft coal. Coal takes up less space than firewood for a commensurate amount of heat produced and can be purchased in bulk, bags or boxes. Coal should be kept dry and covered in a bin or container.

Canned Heat

Canned heat is a jelled petroleum product that comes in a small can, is stable for storage indoors and outdoors, doesn't spill and it lights easily with a match or lighter. All back-pack stoves are made to be used with the jelled fuel because it is light, compact and easy to use. Canned heat can be used for warmth but should not be considered as a major heat source. It is also used for cooking (warming chafing dishes and fondue pots). Canned heat evaporates readily if exposed to air so keep the lid tightly closed when not in use. To extinguish the flame, replace the lid on the container. The shelf life for canned heat is about ten years.

Butane

Butane is pressurized in canisters and there are no liquids to spill. It is safe to use and burns 100 percent clean with no odors, residue or smoke. The canister will burn from two to four hours in a stove, three hours in a heater and five hours in a lantern. Butane is safe to use indoors with proper ventilation. Butane does not work well in cold weather.

Lamp Oil

Using oil lamps for light is a good idea. For the most part, an oil lamp will provide much greater light than a candle. One method to increase the output of light with an oil lamp (and also a candle), is to place a mirror or aluminum plate behind the lamp or candle. The light will reflect off the mirror or plate and provide enhanced light.

Lamp oil is highly refined liquid paraffin oil. It is clean burning, does not leave residual odors or soot, stores well in bottles or containers, and is smokeless when the wicks are correctly adjusted. An ounce of oil in an oil lamp will last approximately five hours. When purchasing lamp oil, make sure you purchase **extra wicks** for the lamp. These wicks can generally be purchased at large department stores and hardware stores.

White Gas

White gas is referred to as *camping fuel* - an unleaded gasoline that is cleaned and modified to operate efficiently in camping equipment and is one-third the cost of propane cylinders. Camping fuel is highly flammable and explosive and caution must be used when pouring the fuel into the gas reservoirs of the equipment.

White gas stoves and propane/butane stoves are similar and work with the same efficiency and results. The lanterns are different in that the base of a white gas lantern is a small tank filled with white gas, compared to a propane lantern, where the base is the propane canister itself. White gas does not burn efficiently which means carbon monoxide fumes could be more dangerous. Use white gas equipment outdoors where there is adequate ventilation.

CHAPTER FIFTEEN

TRANSPORTATION

Transportation is the catalyst of our economy, and our standard of living would collapse if the ways and means for transporting passengers, resources and supplies were disrupted due to compromised transportation infrastructure, vehicles and operations. It is also one of the most vulnerable elements to disaster scenarios. Even a low-level emergency situation, depending on the type of disaster, can have far-reaching affects. Some disaster types are more likely to cause serious repercussions, but depending on the severity of the disaster, transportation systems could be damaged or disrupted for days, weeks, months or even years.

All of the other elements rely on transportation to distribute their components to the population around the world. It is interesting to observe that even if there was adequate – even excessive amounts of merchandise and commodities available for us to consume – without a transportation system to transport and distribute these goods, services and supplies to manufacturing, wholesale, retail and private markets, they would sit dormant in the fields, orchards and the forests, and would remain hidden deep down in the earth, the seas and the oceans.

Transportation is vital for trade and services which in turn establishes civilizations. For example:

- The local grocery store generally maintains a three-day supply of food and bottled water for customers. A panicked population would deplete the shelves within hours. Without additional food and water being transported and delivered to the stores, our commercial food and water source would end.

- The local department store – even the large super department stores – have only a limited supply of items on their shelves, including flashlights, toilet paper, medicines and first aid supplies, matches, and trash bags. A compromised transportation system will cause these items to be grabbed off the shelves by a panicked population in a matter of ~~days~~ - er - ~~hours~~ - er - minutes!

- If the power is out, gas stations would close since gas pumps are dependent on electricity to operate the system. Without gasoline or diesel in the tanks of our semi-trucks, our personal trucks and automobiles, motorcycles, trains, planes and boats – our basic transportation system is grounded.

- If public transportation systems (subways, rail etc.) located in large cities were grounded, millions of people would not be able to get to work or conduct business transactions requiring a physical presence, i.e., buying groceries, picking up prescriptions, buying clothing, etc.

- The military operations in the country would be immobilized if airports, seaports, roads and other transportation infrastructure, vehicles and operations were damaged or destroyed.

- If the power is out, the debit/credit and ATM machines cease to operate and customers are unable to obtain funds to purchase the scarce fuel that may be available to feed our vehicles.

EMERGENCY PREPARATION PRINCIPLES

There are nine principles that should be followed with regards to transportation, including:

- Maintain your automobile or major transportation vehicle on a regular basis. Make sure that full maintenance is performed on a yearly basis.

- Make sure the automobile has an emergency auto kit with supplies.

- Keep the gas tank full in all vehicles used on a regular basis – the general rule of thumb – when the tank is half empty – fill it up.

- Maintain and <u>use</u> a bicycle in the event vehicles relying on gasoline can not be used. Make sure tires are pumped up and oil the chain. Always have spare parts available.

- Begin a regiment of walking on a daily basis to become physically fit and to use your <u>feet</u> (located at the very bottom of your body) - in the event other transportation modes are not available.

- Have comfortable and sturdy walking shoes in good repair and socks without holes to prevent blisters.

- Have adequate equipment such as a garden cart, suitcase stroller, dolly, wheelbarrow, or wagon to transport emergency supplies in the evacuation kits.

- Team members who live in large urban areas and/or rely on <u>public</u> transportation systems should analyze <u>alternatives</u> that can be used in the event of a serious emergency or disaster. Plan in advance by having alternate routes, maps and methods of transport available - including walking.

- Recognize that during a serious emergency, not only would private transportation be impacted, but depending on where the disaster occurs, public transportation would also be damaged or destroyed. Public transportation systems would more than likely be over-crowded and baggage would be limited.

Recognize that special accommodations and advanced planning will be necessary for many citizens, including senior citizens, medical and nursing home patients, disabled, and individuals who rely exclusively on public transportation. Advanced planning will be required to support pets and animals and individuals will also need to be aware that there will be countless pedestrians and bicyclists on the roads to flee disaster situations. Truckers will also pose a unique problem if the large semi trucks are caught on congested freeways and roads will no way to easily leave the area.

CHANGING CONDITIONS

During all disasters, the <u>first</u> priority of government and charitable agencies is the safety and protection of citizens and evacuees. During the initial terrorist attacks in New York City and Washington DC, transportation officials began to implement evacuation plans and organize recovery procedures. In each case, officials were making decisions without full knowledge of rapidly changing conditions and were uncertain of what future events might occur to change the situation. As a result, *safety* and *security* took priority over mobility.

A <u>second</u> priority would be to provide transport mobility for evacuees. With police, fire, and emergency response personnel focused on managing life-threatening situations, the focus on traffic management becomes a secondary concern for responders and during many emergencies, responsibilities for traffic management shifts from local police to citizens. In some cases, team members may observe citizens stepping in to direct traffic at major intersections when police are unable to reach these stations.

IMPACTS TO TRANSPORTATION SYSTEMS

<u>Re-Entering the Area</u>

After a disaster has been contained, reentry of evacuees requires organization. The process for reentry must be coordinated between agencies for the safety of the public and protection of property. <u>Introducing residents into previously evacuated areas is generally not addressed by government agencies</u>.

As a result, there is congestion and confusion as firefighters, utility workers and law enforcement officers are maneuvering around residents, utilities and insurance representatives. Upon returning to your home after an evacuation, there may possibly be chaos and confusion due to lack of communication and poor organization on the part of government officials, charitable organizations and utility workers. Be ready for it.

<u>Transit Decision Problems</u>

Remember - it is extremely difficult – and frankly impossible - to analyze every possible scenario during a disaster situation. **During a serious disaster, government officials responsible for the safety, security and possible <u>evacuation of citizens may make decisions that adversely impact other elements (electricity, communication and</u>**

medication) as well as other modes of transportation. Be ready to deal with inconveniences and threats that may result from poor or fast decisions made by command centers.

GOVERNMENT RESPONSIBILITIES AND MANAGEMENT

Transportation officials in your area should have <u>at least</u> implemented a plan for the flow of vehicles and citizens. As part of the plan, they should <u>identify and publicize to the public *in advance*</u> the (1) designated transportation hubs that will be available during emergency situations, (2) locations where people can assemble and from where they could take public transportation trains or buses out of the city, (3) identify streets to be used only by people on foot, (4) assign staff or citizens at major intersections along these streets to control traffic, and (5) identify which bridges, tunnels or river crossings would be designated for pedestrian and vehicle usage.

Another factor is how prepared <u>federal, state and local officials are to actually *implement* and *manage* transportation issues *during* an emergency</u>. As previously mentioned, although <u>federal</u> and <u>state</u> government agencies may have the perfect transportation disaster plan, the <u>local</u> officials may have an entirely different system or lack of system in place to support transportation needs during an emergency. The overall transportation plan in your area and the ability of local officials to implement and manage the plan will have a direct bearing on how team members are able to evacuate the area, transport to public shelters or reception centers and/or purchase food, water, clothing, flashlights, batteries and other emergency supplies. Depending on whether local officials responsible for emergency transportation have addressed these issues, your chance of successfully evacuating a pending disaster or surviving a disaster could be directly linked to the <u>competence</u> of their plan and processes.

As part of *planning in advance*, team members should learn about <u>any</u> transportation plan for disaster scenarios in their area. Even if an overall emergency plan is available for review, don't be surprised if you discover local officials do not have a <u>detailed or realistic</u> plan in place to handle transportation and the public (including senior citizens, disabled, prison inmates, the homeless or indigent or those without private transportation) during an emergency or serious disaster.

Consider the following questions that should be asked of <u>local</u> officials responsible for transportation issues during a disaster in your area:

- **Are alternate communication devices available to update traffic information** to the general public including cable television, Internet, or a scrolling sign placed at key points on the freeway system? **Have** cameras been installed that monitor freeways and other transportation modes to advise state police on what resources need to be deployed?

- **Are emergency response systems and facilities protected from destruction and disruption?** Emergency <u>telecommunications</u> systems must have built-in redundancy and emergency <u>transportation</u> procedures must have sufficient sources of power and fuel. The key fueling facilities should have installed generators and key intersections should have installed generators to operate traffic signals. If not, evacuation would be impacted due to congestion.

- **Are officials able to communicate the need to evacuate or not to evacuate?** People who do not need to evacuate and do so unnecessarily crowd roads and others who may need to evacuate do not leave the area.

- Can officials **communicate timely information** to all levels concerning **road closures, road conditions, weather, expected travel times, incidents, lane closures and availability of alternative routes**?

- **Are officials prepared for limited use of computer systems and** recognize the use of computers to suggest alternative routes may be limited? Information technology allows agencies to better inform the public of transportation options but information given during a power outage may inform the public of certain closures but because gridlock conditions would be on most roads following loss of power, there would not be many transportation options available.

- **Do officials plan to use ham radio operators, are there enough ham radio operators to provide communication between government officials and the public,** and has law enforcement arranged to make sure operators can reach emergency operations centers? These radio operators would likely run twenty-four hour operations—so every location would need six to ten operators a day!

- **Do officials realize there may be private vehicle restrictions?** Security issues and traffic control may require restrictions on private vehicle usage for weeks or months after a disaster. Increased need for public transportation should be anticipated.

- Has **critical data to support decision-making** been effectively communicated down through the ranks of command? When this information is distributed down to division and group levels, it enables more effective tactical and strategic planning and increases the situation awareness of ground resources.

- Does the overall plan for evacuation include how to **evacuate the general population, elderly and disabled, hospitals, nursing homes, prisons and other institutions with resident populations**? Transit plays a critical and unique role in meeting this need.

- **Does the plan include the use of public shelters or reception centers** and if there are designated public shelters and/or reception centers in the area, has the public been notified of their location and procedures governing their occupancy?

- **Does the plan work in concert with federal and state government and outside agencies? For example,** working more closely with the United States Customs Service to better plan for emergencies that impact the crossing of freight between Canada and the United States.

- During **construction of highways and roads,** have alternate evacuation routes and detours been developed, and is this information provided to the public? If an evacuation route is needed despite the delay due to construction, the use of shoulders as temporary travel lanes could be considered with the aid of law enforcement assistance.

- **Has a public education program been implemented and distributed to increase public awareness of the evacuation plan and how transportation will be involved in evacuations and transport of citizens?**

- **Has low-tech solutions** been included in the plan including facsimile machines, pagers, 800 numbers, conference call lines, older radio systems and previously installed dedicated landlines to communicate within and among agencies? Cell phones, networked phone systems, portable phones and the Internet may experience failures due to loss of electricity or will stop working when limited backup power is exhausted. Officials may have trouble communicating with each other, other agencies and the general public regarding transportation.

- **Has backup power and generators been evaluated for what works and what does <u>not</u> work during an emergency situation?** During several disasters, agencies were stunned by what was <u>not</u> covered by their backup systems. For example, two agencies lost power for the card-key systems that governed access to their offices. Some agencies had backup power for computers but none for air conditioning units needed to cool the equipment. Many agencies had backup power, but it had not been tested under a full load and did not operate as expected. <u>The ability of officials administering transportation to manage effectively relies on critical equipment working properly and consistently during the disaster.</u>

- Has **utility companies been included in the planning process to coordinate restoration of services**? There can be major problems with managing the return of evacuees and restoring utility services. As part of the plan, utility companies, city mayors, law enforcement, fire departments, insurance representatives and other emergency officials and responders should understand their role in returning evacuees to the area and restoring services.

- **Has officials considered an automated public information system** providing a voice or text mail telephone system, an **Internet site, or traveler information** kiosks at rest areas along evacuation routes to relay consistent and trusted messages to the public and w**ill the plan utilize a public information specialist to keep the public informed through use of a public information campaign?**

- **Has officials developed a system to <u>physically</u> deliver messages such as regular mail for internal communication, handouts, maps** and **face-to-face meetings with the general public?** These methods can be far more effective at resolving conflict under stressful conditions than relying on email, radio or telephone - especially at the tactical level.

- **Has officials stored vital documents off site?** The destruction of the World Trade Center wiped out or prevented access to crisis plans, documents and drawings necessary for response and reconstruction. To provide continuity of business and rapid recovery, copies of vital documents should be stored at several physical locations and be available online at secure and password-protected Web sites.

- Is the **Emergency Operations Center stocked with food and water** for transportation staff to use over an extended period of time? Do they have an emergency generator and fuel, flashlights, lanterns, solar battery charger, charged batteries for cell phones, pagers, portable radios, portable computers and a portable AM/FM radio and batteries in order to receive information from the media?

- **Will officials keep employees informed and keep families of employees informed? If the overall plan does not include the human factor, the plan and the implementation of procedures and processes will not work – blood is thicker than water – and the first priority of employees and their families will be to each other – not the general public. Know this. Understand this. Accept this.**

- **Will officials remember to reset equipment when the power comes back on?** When power is restored, signs displaying messages of lane closures or public meeting areas may be obsolete or inaccurate.

- **Will officials use message signs and highway advisory radio (when possible) to communicate with the public?** The most significant contribution from advanced technology for transportation is the use of dynamic and variable message signs and highway advisory radio to provide information to travelers on the closing or condition of roadways.

As you can see from reviewing these questions, there are many issues involved to ensure transportation is efficient, organized and successful during an emergency. The ultimate success of government officials to effectively coordinate transportation issues *before*, *during* or *after* an emergency will directly impact the general population.

HOW TO PREPARE FOR THE TRANSPORTATION ELEMENT

The <u>first</u> order of business is to recognize how vulnerable and fragile transportation is to both natural and manmade disasters. The <u>second</u> order of business would be to prepare to survive <u>without</u> our current transportation system. This is especially true of teams who live in areas with large public transportation systems and the reliance they may have on these systems in getting from place to place.   Prepare to walk and recognize how difficult it may be to walk even short distances during serious disasters. Learn alternative routes and systems to be used to transport team members to safety.

Finally, *prepare in advance* to stock emergency supplies so transportation (if required) can be limited for only short-distance and critical needs. As part of *planning in advance*, ponder alternatives that can be used by the team in getting around during a disaster and remember that one of the best strategies to help eliminate the need for transportation during a disaster is to have adequate supplies available at the primary residence. Possible alternatives include: **Animals** (remember, all animals used for transportation still require fuel!), ATV, **BICYCLE,** Car/Truck (compact) , Catamaran, Golf Cart, Moped, Motorcycle, **Skateboard**, **Raft**, **Roller Skates**, **Row Boat** (transport/fishing), **Sail Boat**, **Ski Equipment**, Snowmobile, **Snow Shoes** and more importantly - **GOOD WALKING SHOES!**

PINTO BEAN PIE

½ cup granulated white sugar
1 cup brown sugar, firmly packed
2 eggs, beaten
½ cup butter, softened
1 ¼ cup pinto beans, cooked and mashed
1 unbaked 9-inch pie shell
Whipped topping (optional)

Beat white sugar, brown sugar, eggs and butter until creamy. Add pinto beans and blend well. Pour into unbaked pie shell and bake at 375 degrees for 20 minutes. Reduce heat to 350 degrees and bake an additional 25 minutes. Serve with whipped topping.

BREAD PUDDING

2 cups milk
1 ½ cups soft bread cubes
1 tablespoon butter *or* margarine
¼ cup granulated white sugar
¼ teaspoon salt
a cup raisins *or* nuts
2 eggs, beaten
Heavy cream (optional)

Heat milk. Add bread cubes and butter or margarine. Add sugar, salt and raisins or nuts to eggs. Slowly stir in some of the hot milk mixture. Add remainder of hot milk. Pour into a greased baking dish and set in a pan of hot water. Bake at 350 degrees for 1 hour or until set. Pour a little heavy cream over each portion, if desired. Serve immediately.

RICE PUDDING

3 eggs
2 tablespoons honey
6 tablespoons granulated white sugar
½ teaspoon nutmeg
1 teaspoon cinnamon
½ teaspoon vanilla
1 cup milk
¾ cup evaporated milk
1 ½ cups cooked rice
½ cup raisins

Beat eggs. Add sugar, honey and spices. Mix well. Stir in vanilla, milk, rice and raisins. Place in 2-quart casserole dish. Bake at 325 degrees for 45 minutes. Stir after 25 minutes.

CHAPTER SIXTEEN

RECREATION

There will be many projects and tasks to do during an emergency situation. During the actual chaos, everyone will be preoccupied with staying alive and after the disaster is over, the population will stick their head out from under the rock where they were hiding, step out into the open, review the situation and begin the undertaking of making a recovery.

The actual location and strength of the disaster will more than likely determine the amount of time and effort needed by each individual to return to normal conditions, but there will be times when the human body will need to rest from the work. Not only will the physical body need to relax, but the mental and psychological spirit will need to recuperate as well. Is recreation absolutely essential to survival? No. You won't hear anyone screaming "The tornado is coming! Quick! Grab the ping-pong paddles!" It is during these times that a form of recreation will be welcome to relieve the team members from the affects of the disaster.

EMERGENCY PREPARATION PRINCIPLES

As we prepare for future disasters, it will be necessary to return to a basic and simple lifestyle when preparing for the **RECREATION** Element. There are several basic principles that would apply when gathering recreational items:

- Items should not require any electricity or batteries to operate
- Items should be geared toward the recreational preferences of team members, i.e. everyone loves to read
- Items should be geared toward the ages of team members
- Items should be non-breakable, compact and easy to store
- Items should provide a balance between cooperative group games, traditional sports and individual play
- Items may be stored for <u>future</u> use in the event of an emergency and not for everyday use
- Some type of recreational item(s) should be included in all emergency pantries
- Include recreational items that already exist in the home as part of the plan

FUN BOXES

The first item of business will be the "Fun Box" that stores the recreational items. The number and size of these fun boxes will depend on the number of team members, the age of members, the significance that recreation plays in their everyday lives, money, and the opinions of how recreation would support an emergency situation. It is important to include a <u>variety</u> of items that can be utilized for recreation. Here are some items that could be easily incorporated into recreational pantries including the following:

- Games (board, arcade, lawn, yard, sport)
- Cards
- Toys
- Puzzles
- Books (including a journal)
- Writing Materials (paper, pens, pencils, etc.)
- Sewing
- Musical Instruments
- Crafts

> Make sure you have several good books to read in your work, auto and evacuation kits for all team members. Make sure that ONE of those books is a first aid book!

<u>Reference Books</u>

There is another type of book that *must* definitely be included in the emergency pantries of all teams – I am talking about *printed copy* <u>reference books</u> that are in good condition and command an accessible location in the primary residence (including the shelter-in-place). These books should be read and studied *prior* to an emergency, should be located in an area that has a high possibility of surviving a disaster and should be easily accessible to all adult team members. Many of these books and pamphlets can be obtained on-line or at book stores offering both new and used books. A valuable resource of information is through federal, state and local agencies including the Federal Emergency Management Administration (FEMA), the Armed Forces, and the extension service at most universities.

The type of reference books and materials to be included on the library shelf in the primary residence include the following:

- **Cookbooks** – these books should include simple and realistic recipes using dutch oven cooking, campfire cooking, wood stove cooking, barbeque cooking, solar oven cooking, canning and freezing, etc.

- **Medical** – these books should include comprehensive first aid methods and techniques, alternative healing, medicines and methods including plants, herbs, vitamins, minerals, salts etc.

- **Gardening** – these books should include comprehensive information on growing and harvesting a vegetable garden, sprouting, and growing fruit trees, berries and grapes. Make sure you have materials that provide information on insect pests, ground preparation and tools.

- **Survival** – these books could include information on survival in <u>specific</u> disaster scenarios including nuclear war, earthquake, biological and chemical warfare and weather related disasters (drought, cold, wind, fire and rain). There are also "how to" books and pamphlets available on how to build a root cellar, how to drain water pipes, etc. It is also important to have books on wilderness survival teaching the types of wild plants that are edible, non-edible and/or can be used for medicinal purposes, the locations and types of shelters that can be built in the wild as well as general rules and guidelines that must be followed for survival in a wilderness environment.

- **Operation** – these <u>manuals</u> should provide detailed and technical information on how to operate, maintain and repair various equipment, tools and machinery in your possession.

- **Maps** – a combination of local and regional maps in your area including a highway map and topical maps.

Remember! **RECREATION** is an element that could be shared between more than one team. For example, if there are five separate teams living in the same neighborhood, each team could be assigned specific recreation items and supplies to include in their primary residence pantry. During a disaster, and when it's time for a break, all five teams could share their recreation items with the other teams. In this way, all five teams can save money by not having to purchase so many recreation items. In the event that one of the teams makes a decision not to share with the others - there is really no major harm done to the other teams - because after all, survival is not contingent on whether you have a board game, guitar, football or deck of cards at your primary residence. Recreation supplies are certainly important, convenient and desired, but may not be considered critical *need* items. However, if your team has small children and/or teenagers, recreation supplies can offer a means to eliminate stress, and boredom for not only the kids, but the adults as well.

LEMON CREAM PIE

½ cup water
2 tablespoons cold water
Dash of salt
a cup wheat flour
a cup dry milk powder
b cup granulated white sugar
1 teaspoon Knox gelatin (a envelope)
1 package lemonade Koolaid (without sugar)
Whipped topping (optional)
1 Crunchy Wheat Pie Crust

Bring to a boil 1 cup water and salt. Make a paste with another ½ cup water and flour. Slowly pour mixture into boiling water mixture, and let cook over low heat for 7-8 minutes stirring constantly. Remove from heat. In small mixing bowl, combine dry milk powder, sugar and 2 tablespoons cold water. Set aside. Soften gelatin in water, put on low heat and stir until dissolved. Add gelatin to milk mixture and stir until thoroughly mixed. Add Koolaid and mix until dissolved. Combine with cooked wheat and mix well. Pour into piecrust and serve with whipped topping, if desired.

CHAPTER SEVENTEEN

PROTECTION

HOW TO PROTECT OURSELVES

We have been warned for years that in the last days, the entire planet would be in crisis and we should prepare ourselves for the time when we would be subject to the affects and consequences of manmade and natural disasters. Unfortunately, it has been somewhat unclear about exactly <u>what</u> type of disaster(s) would be forthcoming, <u>when</u> we should expect them and exactly <u>where</u> on earth they would take place. As we continue to observe the devastating manmade and natural disasters around the world and here at home, we are beginning to understand the significance and wisdom in the counsel of emergency preparation.

When team members address the dilemma of how best to protect themselves from disasters – there are <u>seven</u> general guidelines:

1. *Prepare in advance* and work hard to store a <u>minimum</u> of a **one-year supply** of needed resources, goods and supplies.

2. Make sure all emergency supplies are stored in a *safe* and *secure* location and do not disclose or discuss your emergency preparation supplies with others.

3. **Study**, **learn**, **ponder**, **think**, **analyze** and **discuss** with team members manmade and natural disaster scenarios. Take steps to protect the physical primary residence and surroundings, individual team members and complete the tasks and assignments needed to maintain the *physical*, *spiritual*, *emotional*, *mental* and *psychological* health of team members. Remember - what you don't know - can and will hurt you during a serious disaster.

4. Include **weapons and ammunition** as part of the overall emergency preparation plan to protect survival team members and emergency supplies. This is a sound and sensible strategy. Perhaps the best argument to include weapons and ammunition in the emergency preparation arsenal is to recognize that during some short-term disasters and definitely during medium to long-term disasters– there will be many people who will not be prepared. During desperate times - there will be desperate people - searching for emergency supplies.

5. **NEVER NEVER NEVER** give up your weapons or ammunition to the government, politicians, military or law enforcement - **NEVER**. Under no circumstances or for any reason - **EVER EVER EVER**.

6. **Combine forces with other teams (neighbors, friends, relatives, church)** <u>**IN ADVANCE**</u> to protect homes, neighborhoods and communities from those who would harm team members and property.

7. Recognize that any of these disasters could happen and would more than likely affect you - either directly or indirectly. Don't be naïve into believing you are immune from taking a hit.

TEMPORAL PROTECTION

Temporal protection includes *cannons*, *guns*, *ammunition*, *swords*, *knives*, *grenades*, *bow and arrow*, *slingshots*, *rocks* and *sticks* - in other words - <u>manmade weapons</u>. As part of *planning in advance*, the team should decide whether or not to use these types of weapons during an emergency or disaster situation.

There are countless scenarios when manmade weapons could be justified - and used - to protect the team from groups, gangs or individuals who may elect to use lethal force to take emergency supplies during a short-term emergency or a long-term and serious disaster. As citizens, we have the right to protect ourselves and our supplies from those who would attempt to use criminal and/or unscrupulous

> *The strongest reason for people to retain the right to keep and bear arms is, as a last resort, to protect themselves against tyranny in their government.*
>
> **- Thomas Jefferson**

means to maintain or gain control of the region and/or to obtain emergency supplies for themselves during a crisis environment.

There are basically three types of groups who could potentially pose a threat to teams as follows:

1.   This group comprises one individual or citizen(s) who band together to protect themselves and obtain emergency supplies they need in order to survive.

   o **Law-abiding** citizens who have <u>not</u> prepared in advance, and due to the perception (real or unreal) they are entitled to or need emergency supplies from others in order to survive - resort to unethical, immoral and illegal means to obtain what they need to stay alive. These citizens could be your neighbors, friends, relatives or anyone you pass on the street.

   o **Gangs** who have <u>not</u> prepared in advance, and who have (in the past) continually used intimidation, lethal force, theft and other unlawful means to maintain and control their "turf" and to supplies.

   o **Addicts** who have <u>not</u> prepared in advance, and who have (in the past) continually used theft and even lawful means to support their drug, alcohol and tobacco habit and to get supplies.

   o **Criminals** who have <u>not</u> prepared in advance, and continually use any means to get supplies.

   o **Mentally Ill** citizens who have <u>not</u> prepared in advance, who may or may not have been under a doctor's care, and will take whatever steps are necessary to get supplies.

2.   This group comprises <u>United States Armed Forces</u> (Army, Navy, Air Force, Marines and Coast Guard), National Guard and various <u>law enforcement agencies</u> assigned to federal, state or local jurisdictions.

3.   This group comprises <u>enemy combatants</u> including military forces, terrorists, or citizens from hostile countries.

I believe during a majority of emergency and disaster scenarios, military personnel would give their own lives to protect the citizens of this country. But I also recognize the possibility these same individuals could be commanded, influenced and/or convinced by government politicians, military commanders or even corporate executives to turn their guns on the very citizens they have taken an oath to protect. Remember during the Egyptian uprising when military soldiers were commanded by their own superiors to fire on their own citizenry.

There seems to be a very fine line between (1) limitations and restrictions that must be placed on government politicians to prevent an abuse of power and exploitation of control over the citizens, (2) acceptable role military and law enforcement should play in protecting and/or defending the overall population, a specific group of citizens or even one individual (3) limitations that should be placed on citizens before military or law enforcement intervention is justified and (4) restrictions on citizens by military or law enforcement for illegal, unrealistic, destructive or criminal actions.

That line seems to become even more distorted when one observes the *direction* in which the guns of the military and law enforcement may be pointed and exactly *who* or *what* it is they believe is being protected or defended. Is it the country? Is it the Constitution? Is it the commanders? Is it the citizens? Is it the governor? Is it the members of the Senate and Congress? Is it the President of the United States? Or - is it themselves?

WHAT TO CONSIDER FOR <u>TEMPORAL</u> PROTECTION

- **PREPARE IN ADVANCE**
- **GUNS** (rifles, shotguns, pistols)
- **AMMUNIATION**
- Bullet-Proof Vests
- Camouflage Clothing
- Underground Bunker
- **Locks on Doors and Windows**
- **Safe for Valuables**
- **Security Lighting**
- **Alarm System**
- **Neighborhood Watch Program**
- **Operation Identification**
- Blast/Fallout Shelter
- Gas Masks
- **STRONG TEAM**
- **COMBINE WITH OTHER TEAMS**

CHAPTER EIGHTEEN

INSPIRATION

YOU CAN NOT ACCOMPLISH THIS PROJECT SUCCESSFULLY OR EVEN SURVIVE ANY DISASTER WITHOUT THE HELP OF GOD.

I suppose at this point in time, I should give you a pep talk about how important it is to focus on the goal, plan competently, purchase successfully and store effectively. When I first started to fill my emergency pantries, a serious disaster seemed like an event to happen in the far distant future. It was different back then. The world was a better place to live. More safety. More security. More forests. More space. More unity. Cleaner air. Cleaner water. Less populated. Less hatred. Less violence. Less division. Less crime. . . .

In the Bible and other religious scriptures, we have been counseled by ancient and modern prophets to prepare for the last days. Over the past five decades, we have been counseled by religious, charitable, scientific and community leaders to prepare for future disasters.

No one knows *why*, *when*, *where*, or *how* future disaster scenarios will take place. But most reasonable citizens who read the newspapers, watch the television broadcasts and reports, and simply stop and look around the immediate area and observe world events recognize there have been major changes in the world.

Consider the weather patterns and the ominous transformation in the environment, escalating unrest and crime, financial instability, terrorist attacks, wide spread political divisions among citizens, riots, wars and increased health problems.

Lucifer has been hard at work wreaking havoc and chaos around the world. He has succeeded in creating an increased sense of uneasiness and apprehension in families about the future.

But there is also good news. In the end, Lucifer will not win. Why? **Because there is also a Father in Heaven and a Savior of this world. His name is Jesus Christ, the only begotten Son and Creator of this heaven and earth.** Although the news media wants us to believe all is lost, there are still many good things occurring in this world every day. Through these difficult times, it is important to remember as you look to God for guidance and support, and as you continue to fill your emergency pantries, remember to live each day to the fullest - stop and breathe in the sweet scent of every single rose. Maintain a positive outlook on life while at the same time, recognize the reality of both manmade and natural disasters occurring now and in the future. Trust and have faith in the Lord. And remember God and His son, Jesus Christ are with you - always.

If you are just beginning to get your emergency pantries in order, you may see a foreboding obstacle in the path – lack of time, lack of funds and lack of organizational skills to accomplish the task. As I have been filling my emergency pantries in preparation for the last days, I have discovered that I cannot do it alone but if I continue to look to a Higher Power for guidance and assistance in this daunting task – it is possible.

By systematically and methodically filling emergency pantries, teams will not only have a feeling of accomplishment but will also experience a feeling of independence, self-sufficiency and relief that comes with *preparing in advance* to deal with any future emergency scenario - no matter how big - no matter how small. Your team will be prepared.

Recognize that gathering supplies and resources for emergency pantries is a continual and on-going process. Each team must evaluate their own unique circumstances and based on where you live, current lifestyle and other factors affecting individual situations, review the information contained in this book and make a *realistic* and *smart* decision on what would be good choices for your team.

REMEMBER - YOU <u>CAN</u> DO HARD THINGS – ONE BY ONE - DAY BY DAY. BUT NEVER STOP FILLING THOSE PANTRIES.

The First Presidency of the Church of Jesus Christ of Latter-Day Saints stated on 24 June 1988:

"We continue to encourage members to store sufficient food, clothing and where possible fuel for at least one year. We have not laid down an exact formula for what should be stored. However, we suggest that members concentrate on essential foods that sustain life such as grains, legumes, cooking oil, powdered milk, salt, sugar or honey and water. Most families can achieve and maintain this basic level of preparedness. The decision to do more than this rests with the individual. We encourage you to follow this counsel with the assurance that a people prepared through obedience to the commandments of God need not fear."

Bruce R. McConkie, Apostle for the Church of Jesus Christ of Latter-Day Saints stated in May of 1979::

"I stand before the Church this day and raise the warning voice – it is a voice calling upon the Lord's people to prepare for the troubles and desolations which are about to be poured out upon the world without measure. For the moment, we live in a day of peace and prosperity but it shall not ever be thus. Great trials lie ahead. All of the sorrow and perils of the past are but a foretaste of what is yet to be. And we must prepare ourselves temporally and spiritually. And it may be, for instance, that nothing except the power of faith and the authority of the priesthood can save individuals and congregations from the atomic holocausts that surely shall be. And so we raise the warning voice and say: 'Take heed; prepare; watch and be ready. There is no security in any course except the course of obedience and conformity and righteousness'."

Gordon B. Hinckley, Prophet of the Church of Jesus Christ of Latter-Day Saints stated in October of 1988:

"…I am suggesting that the time has come to get our houses in order. There is a portent of stormy weather ahead to which we had better give heed. We are carrying a message of self-reliance throughout the Church. <u>I urge you to look to the condition of your finances</u>. Set your houses in order. That's all I have to say about it, but I wish to say it with all the emphasis of which I am capable."

L. Tom Perry, Apostle in the Church of Jesus Christ of Latter-Day Saints stated in October of 1975:

"I believe it is time, and perhaps with some urgency, to review the counsel we have received in dealing with our personal and family preparedness. We have been instructed to follow at least four requirements in preparing for that which is to come. Gain an adequate education. Live within your income. Avoid unnecessary debt. Store a reserve of food and supplies. As long as I can remember, we have been taught to prepare for the future and to obtain a year's supply of necessities. I would guess that the years of plenty have almost universally caused us to set aside this counsel. I believe the time to disregard this counsel is over. With events in the world today, it must be considered with all seriousness."

George Q. Cannon, an Apostle of the Church of Jesus Christ of Latter-Day Saints stated:

"The greatest events that have been spoken of by all the Holy Prophets will come along so naturally as the consequences of certain causes, that unless our eyes are enlightened by the Spirit of God, and the spirit of revelation rests upon us, we will fail to see that these are the events predicted by the Holy Prophets."

Ezra Taft Benson, Prophet of the Church of Jesus Christ of Latter-Day Saints stated on 6 April 1965:

"Should the Lord decide at this time to cleanse the Church – a famine in this land of one year's duration could wipe out a large percentage of slothful members, including some ward and stake officers. Yet – we cannot say we have not been warned . . "

ITEM	ELEMENT	NEED/WANT	PRIORITY	HOUSEHOLD TEAM MEMBERS	LENGTH OF TIME	PRIMARY RESIDENCE	PLACE OF REFUGE	AUTO	EVACUATION KIT	WORK	TOTAL ITEMS NEEDED	ON HAND	STILL TO PURCHASE	PACKAGING	UNIT COST	TOTAL COST

ITEM	ELEMENT	NEED/WANT	PRIORITY	HOUSEHOLD TEAM MEMBERS	LENGTH OF TIME	PRIMARY RESIDENCE	PLACE OF REFUGE	AUTO	EVACUATION KIT	WORK	TOTAL ITEMS NEEDED	ON HAND	STILL TO PURCHASE	PACKAGING	UNIT COST	TOTAL COST

ELEMENTS LIST OF SUPPLIES KEY

C - Communication
D - Documentation
FI - Financial Institution
FU - Fuel Consumption

I - Immunization
IN - Inspiration
M - Medication
N - Nutrition

OC - Operations/Clothing
OG - Operations/General
OT - Operations/Tools
P - Protection

R - Recreation
S - Sanitation
T - Transportation

SUPPLIES	EL	SUPPLIES	EL	SUPPLIES	EL
Acco Clips (toilet)	S	Books (reference)	O, R	Cold Press (instant)	M
Activated Charcoal	M	Books (survival, emergency)	OG, R	Comb/Brush	S
Adhesive Tape Rolls	M	Boots (heavy-duty)	OC	Commode	S
Alarm System	P	Bottling and Canning Supplies	N	Compass	OG
Alcohol (Rubbing)	M	Bouillons	N	Compression Socks	M
Allergies (Sinus/Decongestant)	M	Bowls (plastic)	OG, N	Cooking Oil	N
Aluminum Foil	OG	Box Cutter	OT	Cooking Utensils (spatula etc.)	N
Ammonia	S	Brace - ankle	M	Cornstarch	N
Ammunition	P, N	Brace - knee	M	Cotton Balls	M
Analgesics	M	Brace - wrist	M	Cotton Swabs	M
Antacids	M	Briquettes (Charcoal)	OG, N	Cough Suppressants	M
Antibiotic Ointment	M	Broom	S	CPR Microshield	M
Antibiotics	M	Bucket - cleaning (heavy-duty)	S	Crafts	R
Anti-Freeze	T	Bucket - drinking (heavy-duty)	OG	Crimpers	OT
Antihistamine	M	Bucket - toilet (heavy-duty)	S	Crow Bar	OT
Antiseptic Wipes	M	Burn Ointment/Spray/Cream	M	Cups (paper, plastic, metal)	N
ATV	T	Butter Substitute (dry)	N	Deadbolts	P
Axe	OT	Buttons	OC	Debit/Credit Card (kits)	FI
Baby Supplies	OG	Calamine Lotion	M	Deeds	D
Baggies (variety of sizes)	OG	Calendar	OG	Dental Floss	M
Baking Powder	N	Can/Bottle Opener	N	Dental Records	D
Baking Soda	N, S	Candles	OG	Deodorant	S
Bandages - butterfly	M	Canned Heat	OG	Diapers (adult and/or baby)	S
Bandages - elastic	M	Car Registration	D	Diarrhea Medication	M
Bandages - fingertip	M	Carbon Monoxide Detector	P	Dish Rags	S
Bandages - knuckle	M	Card Table	OG	Dishtowels	S
Bandages - strips	M	Cards	R	Disinfectants	S
Bandages - triangular	M	Cash	FI	Divorce Decree	D
Band-Aids	M	Cell Phone	C	Dressings - burn	M
Barbeque Grill	N	Cement Trials	OT	Drink Mix	N
Bath Gel (Shampoo/Soap)	S	Certificate of Deposit	D	Drivers License	D
Batteries (rechargeable)	OG	Chains	T, OG	Drum (heavy-duty 55 gallon)	OG
Battery Charger (Solar)	OG	Chair (folding)	OG	Dry Milk	N
Belt	OC	Checks (checking account)	FI	Duct Tape	OG
Bicycle	T	Chisel	OT	Dust Mask	S, P
Binoculars	OG	Clamps	OT	Dustpan	S
Birth Certificate	D	Cleaning Agents	S	Dutch Ovens	N
Birth Control	M	Cleaning Rags	S	Eggs (dried)	N
Blankets	OG	Clock	OG	Electric Hot Plate	N
Bleach	S	Clothes Line (outdoor)	S	Epson Salt	M
Bolt Cutter	OT	Clothes Pins	S	Extension Cords	OG
Bolts	OT	Clothes Rack (indoors)	S	Eye Drops	M
Bond Certificates	D	Clothes Wringer	S	Eyeglass Repair Kit	M
Bonds	FI	Coat (heavy-duty and/or warm)	OC	Eyeglasses (extra pair)	M
Books (journal)	R	Coins	FI	Eyewash Solution	M
Books (reading)	R	Cold Medicine	M	Facial Tissues	S
Fan (hand-held)	OG	Gloves (Latex)	M	Immunization-Chickenpox	I

SUPPLIES	EL	SUPPLIES	EL	SUPPLIES	EL
Feminine Hygiene Supplies	S	Gloves (light duty)	OC	Immunization-Diphtheria	I
Files (Tool)	OT	Gloves (work)	OG	Immunization-Hepatitis A	I
Fingernail Clippers	S	Glue	OT	Immunization-Hepatitis B	I
Fire Alarm (battery-operated)	P	Gott (hold water)	OG	Immunization-Influenza	I
Fire Extinguisher	P	Grain - Amaranth	N	Immunization-Meningitis	I
Fire Starter	OG	Grain - Kamut	N	Immunization-MMR	I
Fireplace - wood burning	OG, N	Grain - Millet	N	Immunization-Papillomavirus	I
Fireplace Tools	OG	Grain - Pearled Barley	N	Immunization-Pertussis	I
First Aid Kit and Manual	M	Grain - Quinoa	N	Immunization-Pneumonia	I
Fish (dried, canned, etc.)	N	Grain - Rice	N	Immunization-Polio	I
Fishing/Hunting Supplies	N	Grain - Wheat (red)	N	Immunization-Tetanus	I
Flashlight	OG	Grain - Wheat (white)	N	Immunization-Typhoid	I
Flint Striker	OG	Grain- Bulger	N	Immunization-Zoster	I
Flour	N	Grain- Oats	N	Income Tax Returns	D
Fly Swatter	S	Grain- Spelt	N	Insect Repellent / Killer	S, P
Fruits	N	Guardianship Papers	D	Insurance - Auto	D
Fuel Source - butane	FU	Guns	P, N	Insurance - Home	D
Fuel Source - canned heat	FU	Hair Clippies	S	Insurance - Life	D
Fuel Source - coal	FU	Hair Elastics	S	Insurance - Medical	D
Fuel Source - gasoline	FU	Hammer	OT	Insurance - Other	D
Fuel Source - lamp oil	FU	Hand Cart	T	Iodide Tablets (thyroid)	M
Fuel Source - newspaper logs	FU	Hand Dolly	T	Ipecac Syrup	M
Fuel Source - pressed logs	FU	Hand Sanitizer	S	IRA Account Paperwork	D
Fuel Source - white gas	FU	Hand Warmer	OG	Jack	OT
Fuel Source- propane	FU	Hat (heavy-duty and/or warm)	OC	Jacket	OC
Fuel Source- wood	FU	Hat (light-duty)	OC	Jams	N
Funnel (gas)	FU	Hatchet	OT	Jelly	N
Funnel (water)	OG	Heartburn Medication	M	Juicer	N
Fuses	T, OG	Heaters (electric and/or fuel)	OG	Jumper Cables	T
Games	R	Heating Pad	OG	Keys (extra sets)	OG
Garbage Bags - various sizes	OG,S	Hidden Message Box	C	Knife	P
Garbage Bags -13 gal	OG,S	Hoe	OT	Knife or Scapel	OT, M
Garbage Can (large)	OG,S	Home Signal Flag	C	Knife Sharpener	OT
Garden Hose	OG	Honey	N	Ladders	OG
Garden Tools (small)	OT	Hospital Information	D	Lamp Oil	OG
Gas Can (plastic)	OG, T	Hot Dog Sticks	N	Lantern (battery-operated)	OG
Gauze - rolled	M	Hot Drink Maker	N	Lantern (oil)	OG
Gauze - sponges	M	Hot Pads	N	Lantern (propane/butane)	OG
Gauze - squares	M	Hot Press (instant)	M	Lanyards	OG
Gelatin	N	Hot Water Bottle	M	Lawnmower (manual)	OG
Generator (gas)	OG	House Slippers	OC	Laxative	M
Generator (solar)	OG	Hydrocortisone Cream	M	Leases	D
Glass Cutter	OT	Hydrogen Peroxide	M	Legumes - Dry Beans	N
Gloves – (Plastic)	OG	Ice Bag	M	Legumes - Lentils	N
Gloves (heavy-duty and/or	OC	Immunization Records	D	Legumes - Lima Beans	N
Legumes - Soy Beans	N	Nuts (tool)	OT	Quilts	OG
Legumes - Split Peas	N	Nuts and Seeds	N	Radio - CB	C

SUPPLIES	EL	SUPPLIES	EL	SUPPLIES	EL
Level (tool)	OT	Oat Grinder	N	Radio - Ham	C
Light Bulbs (low watt)	OG	Pads - abdominal	M	Radio (battery-operated)	C
Light Sticks	OG	Pads - eye	M	Radio (crank/solar)	C
Lighters	OG	Pads - non adherent	M	Rain Barrel	OG
Lighting (outdoor)	P	Pain Relievers	M	Rain Gear	OC
Lime	S	Paint Brush	OT	Rake	OT
Lip Balm	M	Pancake Mix	N	Ratchets	OT
Living Will	D	Pants and Slacks	OC	Razor	S
Locks	P	Paper	C	Razor Blades	S
Lotion	S	Paper Bags (brown)	OG	Religious Materials	IN
Lumber	OT	Paper Napkins	S	Religious Records	D
Mallet (rubber)	OT	Paper Towels	S	Robe	OC
Maps (driving and topical)	T	Passport	D	Roller Skates	T, R
Marriage License/Certificate	D	Pasta	N	Rope	OG
Matches	OG	Peanut Butter	N	Row Boat	T, N
Mayonnaise	N	Pens/Pencils	C	Rubber Syringe	M
Measuring Cup	OG, N	Permanent Markers	C	Safe	P
Meats (canned)	N	Pet Records	D	Safety Glasses	P
Medical Equipment (walker etc.)	M	Petroleum Jelly	M	Safety Pins	OG
Medication - prescription	M	Photographs - recent	D	Salad Dressing	N
Medicine Dropper	M	Pick	OT	Salt	N
Medicine Spoon	M	Pill Holders	M	Sand paper	OT
Military Records	D	Pillows	OG	Sandbags	OG, P
Mirror	S, OG	Pitch Fork	OT	Sander	OT
Miter Box with Saw	OT	Planers	OT	Savings Account Records	D
Molasses	N	Plastic Grocery Bags	OG	Saw	OT
Mop	S	Plastic Sheeting	OG	Scanner	C
Mortgages	D	Plastic Ties	OG	School Records	D
Motor Oil	T	Plates - paper	N	Scissors	OG, R
Motorcycle	T	Plates - plastic	N	Scrapers	OT
Mouse/Rat (Traps/Solar)	S	Pliers	OT	Screwdrivers	OT
Mouthwash	S	Plow	OT	Screws	OT
Musical Instruments	R	Pocket Knife	OT	Seasonings	N
Nails (various types and sizes)	OT	Popcorn Popper	N	Security Bars (windows/doors)	P
Napkins	S	Pots (grow vegetables)	N	Seeds - garden	N
Naturalization Papers	D	Power of Attorney	D	Seeds - sprouting	N
Nausea Medication	M	Precious Metals	FI	Seeds (for eating, sesame)	N
Needles	S, R	Prescription Lists	M	Sewing Kits (thread, pins)	OG, R
Neighborhood Watch	P	Property Tax Statements	D	Sewing Projects	R
Newspaper Logs	OG	Pruner	OT	Shampoo - lice	S
Notebooks	C	Pruning Saw	OT	Shampoo - regular	S
Noxzema Cream	M	Punch	OT	Shaving Supplies	S
Nozzle	OG	Putty	OT	Shears	OT
Nut Drivers	OT	Puzzles	R	Shirts	OC
Shoe laces	OC	Straws (for drinking)	N	T-Shirts	OC
Shoes - light-duty	OC	Sugar (brown)	N	Tubs (plastic) laundry - 3	S
Shoes - sturdy	OC	Sugar (powdered)	N	Tweezers	M

SUPPLIES	EL	SUPPLIES	EL	SUPPLIES	EL
Shortening	N	Sugar (white)	N	Twine	OG
Shovel (regular)	OT	Sunglasses	OC	Typewriter (manual) and	C
Shovel (snow)	OT	Sunscreen	M	Umbrella	P
Skateboard	R, T	Suppositories	M	Underwear (boxers, panties etc)	OC
Sledge Hammer	OT	Swabs - alcohol	M	Underwear (thermal)	OC
Sleeping Bag (heavy-duty)	OG	Swabs - cotton-tipped	M	Utensils (fork, spoon, knife)	N
Sleeping Bag (light-duty)	OG	Swabs - insect bite	M	Vacuum (manual)	S
Sleepwear	OC	Sweat shirts	OC	Vapor Rub	M
Smoke Detector	P	Sweaters	OC	Vegetables (canned, dried, etc.)	N
Snake Bite Kit	M	Table (small folding)	OG	Vehicle Registrations	D
Snips	OT	Tacks	OT	Vinegar	N
Soap (dish)	S	Tape Measure	OT	Vitamins	M
Soap (hand)	S	Tarp Clips	OG	Wagon	T
Soap (laundry)	S	Tarps	OG	Walkie-Talkies	C
Social Security Card	D	Tarps (outhouse)	S	Washboard	S
Sockets	OT	Tea Kettle	OG, N	Washcloths	S
Socks (heavy-duty and/or warm)	OC	Telephone Book	C	Washers	OT
Socks (light-duty)	OC	Tennis Ball	S	Water - bottled	OG
Solar Camping Shower	S	Tent (heavy-duty)	OG, P	Water - containers	OG
Solar Garden Lights	OG	Tent (light duty) - popup	OG	Water - natural sources	OG
Solar Oven	N	Thermometer (medical)	M	Water Can	OG
Solar Panels	OG	Thermometer (outside)	OG	Water Purification Tablets	OG
Soup Mixes	N	Thermos (insulated)	N	Waxed Paper	N
Spare Tire	T	Throat Lozenges	M	Wedge	OT
Spices	N	Tire Chains	T	Weed Killer Container	S
Spikes	OT	Tire Pressure Gauge	T	Weeder	OT
Splints	M	Tires (for growing vegetables)	N	Wheat Mill	N
Sponges (cleaning)	S	Titles (home, vehicles etc)	D	Wheelbarrow	T
Spray Bottle - Cleaning	S	Toilet Lid	S	Whiskbroom	S
Spray Bottle - Shower	S	Toilet Paper	S	Whistle	C
Sprouting Container	N	Tongue Blades	M	Wicks (for oil lamps)	OG
Sprouting Seeds	N	Toothache Medicine	M	Wills	D
Squares	OT	Toothbrush	S	Wind Turbine	OG
Stapler (heavy-duty)	OT	Toothpaste	S	Windshield Scrapper	T
Staples (heavy-duty)	OT	Toothpicks	S	Wire Screen Mesh (repairs)	OT
Status Letter/Stamp	C	Tourniquet	M	Wound Closures	M
Stock Certificates	D	Tow Rope	OG	Wrenches	OT
Stocks	FI	Towelettes (pre-moistened)	S	Writing Materials	R, C
Stove (butane)	OG, N	Towels - bath	S	Yeast	N
Stove (charcoal)	N	Towels - dish	S		
Stove (coal)	OG, N	Towels - hand	S		
Stove (propane)	OG, N	Toys	R		
Stove (wood)	OG, N	Treadle Sewing Machine	R, OG		

And know that I am with you always; yes, to the end of time.

- Jesus Christ